Gender Equity

Volume 176   Sage Library of Social Research

RECENT VOLUMES IN . . .
SAGE LIBRARY OF SOCIAL RESEARCH

Gender Equity

An Integrated Theory
of Stability and Change

Janet Saltzman Chafetz

Sage Library of Social Research 176

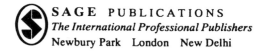
SAGE PUBLICATIONS
The International Professional Publishers
Newbury Park   London   New Delhi

\# 20131005

For information address:

SAGE Publications, Inc.
2455 Teller Road
Newbury Park, California 91320

SAGE Publications Ltd.
6 Bonhill Street
London EC2A 4PU
United Kingdom

SAGE Publications India Pvt. Ltd.
M-32 Market
Greater Kailash I
New Delhi 110 048 India

Printed in the United States of America

Library of Congress Cataloging-in-Publication Data

Chafetz, Janet Saltzman.
   . Gender equity : an integrated theory of stability and change
Janet Saltzman Chafetz.
     p. cm.—(Sage library of social research ; 176)
   Includes bibliographical references.
   ISBN 0-8039-3401-7.—ISBN 0-8039-3402-5 (pbk.)
   1. Sex discrimination against women. 2. Social change.
3. Equality. I. Title. II. Series: Sage library of social
research ; v. 176.
HQ1206.C395 1990   89-10720
305.3—dc20   CIP

92 93 94 15 14 13 12 11 10 9 8 7 6 5 4 3

Contents

This book is dedicated to
Henry Simon and Joshua Aaron Chafetz,
in hope that they are always part of the solution

Preface

This book is a direct outgrowth of a book I published in 1988, *Feminist Sociology: An Overview of Contemporary Theories*, which is a survey of feminist theories that have been developed or used — or could potentially be used — by sociologists since 1970. While writing that book I discovered a large number of quite different theories that address the issue of how gender systems maintain and reproduce themselves, but almost none concerning *how* gender systems change or could be changed. This is a strange omission, given the fact that, by definition, feminists are committed to changing systems of gender that are inequitable to women. Moreover, the theories paid mostly superficial attention to one another. Although most sounded plausible, all seemed substantially incomplete. The need to systematically integrate the variety of perspectives became very apparent to me.

About the time that the book manuscript was completed, I was asked to contribute to a special issue of the *Journal of Family Issues* devoted to the intersection of the economy, the family, and gender stratification. That invitation provided an opportunity to begin to develop an integrated theory of how systems of gender inequality are maintained and reproduced (Chafetz, 1988b). In expanded form, that theory constitutes Part I of this book.

Shortly after, I was asked to write a paper for a volume in an annual series, sponsored by the Theory Section of the American Sociological Association, that would be devoted to feminist theory. This gave me the chance to begin the process of developing an integrated theory of how systems of gender inequality change (Chafetz, 1989). While writing that paper, it became clear that I was integrating much of the theoretical work that had occupied my attention, and that of my coauthor on several projects, A. Gary Dworkin, for nearly a decade. It was exciting to see the various pieces begin to fit together. That paper constitutes the basis for much of Part II of this book.

A major goal in writing this book is to demonstrate both the utility of a variety of the theories about gender published in the past two decades and the need to pay much more attention to their systematic integration. My overriding hope is that, by weaving diverse approaches together, this work will prompt more systematic research devoted to *theory testing* — as distinct from the *application of theory* — to explain a set of empirical data. At the very least, this book provides a summary of what gender sociologists and other social and behavioral scientists have learned in recent years about stability and change in systems of gender inequality.

My thanks go to Mitch Allen, Sociology Editor at Sage, whose early and abiding enthusiasm for this project provided a major incentive to do it. To Rae Blumberg and Ruth Wallace, whose invitations to write the papers that provide the bases for Parts I and II, respectively, go my warmest gratitude. Their enthusiasm for my papers, and concrete editorial suggestions, were both appreciated. Helen Rose Ebaugh gave me feedback on the entire book manuscript, but, far more importantly, provided constant encouragement and support. In addition, Ruth Wallace, Virginia Fink, A. Gary Dworkin, and an anonymous reviewer commented on a draft of the completed book manuscript. Each contributed a number of helpful insights on how to improve the book, and their time and efforts are much appreciated. Jon Lorence and Nestor Rodriguez supplied much-needed and appreciated suggestions and references for Chapter 6. The tedious work of tracking down references and carting books to and from the library was cheerfully supplied by a graduate assistant, Barbara Trepagnier, whose salary was paid by the Department of Sociology, University of Houston. The Public Policy Center, College of Social Sciences, University of Houston, provided funds in support of this project. Lonnie Anderson and Mary Jo Duncan, departmental secretaries, aided me in learning the intricacies of word processing and doing whatever work my inadequate skills could not handle. Without the assistance of my university and these individuals, my work would have been far less pleasant and much more difficult.

—Janet Saltzman Chafetz

CHAPTER ONE

Introduction

The central issues to be addressed in this book are two. *Given a system of female disadvantage* (gender stratification): (1) How do we explain its maintenance and reproduction? (2) How do we explain change in the level of gender inequality? The general answer to the first question will be that the reproduction of gender inequality is fundamentally rooted in the gender division of labor, both within and outside the family and household. Therefore, the answer to the second question must be sought by exploring those processes that contribute to changing the gender division of labor. I will argue throughout the book that women's collective opportunities to enhance their status, relative to men in their society, rest on their increasing access to resource-generating work. However, such access is largely controlled by elites who are male, and it changes primarily in response to forces outside the control of women.

People over the age of 40 who live in advanced industrial societies such as the United States are likely to perceive substantial differences between gender arrangements now and those of their youth. Things have changed, yet much has not. Many changes are more apparent than real. Virtually no scholar would argue that gender equality has been achieved in such nations. Most would agree that some reduction in gender stratification has occurred, although substantially disagreeing about how much and in what ways. In much of the rest of the world women's relative status has remained constant or actually declined in recent decades.

Despite the fact that most scholars with an interest in gender stratification are feminists, relatively little theoretical attention has been paid to the issue of gender system change. Why has female disadvantage declined in recent decades in highly industrialized nations? Why do so many inequities persist? Why has gender stratification increased in some other types of societies and at other times in history? Finally, there has been especially scant attention paid to the question of *how* change in either direction—increased or decreased inequality—comes about. These questions constitute the concerns that prompted this book. Therefore, the majority of attention will be directed toward answering the second question posed at the outset: How do we explain change in the level of female disadvantage?

When feminist activism reemerged in the late 1960s in the United States and elsewhere, many scholars and activists assumed that all societies were gender stratified ("patriarchal"). Others assumed a simple dichotomy between gender-stratified and equalitarian societies (a few, preliterate, technologically simple ones), while a few posited a long-lost, "golden era" of matriarchy (which has never been empirically documented). Since the mid-1970s, anthropologists and sociologists have recognized that gender inequality is a matter of degree. In some times and places, men and women have been nearly equal in their access to societal scarce resources. At the other extreme, there are and have been societies where women are vastly disadvantaged relative to men who are otherwise their social equals (in terms of social class, race/ethnicity, and so on). In no known case has a gender stratification system categorically disadvantaged men relative to women. Most societies fall along a continuum of gender inequality, between the extremes of equality and extensive female disadvantage.

The research upon which scholars have based their conclusion that such variation exists has been primarily cross-sectional. That is, a large number of different societies and communities, each examined at one point in their history, have been found to differ in their degree of gender inequality. Until recently, scholars rarely examined change over time in the gender stratification system of societies. In recent years, a number of case studies of change have been described, mostly concerning technologically simple or Third World societies and communities. The majority have been written by anthropologists and Women in Development specialists. A substantial sociological literature exists documenting specific kinds of gender-relevant changes over the past few decades in the United States and some other industrial nations, and historians have examined changes in Western nations, especially during the nineteenth century. The various descriptions are accompanied by a variety of explanations of the causes of such change. What is lacking in the gender literature is an *integrated*, systematic explanation of the conditions that tend to produce change in the degree of gender stratification. While the main goal of this book is to develop such a general theory, in order to understand social change, it is crucial to understand the powerful mechanisms that, in most times and places, work to perpetuate and reproduce the status quo. Part I of this book presents a general theory of stability in systems of gender stratification. Upon this basis, Part II develops a theory of change in the degree of gender inequality.

In this chapter I will first outline the major issues that theories of stability and change in gender systems should address. Next, some major theoretical perspectives that contemporary gender sociologists have developed will be briefly reviewed. These are partial theories in the sense that they tend to focus on one level of analysis while ignoring or giving short shrift to other levels. Finally, I will present and define the key theoretical constructs to be employed throughout the rest of the book in explicating an integrated theory of gender system stability and change.

GENERAL ISSUES

Levels of Analysis

In the preceding paragraph most gender theories were said to be partial in the sense that they focus largely on only one level of analysis. The first issue, therefore, concerns the meaning of the term "levels of analysis" and my reasons for maintaining that gender theory should integrate them.

Sociologists often distinguish between *micro* and *macro* processes, institutions, theories, and so on. Some have recently introduced *mezo* as an intermediate level. Although the distinction between levels is not precise, a general understanding exists concerning what social phenomena belong in each. The "micro level" refers to intrapsychic phenomena as they are affected by social and cultural factors and to face-to-face interactions between individuals, especially within dyads and small groups. For gender sociologists, the family constitutes the most important micro-level institution. At the other extreme, "macro level" typically refers to societywide (and for some theorists worldwide) phenomena, such as economic and political systems, class and gender stratification systems, and widely accepted ideologies and belief systems. Organizations, communities, and racial/ethnic groups are examples of "mezo-level" phenomena.

Distinctions between levels are fuzzy because they deeply interpenetrate one another. For instance, interaction within the family, ostensibly a micro phenomenon, is shaped by general social definitions and expectations, by economic opportunities, by legal constraints, by racial/ethnic and class phenomena—that is, by macro and mezo processes and structures. Conversely, macro and mezo structures are, in a basic sense, abstractions derived from repeated micro interactions. Almost all that sociologists *directly* observe are attributes, behaviors, and linguistic expressions of individuals. When these are recurrent and patterned—that is, when they reflect properties that, in a consistent fashion, emerge from interaction among group members— a label is assigned to them that is typically macro or mezo in nature. To say that a system of gender inequality exists is fundamentally another way of saying that, in millions of daily interactions between people, women are repeatedly and systematically disadvantaged and devalued relative to men, in a wide variety of different contexts.

Along with age, gender is and probably has always been the most salient marker of human beings in virtually all societies.

Gender appears to permeate all aspects of sociocultural, as well as individual, intrapsychic life. In short, gender shapes and is shaped by processes and structures at all three levels of analysis. Given this, along with the fundamental interrelatedness of the levels themselves, any theory that attempts to explain stability or change in systems of gender stratification must incorporate and integrate structures and processes at all levels. A major goal of gender theory in sociology should be the systematic explication of exactly how micro, mezo, and macro social processes and structures are linked to one another to produce gender systems.

The relative importance of phenomena at each level for perpetuating or changing a system of gender stratification is ultimately an empirical question. In the absence of theory that attempts to integrate the various partial theories, it is difficult to frame research that can help to determine relative importance. For instance, scholars whose frame of reference is primarily micro level often assume that childhood engenderment processes, combined with subsequent reinforcement, constitute the key variables that perpetuate gender systems and, therefore, the most important change targets. Macro theorists often assume that the position of women within a society's economic system constitutes the fundamental barrier to gender equality. Because different people usually work chiefly with only one perspective, it rarely occurs to anyone to frame a research project that explicitly addresses the *relative impact* of engenderment processes and economic opportunities on maintaining or changing the gender status quo. Typically, sociologists *apply* a specific theory, often ex post facto, to a set of findings, rather than testing alternative explanations of a phenomenon. Theory that explicitly incorporates processes at all levels alerts researchers to the need to gather data at all levels. The collection of a broader array of data, in turn, might permit researchers to determine the extent to which some variables explain more variance than others and are thus more central to the maintenance and/or change of gender systems.

In light of these considerations, the theory of stability and change developed in this book calls upon theories at all levels of analysis. One of my major goals is to integrate them in such a manner that future researchers can more readily test the relative explanatory power of the various parts. In the current paucity of such direct tests, I will be eclectic in the theoretical constructs included beyond those that may eventually prove empirically to be necessary.

Why a Theory of Stability?

The main goal of this book is to explicate a theory of change in systems of gender stratification. Why, then, is Part I devoted to the issue of how systems of gender inequality are maintained and reproduced? I begin with the assumption that all aspects of sociocultural life are *not* equal in their ability to stimulate a far-reaching type of social change. Gender stratification systems are interrelated with all other sociocultural institutions and processes. As a feminist, my commitment is to producing a specific kind of social change: a system of gender equality. The question then is this: What specific variables function in such a way that their change triggers larger-scale change in the gender system (in the desired direction)? Change in some variables may have minor impact on the larger system of gender stratification, especially relative to change in other variables. There is another way to say this: What change *targets* are most central, in the sense that, if they change, many other variables are likely to change in the desired direction as a result?

Partial theories presuppose that some type of variable indeed constitutes such a basic target or trigger mechanism (see Chafetz, 1988a). For instance, theories of childhood engenderment assume that systems of gender stratification are maintained primarily by the early transmission of gender norms and engendered personality attributes, which become deeply incorporated in the self-concepts of males and females and affect behaviors and choices throughout life. The implicit, if not explicit, conclusion is that if childhood engenderment processes are changed, other aspects of the gender system will change as a result (including women's roles and status in the economy). Conversely, theorists who argue that women's economic dependence on men is the root cause of their disadvantaged and devalued status perceive change in the structure of labor-force opportunities and rewards as the key target, which will trigger other kinds of changes (including, presumably, childhood engenderment). Those who assume that gender ideology is the key to women's disadvantage suggest yet a different kind of target: developing a feminist consciousness among a maximum number of women.

An integrated theory of the maintenance and reproduction of gender systems identifies potential key targets of change. It also suggests, subject to empirical testing, which are likely to be more central or important in triggering broader system change. Partial theories reflect the idiosyncratic preferences of the theorist, based largely on the personal and educational history of the individual. Integrated theory assumes that all of the partial theories may have important insights into the total process, but whether they do and how much importance are ultimately empirical questions rather than ones of personal predilection.

A theory of change presupposes one or a few specific central targets, which serve as triggering mechanisms, with broader change ramifications than other potential targets. *A theory of the maintenance and reproduction of gender systems* is *a theory of change targets*, because it identifies the critical variables that sustain the status quo and, therefore, must be changed. Conversely, a theory of change targets is also a theory of the maintenance of the status quo.

Issues for a Theory of Change

In the last section I argued that a theory of stability is a necessary basis for the identification of key targets of change. The first issue with which a theory of change must deal is *what* has to change first in order for broader system change to occur. There is no paucity of potential answers to this question in the existing literature (Chafetz, 1988a, chaps. 3, 5).

There is, however, a marked absence of theoretical work on *how* gender systems have, can, or might be changed. In considering this question of process, several specific issues emerge. Change in gender systems can occur in two directions: gender stratification can increase or decrease. One specific theoretical question that must be addressed is, therefore: Under what conditions do women experience an *increase* in their relative disadvantage? Most sociologists today reject conspiracy theories. The idea that a group of powerful men might get together for the express purpose of consciously devising ways to further oppress women is not one that is likely to gain much credence. To answer this question we must, therefore, look to the *unintentionally* negative consequences for women of certain types of economic, political, technological, demographic, ideological, or other kinds of social changes.

When change that *decreases* gender stratification is considered, two possibilities emerge. Just as in the case of increased gender inequality, a decrease may be the unintended result of broader social change. In both cases, theory should identify the most likely *sources* of unintentional change, and the *process* by which the gender system is affected by the broader system change(s). However, change in the direction of greater equality can also be the result of conscious intention. While conspiracy to further disadvantage women is unlikely, change-oriented activism by disadvantaged groups, such as women, has been widespread in the past 150 years. Women's movements have emerged in nations spread across the globe with the express intention of increasing gender equality (see Chafetz and Dworkin, 1986). This second avenue to change toward increased equality raises three more theoretical questions: (1) Under what conditions do intentional change efforts arise and grow? (2) What is the relationship between intentional change efforts and unintentional change in gender systems? (3) What explains the extent of gender system change in a specific place and historical era, especially the extent to which intentional change efforts succeed?

To answer the various theoretical questions outlined in this section, a variety of "partial" theories will be called upon. My goal is to integrate ideas from them into a coherent whole, which can serve as a springboard for systematic research. Preparatory to that, in the next section brief overviews of the major partial theoretical approaches developed and/or used by gender sociologists will be presented (for more detailed discussions, see Chafetz, 1988a).

AN OVERVIEW OF MAJOR ''PARTIAL'' THEORETICAL APPROACHES

Two very different kinds of theoretical approaches to gender issues exist, a difference that parallels a fundamental dichotomy within general social theory. On the one hand, there are theories that stress the *coercive* aspects of gender systems, especially on women. These theories focus on men's ability to maintain their advantages over women by dint of superior power resources: economic, political, ideological, and, to a much lesser extent, physical. On the other hand, there are theories that stress the *voluntaristic* aspects of gender systems by focusing on how women come to make choices that inadvertently contribute to their own disadvantage and devaluation. Each type, and especially the voluntaristic one, usually recognizes the importance of the other—at least in passing. Nonetheless, to date there has been little systematic integration of the two. The coercive theories tend to be macro and mezo level, and they stress structural variables. The voluntaristic theories are micro level and stress the processes by which males and females internalize gender-normative ways of being and behaving. In recent years there has been greater emphasis on structural variables among some micro theorists (and researchers), who thus end up either emphasizing the coercive or beginning the process of bridging the coercive-voluntaristic dichotomy. These few bridging theories, along with a handful of other eclectic theories, will not be discussed in this chapter. Rather, their ideas will be incorporated as needed throughout the rest of the book.

Coercive Theories

Marxist-Feminist Theory

The dominant theoretical approach that emphasizes the coercive aspect of gender systems is that developed by Marxist-feminists (e.g., Sacks, 1974; Eisenstein, 1979; Vogel, 1983; Hartmann, 1979, 1984). While they differ in particulars, Marxist-feminist scholars share a perspective that emphasizes the mutual supportiveness of systems of capitalism and patriarchy in sustaining female oppression. Unlike other Marxists, however, they perceive these two systems as analytically separate, with patriarchy predating capitalism. The demise of capitalism, while necessary, has not been, and cannot be, sufficient to eradicate female oppression (Sacks, 1974; Eisenstein, 1979).

Marxist-feminists argue that capitalism requires two things: (1) the production of surplus value (profit) by labor-force workers who were traditionally male, but are increasingly female as well, and (2) the maintenance and reproduction of a relatively docile labor force, the work accomplished primarily in the unpaid domestic sphere by women. Capitalism seeks inexpensive labor in order to maximize profits. For this reason, women are increasingly employed outside the home, but in low-wage jobs. By paying men more than women, capitalism helps to maintain women's dependence on men and, therefore, stabilizes the family and society (Eisenstein, 1979). Working-class men are "bought off" by the maintenance of patriarchy, which produces advantages for them (compared to women of their social class) in both the world of employment and at home. They are, therefore, less likely to challenge the capitalist system (Hartmann, 1984). As wives, women provide services to their husbands within the household, and in their role of household consumer they support capitalism as well. Furthermore, they maintain and reproduce the labor force without costing capitalism anything.

Because patriarchy is advantageous to capitalism, economic elites propound an ideology supportive of it. Patriarchal ideology is a major lynchpin in maintaining both the capitalistic system and female oppression. This ideology defines women primarily as mothers, which helps to maintain job segregation and low wages for women, as well as women's commitment to unpaid home and family labor (Eisenstein, 1979). Defined primarily as family breadwinners, men devote their energies to producing surplus value for capitalism.

In conclusion, Marxist-feminists argue that female oppression in the contemporary world is sustained by (1) the power of capitalists to protect and enhance their interests, which include low wages for women and unpaid domestic and familial work by women; (2) a patriarchal ideology, developed, supported, and disseminated by capitalists; and (3) the support of male members of the working class for the system of capitalist patriarchy because of the relative advantages—at home and in the labor force—that accrue to them. For Marxist-feminists, the elimination of female oppression requires the demise of both capitalism and patriarchy, as an ideology and as a form of husband-wife relationship. It requires that maintenance/social-reproduction work cease to be the specific province of women, and that women share equally with men the labor involved in production for exchange (Sacks, 1974).

Mezo-Structural Theory

Marxist-feminists are concerned primarily with total societies, that is, their analyses are macro level in focus. They argue that the economic structure of societies is the most important phenomenon for understanding female disadvantage in contemporary societies. Rosabeth Kanter's work (1977) exemplifies a small number of theories that look to organizational structure— or the mezo level—to understand why women are disadvantaged. Kanter focused on three variables to explain the work behaviors and motivations of people within an organization: (1) the extent to which employees are in a position from which further upward mobility is possible versus being "blocked"; (2) the extent to which employees possess the power necessary to accomplish their goals; and (3) the relative number of people in a work peer group of one's own "social type" (in this case women) versus some other "type" (men). Worker commitment and productivity, as well as future opportunities for mobility and empowerment, are enhanced when they are empowered, have mobility opportunity, and are not "tokens" (i.e., of a scarce type).

Kanter argues that regardless of personal attributes, including gender, people respond in a similar fashion when their employment situations are similar. However, men and women typically do not enjoy similar levels of opportunity and power, and in responsible, prestigious, and high-income jobs, it is women who are likely to be tokens. Therefore, the work behavior and commitment of women and men come to differ as a result of their different positions within an organization. In turn, the differential outcomes reinforce stereotypes about gender and work, helping to maintain a system that places men and women in different organizational positions.

In general, the mezo-structural approach argues that differences in men's and women's attitudes and behaviors are produced by the fact that they play different and unequal social roles. In turn, the differences produced in this way enhance the likelihood that roles will be distributed differentially on the basis of gender, to the continuing disadvantage of women (see also Miller et al., 1983; Kohn and Schooler, 1983; Epstein, 1988, chap. 4; Chafetz, 1984; Barron and Norris, 1976; Schur, 1984, pp. 38–42).

Micro-Structural Theory

The micro-structural approach focuses on how gender inequality generated at the mezo and macro levels produces inequality in direct male-female interactions, especially those between husbands and wives. The major theoretical orientation used for this type of explanation is Exchange Theory (e.g., Curtis, 1986; Parker and Parker, 1979; Chafetz, 1980).

Exchange Theory argues that, for relationships to continue over time in a stable fashion, partners must provide for one another approximately equal values. When one partner has access to superior resources needed or desired by the other, something must be offered in return to balance the exchange, if the relationship is to be sustained. The partner who has less access to valued resources balances the exchange by offering deference to, or compliance with, the requests of the provider of resources (Blau, 1964; Parker and Parker, 1979). In gender stratified societies, men typically have greater access to the scarce and valued resources upon which women—especially wives—are dependent. Therefore, women come to offer deference and compliance to men.

Curtis (1986) makes a distinction between economic and social exchange, arguing that the latter is characteristic of spousal exchanges. Economic exchange is based on an enforceable agreement between parties and relies upon an impersonal system of enforcement. The details of what is to be traded for what are specified at the time of the transaction. Social exchange consists of the exchange of gifts and favors and is implicit rather than explicit. It relies "on the debtor's good will at some time in the future" (Curtis, 1986, pp. 175–76). Trust in the individual is the basis of this type of exchange. Social exchange establishes a diffuse debt for the recipient of gifts and favors, one that can be called in at any later time. Moreover, it is never clear when the debt has been discharged. The result is that the person who accumulates social debts acquires interpersonal power, in a manner far exceeding the power of one who acquires only economic debts. Because of their extrafamilial roles, husbands are likely to acquire resources superior to those of their wives and are thus likely to be the ones who acquire such interpersonal power over their spouses.

Some other theorists begin by assuming that men possess superior power in their interactions with women, and these theorists explore the results of this power asymmetry in terms of the nature of male-female interactions. For instance, Fishman (1982) argues that men use their power to force women to work at interaction with them, in an unreciprocated fashion. The result is that "the definition of what is appropriate conversation becomes the man's choice. What part of the world interactants orient to, construct, and maintain the reality of, is his choice, not hers" (1982, p. 178; see also West and Zimmerman, 1977; Ferguson, 1980).

Voluntaristic Theories

The theories reviewed in the last section all emphasize that gender inequality is sustained primarily because men have the wherewithal to do so, regardless of what women may desire. Structured inequality, by which men acquire resources superior to those available to women, allow men to coerce or bribe women into the behaviors they desire. Yet in most times and places people do not perceive such coercion and women do not consciously think that they are more oppressed than men. The voluntaristic theories address how and why women come to want to do that which they would be constrained to do anyway. I am *not* suggesting that the voluntaristic theories "blame the victim" or assert that women are responsible for their own disadvantages. They all recognize that behind the processes upon which they focus there exists an inequitable gender system. Rather, they take that system as a given and go on to explore its system-maintaining social psychological effects, especially for women.

Feminist Neo-Freudian Theory

There are a number of scholars who have developed feminist versions of Freudian theory, but by far the most influential in sociology has been Nancy Chodorow's work (1978). She begins with the assertion that the division of labor places child rearing overwhelmingly in the hands of women. This fact has vastly different ramifications, depending on the sex of the child, especially in terms of the "relational capacities" of each gender. The fact that women "mother" (i.e., are primary caretakers and love objects of infants and young children) produces daughters, but not sons, who want to be primary child rearers. It does so because females come to value relationships with others as central to their lives; they spend their lives preoccupied with issues of love and symbiosis. This also affects the kinds of labor-force positions (those working with and helping people) women seek, if they even seek work outside the home. Conversely, the fact that women constitute the primary child rearers results in sons who are oriented to individuating themselves and establishing strong ego boundaries. Such sons become men who are fearful of women, misogynistic, and insistent upon male superiority and dominance. Males spend their lives denying connectedness with others, and seeking to succeed in the public sphere of life.

Chodorow traces in detail the different developmental processes that boys and girls undergo during the preoedipal and oedipal stages of childhood, contingent upon having a female as primary love object. It is not necessary to review them here. The important point is that, from this perspective, the results outlined above occur unconsciously. They result regardless of conscious efforts by adults to teach other behaviors and orientations to their children, simply from the different developmental tasks girls and boys confront, depending on whether their primary love object is of the same or the other gender. By becoming deeply embedded in the unconscious personality structure of each gender, the division of labor and gender inequality are, therefore, the automatic results and reinforcement mechanisms of the very system that produces them.

Socialization Theory

Unlike Neo-Freudian Theory, the various approaches that are termed "socialization" theories concentrate on the more conscious and purposive efforts of especially adults to teach children socially defined, gender-appropriate ways of thinking, feeling, and acting. This perspective includes both Symbolic Interaction Theory, as developed by sociologists, and Social Learning and Cognitive Development theories, which are primarily the province of psychologists. Although they differ in specifics, these theories focus on how, as children, people internalize socially defined norms for their gender and make gender a fundamental component of their self-concept. The key processes are rewards and punishments (both direct and vicarious) by "significant others" and, especially, modeling the behaviors of people with whom the child identifies (e.g., Cahill, 1983; Lever, 1976; Constantinople, 1979; Lewis and Weinraub, 1979). Aside from parents, peers are seen as fundamental to the process. In addition, media, games, sports, schools, clothing styles, language, and a host of other social and cultural phenomena are viewed as contributing to it.

The gender socialization approach assumes that adult behaviors, attitudes, priorities, and choices are to be understood largely as direct expressions of internal conceptions of the self. To the extent that the adult generation "successfully" socializes children to socially acceptable conceptions of gender, those children will mature into adults who will make choices consistent with their gendered self-identity. In this way, the gender system is replicated from one generation to the next.

Everyday Life Theory

The gender socialization theories focus on childhood engenderment processes. Another set of theories, reflecting Symbolic Interactionism, Ethnomethodology, and the Dramaturgical Approach, address the processes by which adults seek ongoing confirmation of their gendered self-identity and inadvertently recreate social definitions of gender itself. For instance, Goffman (1977) argues that both men and women require members of the other gender to validate their gender identities. They do this by giving one another opportunities to display those behaviors socially defined as specific to one gender. He then goes on to describe some concrete, typical examples from contemporary America, which permit that display. In general, Goffman argues that people are constantly involved in the work of producing gender differentiation while pursuing affirmation of their own sense of identity. For men, this quest entails demonstrations of strength and competence. However, for women it entails demonstrations of weakness, vulnerability, and ineptitude (see also Haavind, 1984).

More recently, West and Zimmerman (1987) extended Goffman's insights. In addition to recognizing that people organize their activities to express gender in normative ways, they argue that people are predisposed to perceive and interpret the behaviors of others as expressions of gender. They assert that virtually all activities can be, and usually are, assessed according to their gender content. Such behaviors and interpretations create and legitimate gender itself.

Summary

In this section several widely employed, partial theoretical approaches to issues of gender have been reviewed (for a more complete discussion of these and other feminist theories in sociology, see Chafetz, 1988a). The division into coercive and voluntaristic types should not be taken as hard and fast. Elements of each are found in both, but the emphasis varies. Likewise, divisions within each type are not hard and fast. The voluntaristic theories are all micro level in their primary focus. The coercive theories tend to be more mezo and macro level in focus but also include micro-level theories. What all the partial theories lack are *detailed and systematic* ties to other types and levels of analysis.

KEY THEORETICAL CONSTRUCTS

The various partial theories tend to develop their own vocabulary of concepts or theoretical constructs. Some of these concepts are shared by several theoretical approaches. However, they are frequently defined or used in ways that differ, subtly or substantially, from one perspective to another. In order to develop an integrated theory, clearly defined constructs are required that neither automatically or implicitly convey priority to any one partial theory nor preclude the insights provided by any of the theories. In addition, recall that one of my major purposes in proposing an integrated theory is to encourage systematic empirical testing of the relative importance of different variables representing diverse theoretical approaches. Many of the commonly used terms, such as "patriarchy," "female oppression," "sexism," and "gender roles," do not readily lend themselves to concrete operationalization, but do lend themselves to the problem of reification. They also tend to divert attention away from variability, making it difficult to explain the variation implied by change. In the remainder of this section the most central theoretical constructs to be employed throughout this book will be defined. Each time they are used, they are meant to be understood as defined here. Those used only in one section of the book will be defined at the point they are introduced.

Gender

Over the past twenty years there has been some confusion concerning the words "sex" and "gender." Sex has come generally to mean biological differences (at a minimum, chromosomal, hormonal, and morphological) between males and females. Gender has come to mean the socioculturally constructed components attached to each sex. The term "gender" will be used throughout this book to distinguish between males and females. By using this term I am conveying my opinion that, for the theoretical questions addressed here, biology does not constitute a relevant variable. Rather, it is sociocultural definitions of, and reactions to, biological sex that produce and reinforce inequality between males and females. Biological differences—whatever they may be—are basically constant across historical time and space. The phenomena of interest in this book are aspects of gender systems that can and have varied and, therefore, must be explicable by phenomena that vary.

Gender System

Gender permeates all aspects of sociocultural and personal life in most societies. The term "gender system" refers to the sociocultural status quo in stable systems, and to the status quo ante in changing systems, as it relates to gender. When the term "gender system" is used, it includes systems of gender stratification and differentiation, as well as the gender division of labor, gender social definitions, and power inequities between the genders, each of which will be defined shortly.

Gender Stratification

"Gender stratification" refers to the extent to which males and females who are otherwise social equals (e.g., in terms of age, social class, race/ethnicity, and religion) are equal in their access to the scarce and valued resources of their society. The higher the level of gender stratification, the greater the inequality between males and females as general categories. Empirically, gender stratification has always meant some degree of female disadvantage. In no known society has a system of gender stratification favored females, although systems approaching gender equality have been known to exist (see Chafetz, 1984, chap. 1).

The scarce and valued resources that may be unequally distributed by gender include at least the following: material goods, services provided by others, leisure, prestige-conferring roles, health care and nutrition, personal autonomy, physical safety, opportunities for psychic enrichment and gratification, and opportunities for education and training. Money is a generalized resource that may be used to acquire most, if not all, of the scarce values listed. Relative access to it by men and women is, therefore, an excellent indicator of gender stratification in modern, complex societies. However, access to these scarce values may be independent of access to money in many, especially simple, societies, and differential access to some may be acquired regardless of personal income even in modern, complex societies. Money is, therefore, insufficient as a sole indicator of gender stratification.

The degree of gender stratification is not uniform throughout a complex society. It varies by social class and possibly by race/ethnicity or religion (see Almquist, 1987; Blumberg, 1984). My focus will be primarily on the societal level. Undergirding all systems of stratification is inequality of power and authority, which are themselves scarce and valued resources. In this book, however, these are treated as separate constructs rather than as dimensions of gender stratification. They will be defined shortly. Three terms will be used as synonyms for gender stratification: degree of gender inequality, gender equality, and female disadvantage. In this book I am not attempting to explain the degree of gender stratification (see Chafetz, 1984, for such a discussion). Rather, some degree of female disadvantage is assumed and the questions raised concern what maintains and changes its level.

Gender Differentiation and Engenderment

Adult males and females in most societies differ from one another, *on the average*, in one or more of many types of traits: cognitive skills and style, basic personality, emotional expression, self-concept, priorities among various social roles, task competencies, preferences, aspirations, motivations, language usage, and so on. This does not mean that there are in fact sharp differences between all or most males, on the one hand, and females on the other. Rather, there are differences in categorical averages, which may be minor or quite substantial (see Chafetz, 1978, chap. 2). "Degree of gender differentiation" refers to the number of traits upon which males and females differ, and the extent to which the genders differ on those traits. The process by which males and females as individuals come to be gender differentiated is referred to as "engenderment." Major theoretical issues concern how engenderment occurs, and what the ramifications of gender differentiation are for gender system maintenance and change.

Gender differentiation does not, conceptually, imply inequality. To say that two categories differ does not logically convey that one is valued or rewarded more highly than the other. Empirically, however, gender differentiation and gender stratification are closely related to one another (Sanday, 1974). Another major theoretical and empirical issue, therefore, concerns the processes by which "different" becomes translated into "unequal." That is, how do female traits come to be devalued relative to male ones?

Related to this is the issue of how gender inequality produces gender differentiation.

The Gender Division of Labor

Sociologists and anthropologists have long recognized that in almost all societies men and women do at least somewhat different kinds of work. The tasks for which each gender is responsible may overlap or be totally segregated. Moreover, with a few very important exceptions, the precise nature of what constitutes men's tasks versus women's varies extensively cross-culturally. Such variability is especially noticeable when comparing societies with fundamentally different forms of technology and economic bases (e.g., foraging, pastoral, horticultural, agrarian, industrial). For instance, in one society or societal type (e.g., horticultural) women may be responsible for growing most or all of the food, while in another (e.g., most agrarian societies) men may be, and in yet others (e.g., rice-growing agrarian societies) both are involved in food growing but their specific tasks differ.

The important cross-cultural uniformities in the gender division of labor are two. First, women are uniformly more responsible than men for the work of child rearing, food preparation, and care of the domicile. Men's participation in such tasks ranges from none at all to substantial, while women's participation is uniformly high. Second, men always participate in a variety of the extradomestic tasks of their societies in those realms that in complex societies are differentiated as the economic, political, religious, educational, and other culture-producing spheres of activity. Women's participation in such work varies from practically none to substantial. The following generalization about the gender division of labor can, therefore, be made: *Women tend to shoulder the bulk of the responsibilities associated with children and the household, and vary in the extent to which they participate in other types of work; men are universally involved in extradomestic work tasks, and vary in the extent of their domestic and child-rearing work.* In general, the more men monopolize extradomestic work tasks, the more women monopolize the domestic/child-rearing tasks, and vice versa (Chafetz, 1984, pp. 58–60). The "gender division of labor" is, therefore, a variable: the extent to which the work activities of men and women in a society—both within and outside the household and family—are gender segregated. The general theoretical issues concern how the gender division of labor affects and is affected by gender inequality, and what causes it to change.

Just as gender differentiation does not logically imply inequality, neither does the gender division of labor. That men and women do different kinds of work is not tantamount to saying that the types of work done by one are superior in any fashion to the types done by the other. But again, empirically the two are indeed related. This raises another theoretical and empirical question: How do the tasks done by men come to be more highly valued and rewarded than those done by women?

Power and Authority

"Power" is defined in the Weberian sense as the ability of persons or groups to command compliance from other persons or groups, even in the face of opposition. Power requires resources superior to those controlled by compliers. Power wielders must have at their command something that compliers value and need or want and cannot otherwise get in sufficient quantity. It might be money or material goods, approval or love, services, safety from physical harm, or the like. Stated otherwise, power wielders have—or are at least thought by compliers to have—the wherewithal to bribe or punish those who come to comply with their demands. The degree to which some are able to extract compliance from others is a variable, one dependent upon the extent of the discrepancy between power-relevant resources available to different actors. *All systems of stratification are, by definition, systems of power inequity.* However, the bases (types of resources) and degree of the power inequity differ from one form of stratification to another, and from one society or time to another. *By definition a system of gender stratification implies superior power for men.* The theoretical and empirical issues are as follows: What constitutes the basis of superior male power and how do males acquire superior power resources? How do men use their power to maintain the status quo, and under what conditions is their relative power advantage over women reduced?

"Authority" is also defined in its Weberian sense as legitimated power. "Legitimacy" refers to a perception on the part of both the power wielder and the complier that the former has the right to make binding decisions or issue commands, and the latter, the moral obligation to comply with them. Stable power relations tend to be legitimated over time, but even if legitimacy is withdrawn, most often those in authority also possess superior power resources upon which to fall back. The legitimacy of male power is rooted in gender ideology, which will be discussed shortly. The theoretical issues concern both the processes by which male power is converted into authority and those that sometimes work to produce widespread rejection of the legitimacy of male power.

Power and authority exist at all levels of analysis. At the micro level, power exists when husbands, or any individual males, can extract compliance from wives or other women with whom they personally interact. When women feel duty-bound to comply with the requests or demands of male interaction partners, authority exists. Again, the main theoretical issues concern the bases for such power and authority: How is it that, as individuals, men possess greater power resources than women? How do women come to feel duty-bound to comply with the demands made by male interaction partners? There is also the theoretical question of how males use their micro-level power/authority to sustain their advantages, and the conditions under which women gain in their power resources at the micro level.

At the mezo and macro levels, power and authority accrue specifically to those who are incumbent in elite roles, particularly in dominant social institutions. In modern industrial societies, political and economic organizations constitute the dominant social institutions, with religious, educational, and other culture-producing organizations constituting secondary but nonetheless important ones. In gender-stratified societies, elite roles are and have been overwhelmingly filled by men. Elite incumbents may have other common attributes in given societies (e.g., racial, religious, class background), but their maleness is historically and cross-culturally nearly uniform. "Elite roles" are those whose incumbents control the resources of their organizations (including, in the political realm, those of entire nations). They serve as societal gatekeepers, distributing concrete opportunities and rewards. In some cases, elites may be free to overtly use particularistic criteria in awarding the resources and opportunities at their command. They may, therefore, unabashedly give preference to their "own kind"–which, among other attributes, includes maleness. Most often, however, especially in contemporary industrial societies, elites need to justify and legitimate the criteria upon which they distribute the socially valued rewards at their command. This brings us to the last set of theoretical constructs to be defined in this chapter, those that refer to definitional phenomena.

Gender Social Definitions

Social definitions are beliefs, values, stereotypes, and norms that are widely shared by societal members. They arise over time and at any given time reflect historical as well as contemporary phenomena. Elites play a disproportionately strong role in sustaining old and establishing new social definitions, in their roles as decision makers of powerful organizations and institutions. Because in gender-stratified societies elites have long been overwhelmingly male, social definitions are androcentric in content. That is, elite individuals define the world and are in a position to impose those definitions on others, from their own perspective. That perspective is masculine, regardless of what else it may also be. A gender-stratified society's conceptions of the true, good, important, valuable, beautiful (and their opposites) will necessarily reflect primarily the experiences and perceptions of its dominant male members, past and present (see Reskin, 1988). Moreover, while it is debatable whether elites *self-consciously* propound social definitions in order to sustain and legitimate their own privileged positions, one thing is probably not debatable: Elites rarely support social definitions that seriously challenge their status and perquisites. There are three kinds of social definitions of importance to understanding gender system maintenance and change: gender ideology, gender norms, and gender stereotypes. As a general principle, which will be elaborated in a later chapter, I suggest that all three types will support male advantage. All three will be conceptualized as varying on two general dimensions: the extent of societal consensus and the degree to which the genders are defined as different.

Ideologies are coherent belief systems that orient people to a particular way of understanding and assessing the world; provide a basis for evaluating events, behaviors, and other social phenomena; and suggest appropriate behavioral responses (or nonresponses) to them. Ideologies may be secular or religious in their basic justification or legitimation mechanisms. "Gender ideologies" are defined as belief systems that explain how and why males and females differ; specify on that basis different (and inevitably unequal) rights, responsibilities, restrictions, and rewards to each gender; and justify negative reactions to nonconformists. Gender ideologies are virtually always grounded in religious principles ("God said . . .") and/or conceptions of biologically inherent, "natural" sex differences. Because of this, clergy, and in the past few centuries scientists and physicians, have played major roles in the development and dissemination of gender ideologies. Gender ideologies vary in the extent to which they legitimate female disadvantage and in the degree to which societal members share a consensus about them.

Social norms are widely shared expectations of proper behavior for people who occupy given roles or statuses, or find themselves in specific settings or situations. They may or may not be codified into law. "Gender norms" refer to behavior that is expected of people on the basis of the status to which they are assigned, given their sexual biology. They vary over time and space in two ways: the level of consensus among societal members and the number of behaviors that are defined as gender-specific. To the extent that consensus is widespread concerning proper behavior for people on the basis of biological sex, the violation of gender norms will be perceived by others (of both genders) as deviant behavior and negatively sanctioned. The likelihood and severity of negative sanctions, in turn, reflect the strength of gender norms. While the specific content of gender norms varies widely over time and space, I suggest that the underlying themes are relatively constant in gender-stratified societies. Appropriate behavior for men is defined as that which helps to sustain their commitment to gender-specific work tasks and aids in their exercise of power/authority over women. For women, it is also that which helps to sustain commitment to their traditional work tasks as well as their deferential behavior toward men. In addition, in gender-stratified societies men will want to be sure of the paternity of their offspring, especially their sons. Such assurance requires restrictions on female sexuality. Gender norms for women – but not necessarily for men – will, therefore, include behaviors directly and indirectly related to chastity.

Earlier, gender differentiation was defined as *real* differences, on the average, between men and women. Regardless of the reality of such differences, there usually exist *beliefs* or perceptions that the genders are fundamentally different on a variety of traits. These beliefs constitute "gender stereotypes" when they are shared by collectivities. Societies vary in the number of stereotyped beliefs they hold concerning males and females and the degree of consensus among societal members concerning them. Again, the specifics undoubtedly vary across time and space, but I suggest that the same themes operative for gender norms underlie gender stereotypes in gender-stratified societies.

In some times and places, a substantial number of the members of a disadvantaged group come to question and subsequently reject dominant social definitions pertaining to them and the socially dominant group. They develop – usually in the process of social movement formation – a set of counterdefinitions. This counter set rejects the ideology and stereotypes as false and encourages people to violate norms that are redefined as vehicles for their oppression. In short, the legitimacy of the social definitional system is questioned and then withdrawn. It is typically replaced by a set of counterdefinitions that includes different norms, ideology, and possibly stereotypes. When women do this it is called "gender consciousness." It is the gender parallel of the proletariat class consciousness of which Marx spoke. No less than gender social definitions, gender consciousness is a social phenomenon. Both the rejection and the reconstitution are accomplished and shared by collectivities of women (along with some male allies). Variation exists in the number of people who share a gender consciousness and in the radicalness of the rejection and reconstitution. The theoretical issues that arise from this discussion of social definitions are these: How do social definitions normally function to sustain systems of gender stratification? Under what circumstances are they rejected and replaced by gender consciousness?

Micro-Definitional Power

The earlier discussion of power focused on resource power. The earlier discussion of definitional phenomena focused on the mezo and macro levels of widely shared ideologies, norms, and stereotypes. The two constructs intersect in the concept of "micro-definitional power." Although rooted in resource power, micro-definitional power is conceptually different. It is the power to define the reality or situation to which people who are interacting orient themselves; what is and is not worthy of notice and especially discussion; what is and is not "proper" behavior in the concrete interaction situation. In short, it is the ability to shape what transpires during an episode of interpersonal interaction. Because it is heavily rooted in resource power, which in turn accrues disproportionately to men in gender-stratified societies, micro-definitional power also tends to belong primarily to men in male-female interactions. If men possess greater power to orient interactions with women, especially their wives, in terms of their

own interests, values, beliefs, and perceptions, then the following theoretical questions arise: What is the impact of this kind of
power on the gender division of labor, especially within the family? Does male micro-definitional power help to substantially bolster gender social definitions and reduce the likelihood of the
development of gender consciousness?

CONCLUSION

In the process of defining the key theoretical constructs, a
number of theoretical issues were raised. These questions, which
will be addressed in the process of explicating the theory during
the next seven chapters, are listed below. It is important to
remember that the theory to be developed *presupposes* a system of
gender stratification but does not address how that comes into
existence. Causal and maintenance mechanisms may be very
different. Therefore, understanding one does not imply that the
other is understood. In turn, a system of gender stratification, *by
definition*, implies superior male power, specifically at the macro
level (i.e., at the same level of analysis as the construct "system of
gender stratification").

(1) How does engenderment occur? What role does gender
inequality play in this?

(2) How do the different gender traits become translated into
unequally valued traits?

(3) What are the major ramifications of engenderment for gender system maintenance and change?

(4) How does the gender division of labor affect the level of
gender stratification, and vice versa?

(5) How do male tasks come to be more highly valued and
rewarded than those done by females?

(6) What causes change in the gender division of labor?

(7) What are the resource bases of superior male power, specifically at the micro level, and how do males acquire greater access
to them than females? (The issue does not arise at the macro level

because superior male power is a given, by definition, in gender-stratified societies.)

(8) How do men use their power as individuals, and at the macro level as elites, to maintain the gender system?

(9) Under what conditions are men's relative power advantages over women, at both the micro and the macro levels, reduced?

(10) How is male power converted into authority, at both the micro and the macro levels?

(11) Under what conditions do women reject the legitimacy of male power?

(12) How do gender social definitions contribute to the maintenance of gender inequality?

(13) What causes the development of gender consciousness in rejection of gender social definitions?

(14) What is the effect of male micro-definitional power on the gender division of labor within the family?

(15) What is the relationship between male micro-definitional power and individual women's acceptance of gender social definitions versus their conversion to gender consciousness?

The questions enumerated above will not be answered in the order posed. Their answers will be a by-product of the achievement of the central goal: the explanation of how systems of gender inequality are maintained and changed. Answers to those questions that deal with stability will be summarized at the end of Part I, and those dealing with change, at the end of Chapter 8. Stability and change in gender systems are fundamentally macro-level issues. Nonetheless, it should be apparent from the discussion of key constructs, and the theoretical issues that emerged from that discussion, that no level of analysis can be absent from a full rendering of a theory designed to explain them.

Overview of the Book

The remaining nine chapters are divided into two separate parts. In Part I a theory of the central processes that maintain and reproduce systems of female disadvantage is presented. The coercive elements of system maintenance constitute the focus of Chapter 2, where the gender division of labor and male macro-level power emerge as the key explanatory constructs. Chapter 3 concentrates on the voluntaristic components of system maintenance, with an emphasis on gender social definitions and engenderment processes. In the fourth chapter the theoretical arguments developed in Chapters 2 and 3 are woven together into a general theory of how systems of gender stratification maintain themselves. In this model greater emphasis is placed on coercive than on voluntaristic phenomena. Throughout Part I the level of stability in gender systems is systematically exaggerated as a device to help clarify the fundamental processes that contribute to system maintenance.

Part I serves as a springboard to the much longer Part II, where gender system change constitutes the focus of attention. Chapter 5 is the bridge between the two discussions. I use the theory of stability to identify four potential change targets that could serve as triggering mechanisms for broad-scale gender system change. The conclusion of this chapter is that the best candidate to serve as the major independent variable in a theory of change is the gender division of labor. Chapter 6 explores unintentional change in gender systems resulting from demographic, economic, and to a lesser degree political phenomena. Change in both directions, increasing as well as decreasing gender stratification, is viewed primarily as the result of the impact of these macro-system phenomena on the nondomestic gender division of labor. The chapter concludes with a model of the process by which a decrease in women's access to resource-generating work affects other elements of the gender system (e.g., micro power relations, gender social definitions, engenderment) as gender inequality increases. Intentional change efforts to reduce female disadvantage constitute the topic of Chapter 7. The central focus of this chapter is on women's movements, but the efforts of male political elites to produce such change in some times and places are also explored. Change in the gender division of labor is defined as central for the emergence, growth, and success in goal achievement of women's movements. In Chapter 8, the ideas from Chapters 6 and 7 that pertain to the reduction of gender inequality are integrated into a general model. Macro-structural changes, primarily in economic, technological, and demographic variables, are shown to trigger a change in the gender division of labor, by which women increase their access to resource-generating work roles. In turn, this change leads to the emergence and growth of women's movements. Such movements, together with the unintended effects of changes in women's work roles, set in motion a series of other changes in the gender system, which reduce the level of gender inequality: changes in gender social definitions, engenderment, micro power relations, and so on. The integrated model is systemic and includes considerable feedback mechanisms. It would, therefore, appear that, once a process of change began, it would continue indefinitely until gender equality was reached. In Chapter 9 the reasons why this does not occur are explored. Attention is focused on why both women's movements and public and elite support for gender system change inexorably wane. In the Epilogue the issue of gender equality in elite, gatekeeping, resource- and opportunity-distributing, and social-definition-making roles is addressed, along with the prospects for future women's movement activism. Two very different scenarios for coming decades in the United States are presented.

PART I

Gender System Stability

CHAPTER TWO

The Coercive Bases of Gender Inequality

The issue for this and the next two chapters is this: Given a system of gender stratification, how is it maintained and reproduced over time? Based on the discussion of key theoretical constructs in the last chapter, I begin with two assumptions: (1) By definition, a system of gender stratification implies superior male power resources at the macro level; and (2) there exists a gender division of labor by which, at a minimum, women are more responsible than men for child rearing and other family and household work. These two concepts—gender power inequity and gender division of labor—constitute the starting point for an analysis of the coercive aspects of gender system maintenance, the topic of this chapter.

THE GENDER DIVISION OF LABOR AND RESOURCE POWER

In this section I explore how the gender division of labor recreates itself, first, through micro processes within the family, and, second, through mezo and macro processes outside the household.

Micro Processes

Any division of labor requires some degree of cooperation and interdependence among people who specialize in performing

only some of the tasks necessary to sustain life. In turn, interdependence implies exchange, whereby specialists swap goods
and services (or their equivalence in money) with one another, so
that all can achieve satisfaction of their needs and, to varying
degrees, their wants.

Since the inception of agrarian and pastoral forms of economic
production (if not in many technologically more simple, horticultural societies), there has been extensive, although variable
amounts of, gender stratification. In most gender-stratified societies the gender division of labor has disproportionately placed
males, relative to females, in work roles that generate direct access to material resources, including but not restricted to money.
In most agrarian and virtually all pastoral societies, men perform
the bulk of the labor involved in producing (as distinct from processing and preparing) food. Ownership and especially control
of the means and products of production often accrue to a relatively small minority of people, but that minority is overwhelmingly male (see Chafetz, 1984; Martin and Voorhies, 1975;
O'Kelly, 1980). Even if male producers do not control the means
and products of production, they typically receive some quantity
of produce and/or money for their labor (with the exception of
slaves, for whom this theory is not relevant). In industrial societies, at least until very recently, men have constituted the primary
paid labor force, and a minority of mostly men constitute those
economic (in capitalist societies) or political (in socialist ones)
elites who control the means and products of production. Where
women produce goods for other than household consumption,
or enter the paid labor force, in all of these types of societies the
tasks for which they are responsible usually generate fewer
resources than those for which men are responsible.

Because men constitute the primary extradomestic work force,
the remaining tasks that must be accomplished—those involved
in child rearing and family/household maintenance—become the
specialty of women. Women's first (but not necessarily only) priority has been to work within the domestic sphere. However, this
work produces no *direct* access to money or other material goods.
Women may garden, create handicrafts, or provide services for

nonfamilial members (e.g., take in boarders, laundry, others' children; see Strasser, 1982). In this way, they may earn money or produce material goods for sale or exchange. However, when they do these things, they are engaged in one of two types of work. To the extent that they produce goods for family consumption (food, clothes, or other handicrafts), they are not acquiring resources that can be exchanged with others outside the family. They are engaged in subsistence production, which garners few rewards and little social recognition in societies whose economies are structured around surplus production and exchange (see Chafetz, 1984; Blumberg, 1988). To the extent that they market the goods and services they produce, they are adding the equivalent of a labor-force job to their domestic work load. Especially in modern, highly industrialized societies, women increasingly do this in a more formal and obvious way by assuming positions in the paid labor force. However, when they do so, they do not abrogate responsibility for domestic and familial labor (for a review of the family division of labor literature, see Coleman, 1988). In dual-earner families today, women perform the overwhelming majority of such work, while their husbands contribute very little more to child rearing and especially to housework than the husbands of women who are not in the paid labor force (see Berch, 1982; Schwartz, 1980; Huber and Spitze, 1983; Coverman and Sheley, 1986; Berk and Berk, 1979).

In terms of Exchange Theory, men in these kinds of societies (that is, at least in agrarian, pastoral, and industrial ones) bring in to the family a substantial majority, and in some cases virtually all, of the material resources needed for the survival of its members. Depending on the nature of their work, and hence the level of material rewards, men also provide most of the resources necessary to acquire those things desired—although not necessarily needed—by family members. They can, therefore, establish a diffuse debt by providing for their wives the gifts of which Curtis (1986) speaks (see Chapter 1). To balance the exchange, women provide services to their husbands, in terms of caring for the husband's personal needs, those of other family members, and for the physical household and the objects it contains. But this exchange is unequal. As individuals, women are substantially dependent upon their husbands in order to acquire access to material goods, a dependence not readily replaced with people other than husbands in most gender-stratified societies. Even where government allowances can substitute for husbands in the provision of resources (e.g., family allowances, welfare), in most cases they are far lower than the average male wage and may be no higher than poverty level. However, given their substantially greater access to material resources, many men could purchase or barter for at least the necessary services provided by their wives. While the quality of men's lives might decline if their wives withdrew their services, this is less costly to them than the problems wives confront if material support by their husbands is lost or withdrawn (see Weitzman, 1987). Moreover, in most gender-stratified societies it is probably easier for a divorced man to remarry than his former wife, and in many societies men but not women have been able to marry additional spouses.

Recall the discussion of Exchange Theory in Chapter 1. When husbands provide more valued and scarce (i.e., more irreplaceable) resources to the family than do wives, wives balance the exchange by offering deference to, or compliance with, the demands of their spouses. The extent to which wives defer and comply is thus, at least in part, a function of the extent to which husbands contribute a disproportionate amount of the material resources brought into the family (see Blumberg, 1984, 1988). Where women bring in no such resources, their deference and compliance is greatest. The higher the ratio of women's material resource contribution to men's, the less the deference/compliance of wives to their husbands. In summary:

Proposition 2.1. The greater the gender division of labor concerning work roles to which accrue material resources (i.e., the macro division of labor), the greater the micro power resources available to husbands relative to their wives.

Proposition 2.2. The greater the micro power resources available to husbands relative to their wives, the more wives defer to, and comply with, the demands of their husbands.

England and Kilbourne (forthcoming) point to additional reasons why the exchange between husbands and wives is unequal when husbands provide most or all of the material resources and wives are full-time homemakers. First, the beneficiaries of women's services are children and other relatives, in addition to husbands. Therefore, men may fail to perceive or define some portion of women's work as part of an exchange between themselves and their wives. In addition, the investments wives make in their domestic work are more relation-specific and less liquid than those their husbands make in nondomestic work. Women learn how to please a specific person by cooking his favorite foods, caring for his possessions as he wants, and so on. Unlike most nondomestic work skills, these are not relevant to a different exchange partner. Even more general skills (e.g., cooking, cleaning) can only be transferred to another marriage. The skills developed through nondomestic work are usually transferable to other employers, and even to other types of occupations, and the resources earned are readily transferable to another marriage. Because women's skills are minimally liquid, they have a higher stake in maintaining a marriage than do their husbands, whose resource accumulation from work is far more liquid. As Willard Waller originally noted over half a century ago in his "principle of least interest," the spouse whose commitment to the relationship is least gains power over the more committed spouse (see Waller with Hill, 1951).

The extent to which the services wives provide are valued by their husbands undoubtedly varies cross-culturally and historically. In the nineteenth century, as industrialization removed from the home to the factory such work as basic food processing and candle, soap, cloth, and clothing manufacture, the perceived worth of women's domestic contributions probably declined. This perception has been further exacerbated in this century by the introduction of "labor-saving" appliances and convenience foods. Full-time homemakers today work as many hours as did their grandmothers (Strasser, 1982), but the nature of their labor is very different. Shopping and marketing, chauffeuring children and providing them "enrichment" (e.g., trips to museums, the zoo; the provision of lessons; adult-run clubs and sports such as

scouts), attending to the emotional needs and arranging the
social lives of family members, tending to the health and education of children, connecting the family to community agencies
and services – these have become central (and time-consuming)
tasks for modern homemakers in wealthy societies. They are
often important to the maintenance of high status or the achievement of upward mobility for the family. Nonetheless, they are
probably less often perceived by husbands, and possibly by
wives themselves, as "real work" than the kinds of physically
onerous labor women did 100 years ago. In turn, the exchange
between marital partners appears even more unbalanced and in
need of recompense by wives in wealthy modern nations than in
other times and places. Such recompense comes in the form of
deference by wives to husbands.

What do men do with their greater micro-level resource
power? Many things, but one that is particularly important to
sustaining the gender division of labor. Much of the work of
child rearing and care of family members and household is
highly repetitive, dull, dirty, and generally undesirable. Meals
must be produced several times each day. Clothes, dishes, and
other physical objects must be cleaned – some daily, others regularly, if less frequently. Sick people, babies, and toddlers must
have virtually all their physical needs met many times each day.
Other tasks are more fun, such as playing with older children
and shopping. Given their power, men are in a position to decide
to which, if any, of these tasks they will contribute. In the next
chapter the argument will be developed that men usually do not
need to use their power in order to avoid doing most familial and
domestic work. Nonetheless, regardless of their wives' wishes,
men typically have the wherewithal to not do work within the
home and family that they do not want to do. The result is three-
fold: (1) men do very little such work; (2) what they do is more
occasional than women's work (e.g., car care, bush trimming,
lawn care); and/or (3) they do tasks that are less dull, dirty, and
repetitive, and more intrinsically interesting (see Coleman, 1988;
Berk and Berk, 1979; Hood, 1983; Meissner, 1977).

Men can also use their superior micro power to determine

whether or not their wives supplement their work within the household with work outside. Again, they may not need to exercise power to keep women home or employed outside only part-time, a topic for the next chapter. The point here is that they possess the power to do so, regardless of their wives' wishes. If a man wishes to maintain a specific quantity and quality of services provided by his wife, given superior power, he can insist that she absent herself from economic activity for exchange or pay or assume only part-time work. If women absent themselves from work outside the home, the relative power advantage of husbands over their wives is maintained, because women continue to be dependent upon resources provided by their husbands. If women assume a commitment to work outside the home, given a system of gender stratification, as the Marxist-feminists argue, the material rewards they receive are likely to be less than those that accrue to their husbands. This discrepancy is especially true where wives assume part-time work outside the home. When women work outside the home the micro power of husbands is, therefore, reduced, but it is far from being eliminated (see Blumberg, 1984, 1988). Because of this, men are still able to impose upon their wives the overwhelming responsibility for familial and household work, by refusing to participate or doing so only minimally and according to their task preferences. When women work outside the home, they, therefore, assume a double workday, one not faced by their husbands.

The fact that wives employed outside the home maintain primary—if not overwhelming—responsibility for the family and household adversely affects their economic opportunities (Sacks, 1974; Hartmann, 1984; Schlegel, 1977; Curtis, 1986, p. 180). Women may select jobs at a lower pay or offering less opportunity in order to have more flexible hours or to be in close proximity to home or their children's school. It is unlikely that women can effectively compete with men for desirable and well-rewarded jobs if the former, but not the latter, are also responsible for another, substantial set of work tasks. Women's time, energy, and attention are divided where men's are not. Shelton and Firestone (1989) found, after controlling for a variety of work-relevant variables, that household labor time directly accounts for 8.2% of the gender pay gap in the United States. Relative to men, women will also have less time to devote to skill enhancement or to cooperative efforts such as unions that might enhance their rewards from extradomestic work. We have thus come full circle: An inequitable gender division of labor outside the home is maintained because the superior micro power resources it provides to husbands permit men either to keep women out of extra familial work or to keep them at a competitive disadvantage because of their mostly unshared domestic responsibilities.

Proposition 2.3. The greater the level of wifely compliance with the demands of husbands, the less husbands contribute to family and home work, and especially the less they contribute to the repetitive, onerous, and dull tasks of family and household labor.

Proposition 2.4. The less husbands contribute to family and household labor, the less wives are able to compete with men for resource-generating work outside the home, and, therefore, the greater the macro-level gender division of labor.

The argument to this point, as represented by the four propositions, can be depicted graphically as a process model of stability in the gender division of labor, as in Figure 2.1.

Macro and Mezo Processes

In the last section I argued that, starting with a macro-level division of labor that places material resources disproportionately in the hands of men, micro-level processes between husbands and wives reinforce that division of labor. Sooner or later most women become wives, especially in gender-stratified societies where women's opportunities to be economically self-sufficient are substantially limited. Given their heavy domestic responsibilities as wives (or as divorced mothers), most women will be especially unable to compete successfully for elite roles in dominant social institutions and major organizations. The macro power resources that accrue to political leaders, judges, high-level managers and officers of economic and professional organi-

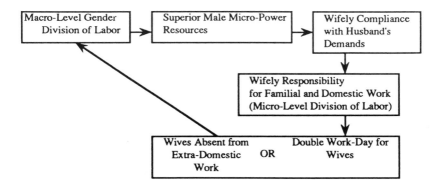

Figure 2.1. A Model of Stability in the Gender Division of Labor, with Focus on Micro-level Power Resources

zations, union officials, educational administrators, clergy, and so on will, therefore, accrue primarily—if not exclusively—to people who are male. That is, some men will get to decide who gains access to various educational and training opportunities, who gets to fill various social roles outside the family and home, and who is promoted into yet more highly rewarded positions.

For at least three different kinds of reasons, male elites will tend to favor other males over females in distributing opportunities and rewards. First, especially in situations of uncertainty or risk, elites think that they need to be able to personally trust their immediate subordinates and peers. Most organizations exist in an environment of chronic uncertainty. Trust is most easily extended to those most similar to oneself—those whose attitudes, priorities, values, and behaviors are presumed to be predictably similar to one's own (Kanter, 1977). Because elites are overwhelmingly male, one fundamental trait—but not the only one—on the basis of which they will feel similarity, hence trust, is maleness.

Second, given gender social definitions, especially gender stereotypes, elites are likely to believe that women lack the personal traits required to fill positions of responsibility, which are also positions to which accrue substantial rewards. Further, gender social definitions encourage elites to presuppose that women do not want responsible positions, and that women's priorities place family above extradomestic work. They are thus likely to question the level of commitment of women to work outside the home (Coser and Rokoff, 1982).

The third reason relates to the psychology of men as described by Chodorow (1978; see Chapter 1). She argues that, for males, major results of the fact that their primary love object is female are misogyny and the need to dominate women. If indeed these psychological propensities are widespread among men in gender-stratified societies, then male elites would presumably restrict women to low-level positions over which they clearly dominate. Recently, Coltrane (1988) systematically tested Chodorow's thesis on a sample of 90 nonindustrial societies. Multivariate analysis demonstrated that the more contact fathers have with their young children (that is, the lower the gender division of child-rearing labor), the more women are found in public decision-making roles (see also Sanday, 1981). Coltrane interpreted his findings as substantial support for Chodorow's thesis. Elite men may justify their exclusion of women from well-rewarded work roles with reference to social definitions, but a more basic cause may be a deep-seated, largely unconscious need to dominate and devalue women. For any or all of these reasons, male elites can be expected to distribute opportunities and rewards unequally on the basis of gender.

Proposition 2.5. The greater the macro and micro gender division of labor, the more frequently males are the incumbents of elite roles, to which macro power resources accrue.

Proposition 2.6. The more male the composition of a society's elite, the more the distribution of opportunities and rewards in nondomestic spheres will favor men over women.

The mezo-structural approach reviewed briefly in Chapter 1 argues that the characteristics of social roles create the characteristics of role incumbents. To the extent that men and women occupy different roles that are unequal in terms of power, opportunity, and rewards, their work behaviors and attitudes will come to differ (Kanter, 1977; see also Epstein, 1988; Miller et al., 1983; Nielsen, 1978). Productivity and work commitment are heightened among employees who occupy positions from which upward mobility is possible and who are empowered. Workers in dead-end jobs emphasize nonemployment aspects of their lives over their paid work, and value on-the-job sociability more than the work itself. Workers who are poorly paid, heavily supervised, and have no opportunity to advance are likely to change jobs frequently (Barron and Norris, 1976, p. 50). Moreover, in the case of women, when it becomes financially feasible, they may absent themselves entirely from extradomestic work that offers so few rewards (Glass, 1988). Lack of commitment, frequent job changes, and frequent absence from the labor force in turn create a negative impression on actual or potential employers, who are not likely to offer such workers a job or promotion entailing any responsibility or much by way of material rewards. Stuck in low-paid, heavily supervised jobs, women are, therefore, likely to respond in ways that maintain or exacerbate their disadvantaged position. In short, lack of opportunity and poor rewards breed more of the same for women in work roles outside the home.

Conversely, given greater opportunities, power, and rewards, men tend to develop attitudes and behaviors that expedite their future opportunities for gaining rewarding positions. Again, we have come full circle: An inequitable gender division of labor produces an elite overwhelmingly comprised of men, who distribute extradomestic roles in such a manner as to reproduce the inequitable gender division of labor.

Proposition 2.7. The more disadvantaged women are, relative to men, in acquiring resource-generating, extradomestic work roles, the more the work attitudes and behaviors developed at work will result in their continuing disadvantage in competition with men.

Proposition 2.8. Conversely, the more advantaged men are, relative to women, in acquiring resource-generating, extra-domestic work roles, the more the attitudes and behaviors developed at work will result in their continuing advantage in competition with women.

The argument presented in this section, as expressed in propositions 2.5–2.8, can be depicted as a process model of stability in the gender division of labor, as in Figure 2.2.

RESOURCE AND DEFINITIONAL POWER

In this section the relationship between male superiority in resource power and definitional power is explored, in both cases at the macro and the micro levels. As in the last section, the processes are circular, with power inequity functioning to sustain itself.

Micro Processes

In the last section I argued that one use to which men put their superior resource power at the micro level is to maintain a household division of labor that places most of the tasks, and especially the more onerous ones, in the hands of women. Men are also able to convert resource power into micro-definitional power (Ferguson, 1980; McConnell-Ginet, 1978; Fishman, 1982; West and Zimmerman, 1977; Sattel, 1976). A growing body of empirical literature from the United States supports this assertion. West

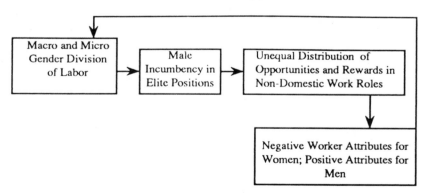

Figure 2.2. A Model of Stability in the Gender Division of Labor, with Focus on Macro/Mezo-Power Resources

and Zimmerman (1977) found that men interrupt women more frequently than vice versa, using interruptions to control the content and direction of a conversation. Other research has shown that women must actively work to gain the attention of male interaction partners, using questions and statements such as "Listen, this is interesting . . ." to preface their remarks (e.g., Fishman, 1982; Lakoff, 1975). Typically, men simply make assertions. Men less frequently than women support their conversational partner with little verbal and nonverbal forms of encouragement, such as "right," "uh huh," "then what happened?" and head-nodding and smiling (e.g., Fishman, 1982; Mayo and Henley, 1981; Henley, 1977). In all of these ways, men typically shape the definition of the situation and reality to which interaction partners orient themselves and the length and content of the interaction, all presumably in a direction that interests them.

Given micro-definitional power, how are men likely to use it? One very important way is for the reinforcement of their power and perquisites. To the extent that men profit from the gender system status quo, they are likely to use their definitional power to reinforce and legitimate gender social definitions. In turn, as I suggested in Chapter 1 and will discuss more fully in the next chapter, gender social definitions support the gender division of labor and female deference to men. The more isolated women are from others, the more likely that their male interaction partners' definitions will be the only ones available to them, and, therefore, the more likely those definitions will be accepted as valid and true. Full-time homemakers, especially in industrial societies where nuclear families are relatively isolated, are likely to be substantially deprived of contact with adults other than their husbands and some other women in the same, homemaking position. They are most prone to accepting their husbands' definitions of reality (see Bell and Newby, 1976). Women who work in traditionally female labor force jobs in direct interaction primarily with men in superordinate positions may also be especially vulnerable to this process (see Kanter's discussion of private secretaries, 1977).

Proposition 2.9. The greater the micro-level resource power advantage of men, the greater their micro-definitional power in interactions with women (especially their wives).

Proposition 2.10. The greater the micro-definitional power of men, and the more isolated from other adults their female interaction partners are, the more likely those women are to accept male definitions of reality.

To the extent that women accept the definitions of reality and proper behavior imposed by their male interaction partners, especially husbands, they are likely to choose to work at gender traditional tasks, including, especially, those involved in the household and for the family. At this point, the voluntaristic dimension of gender system maintenance begins to enter the picture, a dimension to be developed more fully in Chapter 3. To complete this discussion of the micro-level relationship between the two forms of power, it suffices to say that such choices by women, in turn, support male advantage in access to resource power. We have again come full circle.

Proposition 2.11. The more women accept male interaction partners' definitions of reality, the more likely they will be to choose to perform gender traditional tasks, especially, but not exclusively, within and for the household, thereby supporting the gender division of labor.

Proposition 2.12. The greater the gender division of labor, the greater men's resource power at both the macro and the micro levels.

A process model that summarizes how propositions 2.9–2.12 are related and function to sustain the status quo appears in Figure 2.3.

Mezo and Macro Processes

The gender division of labor provides most males with resource power superior to that of their wives. At the mezo and macro levels, however, only a relatively small proportion of men control substantial resource power, namely, those who fill elite

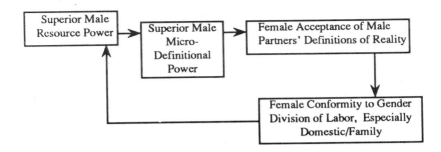

Figure 2.3. A Process Model of the Relationship Between Micro-Level Resource and Definitional Power

positions. By definition, elites have resource power superior to all others in their society, regardless of gender. As mentioned in Chapter 1, in gender-stratified societies, those who fill elite positions are overwhelmingly male. I also suggested that, just as men use resource power at the micro level to impose their definitions of reality on female interaction partners, at the mezo and macro levels elite men use their resource power to impose their definitions on members of organizations, communities, and societies (see also Epstein, 1988).

Gender social definitions reflect the experiences and perceptions of those who formulate, support, and impose them on societal members, that is, elite men (Sacks, 1974; Eisenstein, 1979; Vogel, 1983; Hartmann, 1984; Bennholdt-Thomsen, 1984; Ferguson, 1980; Schur, 1984). Contemplate Western societies' evaluation of regular meal cooking versus restaurant cooking; creation with clay or fabric versus creation with paint or stone. The first of both pairs have traditionally been done by women. In the case of routine cooking, it receives little prestige. Pottery and sewing are termed "crafts." The second of both pairs have traditionally been done by men. Chefs, painters, and sculptors (i.e., "artists") enjoy greater social recognition and rewards for their labors than do cooks and crafts workers, holding quality constant. These are minor examples of a very widespread phenomenon: the tendency for social definitions of the good, beautiful, true, and worthy to be skewed to the advantage of whatever tasks and traits are associated with maleness in a given gender-stratified society. If the feminine is thought to be nurturant and emotionally expressive, then instrumentality and cognitive rationality will be associated with maleness and be more highly valued socially. In short, maleness itself is more highly valued than femaleness, regardless of the specific attributes attached to each in a given time and place (see Schur, 1984).

Gender social definitions also define the gender division of labor as right and proper. As should be apparent by now, that division of labor profits men in general—and elite men most of all, if the Marxist-feminists are correct. In this way, gender social definitions serve to legitimate a system of unequal opportunities and rewards for men and women. Women receive fewer of both because, relative to men, they have attributes that make them less worthy, according to gender social definitions.

Proposition 2.13. The more male the composition of social elites, the more social definitions value highly those attributes associated with maleness.

Proposition 2.14. The more social definitions value highly those attributes associated with maleness, the greater the legitimacy of a gender-based system of unequal opportunities and rewards.

Proposition 2.15. The more social definitions value highly those attributes associated with maleness, the more devalued is the work done by women, simply because it is done primarily by women.

This last proposition constitutes part of the answer to a question often posed: Is work done by women devalued on that basis, or are women, because of power inequities, only permitted access to devalued work roles? Both appear true. The research literature concerning "comparable worth" or pay equity suggests that, all else being equal, the simple femaleness of an occupation lowers the rewards that accrue to it (for a review of this literature, see Acker, 1987). Given gender social definitions that devalue femaleness, when a form of work is done largely by women, it will be devalued on that basis (Reskin, 1988). However, the arguments made earlier also suggest that men can, and typically do, act in ways—at all levels—to keep women from assuming work roles that generate substantial power resources and are thus likely to be valued highly. Despite their differences, in both cases the fact that women do devalued and underrewarded work results from superior male power. It is the power to devalue that which women do, and/or to ensure that women do not gain access to work that is highly valued.

Finally, given both the devaluation of women's work and the legitimation of unequal opportunities and rewards on the basis of gender, the actual system of unequal distribution is strengthened. As noted earlier, such inequality creates processes that, in turn, reinforce the gender division of labor and male superiority in resource power.

Proposition 2.16. The greater the devaluation of women's work, and the legitimation of unequal opportunities and rewards based on gender, the greater the actual inequality in the distribution of opportunities and rewards, hence the greater the macro-level gender division of labor and male superiority in resource power.

A summary process model of this section, and propositions 2.12–2.16, appears in Figure 2.4.

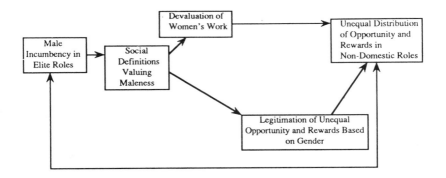

Figure 2.4. A Process Model of the Relationship Between Male Macro-Resource Power as Expressed Through Elite Incumbency, and Social Definitional Power

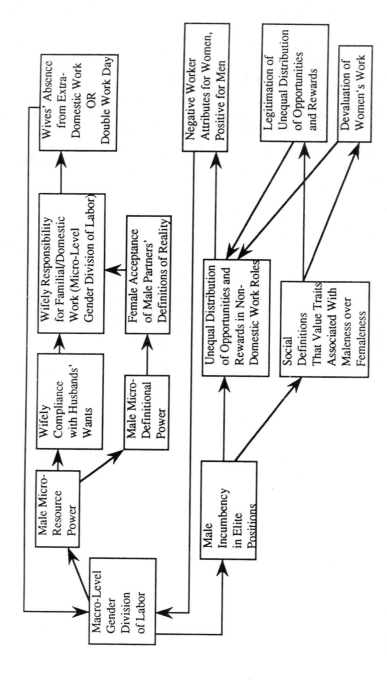

Figure 2.5. Summary Process Model of Coercive Aspects of Gender System Maintenance

CONCLUSION

Figures 2.1–2.4 are integrated in Figure 2.5, which summarizes the argument concerning the coercive bases of gender system maintenance in gender-stratified societies. The chart clearly depicts my central theoretical logic: Given a gender division of labor and superior male macro-level resource power, as reflected through male incumbency in elite positions, a set of processes result that function to sustain them, to the disadvantage of women. These processes are both "real" and definitional and pertain to all levels of analysis.

Unlike the charts, which represent process models, the propositions have been stated quantitatively, implying *variation* in the level of each theoretical construct. The lower the values on the variables, the less the system-maintaining effects would be. Stated otherwise, I have rather consistently overstated the power of each construct in its effects, an overstatement depicted in the process models. In reality, men rarely have unilateral or complete micro-level power—resource or definitional—over women, even over wives who earn no money at all. Elites do not have unilateral power to develop and disseminate social definitions or even usually to distribute opportunities and rewards according only to their own preferences. The overstatement is necessary to make clear the central theoretical logic of gender system maintenance. In reality, gender systems are probably never totally stable, because the constructs do not, in fact, take the extreme values implied in much of my discussion. This caveat applies as well to the next two chapters.

CHAPTER THREE

The Voluntaristic Bases of Gender System Inequality

The coercive aspects of gender system maintenance are not only rarely obvious to most societal members of either gender, in relatively stable systems they are more often potential than real, especially at the micro level. It is primarily during times of change that they become relatively clearly perceived. Once perceived, coercive forces are often more fully activated in response to resistance to the status quo. In stable systems, the reason that the coercive elements tend to be ill-perceived and often unused is that people of both genders tend to make choices that conform to the dictates of the gender system status quo. Stated otherwise, they make choices consistent with gender social definitions. In this chapter, I explore the processes that produce such choices, especially for women, for whom the choices function to maintain a disadvantaged status. It is scarcely problematic that most men make choices that reinforce their advantaged status, especially when those choices are also normative. Before getting to that, however, further discussion of the content and interrelatedness of the three types of gender social definitions, beyond that in the last two chapters, is necessary.

GENDER SOCIAL DEFINITIONS AND THE MAINTENANCE OF GENDER INEQUALITY

In Chapter 1 three types of gender social definitions were presented: gender ideology, norms, and stereotypes. Each can vary along two dimensions: the level of societal consensus and the extent to which gender differences are presumed. Gender ideologies serve to justify or legitimate differential — and unequal — rights, responsibilities, restrictions, and rewards for men and women by "explaining" how and why they differ. How many such distinctions are legitimated varies, but in gender-stratified societies there will be at least some. There will also be substantial, although rarely total, societal consensus about them (see Chafetz, 1984, chap. 2; Sanday, 1981). Gender norms specify particular behaviors for males and females. The number of such behaviors, as well as the degree of societal consensus about them, both vary. Nonetheless, in gender-stratified societies there will be at least some behaviors so designated by a substantial proportion of societal members. Likewise, gender stereotypes, or beliefs concerning gender differentiation, will vary in the number of traits and level of agreement among societal members. Nonetheless, the levels of neither dimension will approach zero.

Gender ideology constitutes the basis for the other two types of social definitions. Gender ideologies are more stable and resistant to change, because they are typically embedded in yet broader belief systems, especially religions, along with overarching sociopolitical and cultural views of the world. A given gender ideology is likely to be sufficiently flexible to survive minor to moderate changes in the specific content of gender norms and stereotypes. For instance, suppose a deity is believed to have mandated that men's primary obligation is to the world outside the home and family, and women's, to family members. Let us further suppose that a change in the economy occurs such that large numbers of women who were heretofore full-time homemakers and family caretakers must take paid employment outside the home in order for families to avoid poverty. This new situation requires change in gender norms concerning the exact nature of women's work obligations, and probably in gender stereotypes about women's abilities to perform various tasks. But the ideology need not change. Women continue to be seen as serving family members, but in a different context. Their orientation is still defined as familistic, regardless of where they actually labor, so the ideology can remain in tact.

Given gender stratification, gender ideologies typically legitimate male authority—micro and macro—over women. Especially the major world religions, which all arose in highly gender-stratified societies, explicitly grant men dominion over their wives and other family members (see Chafetz, 1984, chap. 2). Gender ideologies often enumerate rights specific to women, which are required for their protection precisely because men have substantially more power and authority (Curtis, 1986, p. 173). They typically define the outer boundaries of men's use of their power/authority, by proscribing or restricting certain male behaviors. Men may be restricted in their ability to divorce or at least be required to continue supporting the family financially; they may be restricted in their ability to physically chastise their wives or to deprive them too much of basic resources needed for survival. It is possible that the more disadvantaged their status, the more the gender ideology of a society will specify concrete, protective rights for women.

Gender ideologies are also likely to include certain rewards for women, courtesies offered as recompense for their otherwise devalued and disadvantaged status. Substantial deference to mothers or to virgins constitutes an example of this. Women are likely to be ideologically placed upon a pedestal, but only if they are "good women" who subscribe fully to gender social definitions. The pedestal is, in fact, a "gilded cage." Women's rewards are thus primarily symbolic in nature.

Gender ideologies are likely to specify responsibilities for men (e.g., service in the defense of nation or religion, extrareligious obligations such as in Orthodox Judaism) that are more onerous than those prescribed for women. However, these are recompensed with more concrete and meaningful rights and rewards than those offered to women, and include dominion over women.

Women are likely to face far more ideologically rooted restrictions on their behavior and demeanor than are men, especially concerning sexuality. Virtually all gender ideologies in substan-

tially gender-stratified societies insist on female chastity, probably to ensure that men are secure in the knowledge of paternity
of their own offspring (heirs). An implicit (if not explicit) sexual
double standard is widespread. To ensure chastity, all manner of
other restrictions are often imposed specifically on women (e.g.,
purdah, chaperoning, veiling, "modest" clothing and behavior).
Gender ideology, along with gender norms, usually also pre-
scribe heterosexuality, that is, restrict the expression of homosex-
ual and lesbian impulses. In restricting same-sex relationships,
the interdependence of the genders and the gender division of
labor that undergirds gender stratification are reinforced (Johnson, 1988; Rubin, 1975).

In general, gender ideologies provide for women fewer responsibilities and more restrictions than for men. Their rewards
are more symbolic, and their rights protective, while the rewards
and rights of men are more "real" and positive. Finally, men face
not only fewer restrictions but those they do have often address
the potential abuse of their rights and reward advantages (for a
similar analysis, see Polk and Stein, 1972; Chafetz, 1978, p. 51).

From the discussion of gender ideology it is clear that, to a
greater or lesser extent, specific gender norms are often incorporated directly into the ideology (e.g., proper sexual conduct,
especially for women; male courtesies toward women who behave "properly"; female obedience to men; and, often, specifics
about the gender division of labor). Most gender norms, however, are derived from general ideological principles and are
more responsive to contemporary conditions than are gender
ideologies, which tend to have deep historical roots. For instance,
gender ideology usually requires of women modesty, chastity,
and deference and obedience to men. In the nineteenth and most
of the twentieth centuries, especially in Anglo-Saxon and many
Western European societies, these requirements were rendered
into a detailed set of concrete norms focused on the concept of
"ladylike behavior." Regardless of the historical implications of
the word "lady," it was not class-specific (Fox, 1977, p. 809). This
fact is reflected in the absurd American euphemism for female
domestic workers: "cleaning ladies." Conformity to a set of spe-

cific behaviors and restrictions, expected in all contexts and throughout the life span, constituted the requisite for definition as a "nice girl" or "lady." Ladylike behavior entailed such things as restrictions on modes and times of travel (e.g., daylight unless accompanied by a man) and on entrance into certain places (e.g., not bars) (Fox, 1977), as well as dress norms and rules pertaining to how to sit, walk, and so on. In her analysis of the way men and women use the English language, Lakoff (1975) reached the conclusion that speaking norms for women center on ladylike or polite forms of communication. Voice tone and loudness, specific forms of sentence construction, the use of euphemism, the nonuse of slang and especially curse words, adjective choice, and politeness ("please," "thank you," "excuse me") are all involved in ladylike speech. In turn, these forms of language usage convey a lack of assertiveness and power. Men are rarely enjoined to be "gentlemen," and those described as such are usually from the upper reaches of the socioeconomic hierarchy ("gentleman janitor"?). Moreover, to be a gentleman does not imply deferential or powerless behavior.

Given at least a moderately strong gender ideology, gender norms will usually specify behaviors congruent with the gender division of labor. Women are enjoined to be committed mothers and homemakers whose first priority is the family. Moreover, they are to pursue, if any, only those work roles outside the domestic sphere that are gender-typed as female, and often represent extensions of women's wifely and motherly responsibilities (e.g., work with the young and sick; supportive work for male superordinates) (Bennholdt-Thomsen, 1984; Coser and Rokoff, 1982). Men are almost everywhere enjoined to be prepared to defend their societies in warfare and to be committed workers in nondomestic work roles.

Gender norms for women's work are probably less class-specific than for men's. Regardless of social class, all married women are expected to perform nurturant roles associated with the family, and, even if their families are wealthy enough to hire domestic servants, women have the responsibility for ensuring that domestic tasks are done and supervising those who do them. When women work outside the household, their jobs are probably less class-stratified than are men's. Traditionally, women have not been able to convert educational credentials into job opportunities in anything approaching the extent that men have. For instance, in the mid-1970s in the United States, college-educated women earned about the same wages as men with some high school but no diploma (U.S. Bureau of the Census, 1976, p. 413; see also Featherman and Hauser, 1976; Treiman and Hartmann, 1981). The situation is even more extreme in Japan (Cook and Hayashi, 1980; Condon, 1985). College-educated women have frequently filled the same clerical and low-level white-collar jobs as their high school-educated sisters in industrial societies. Distinctions between nurses with one year of post-high school training and those with bachelor's degrees or postgraduate education are often not made—except by the better educated nurses. In short, gender norms are of overriding importance for women. For men, they are likely to coexist equally with class norms. As Schur (1984) argues, for women, but not men, gender is the master status.

At least some gender norms are likely to be codified into law and given the full and formal weight of governmental sanction. In various times and places, unlike their male peers, women have been *legally* barred from certain types of work; executed for adultery; required to assume "modest" attire; placed under special restrictions concerning their political behaviors; permitted to attend only inferior, gender-segregated schools; barred from establishing their own legal residences; denied the opportunity to gain credit or even to control their own income. When gender norms gain the status of law, they take on a far more powerful role in reinforcing the gender system status quo than when they remain informal. They become part of the coercive forces that maintain the gender system. Conversely, in remaining silent about various customs, the legal system may also support normative definitions that reinforce gender inequality: foot-binding, widow suicide, educational and employment discrimination, sexual harassment, wife-beating, and marital rape. Laws—and their absence—may reflect informal gender norms, but just as clearly laws contribute to their creation and maintenance (see Epstein, 1988, chap. 6).

Gender ideology and norms contribute to the perception of gender differentiation, that is, to gender stereotypes. It is a small step from saying that people ought to behave in specific ways and have certain attributes to believing that most in fact do so. As suggested above, for women, but not men, gender constitutes a master status. Stereotypes in general, but especially those attaching to a master status, tend to prompt selective perception that focuses attention on phenomena supporting the stereotype and that screens out disconfirming evidence. Women are, therefore, likely to be "seen" as that which, given stereotypes about them, they are supposed to be (see Schur, 1984, pp. 28–29; also Kanter, 1977), thereby constantly providing "evidence" that the stereotypes are "true." Further, if the stereotypes are "true," then gender norms and ideology must be appropriate and true as well.

To summarize this discussion concerning the relationships between the three types of gender social definitions:

Proposition 3.1. The stronger the gender ideology on both dimensions, the stronger the gender norms on both.

Proposition 3.2. The stronger the gender ideology and gender norms on both dimensions, the stronger the gender stereotypes on both, and vice versa.

Finally, gender social definitions serve to justify and legitimate the gender division of labor at both the micro and macro levels, as well as unequal opportunities and rewards in nondomestic work roles and male incumbency in elite positions, as generally suggested in the last chapter (see also Reskin, 1988). They do this by "explaining" and "proving" that men and women are fundamentally different, that the attributes associated with maleness are more important to the world outside the family, and, therefore, that society "requires" these structural arrangements. In this way, gender social definitions contribute to the maintenance of the very structures of gender inequality that function, directly and indirectly, to produce them. Therefore, Propositions 2.14 and 2.16, which pertain to the unequal distribution of opportunities and rewards, can be restated as:

Proposition 3.3. The stronger the gender social definitions on both dimensions, the greater the inequality in the distribution of opportunities and rewards in nondomestic work roles.

To this can be added:

Proposition 3.4. The stronger the gender social definitions on both dimensions, the greater the male incumbency in elite positions, and vice versa.

Proposition 3.5. The stronger the gender social definitions on both dimensions, the greater the gender division of labor at both levels.

A summary process model incorporating Propositions 3.1–3.5 appears in Figure 3.1.

THE PROCESS OF ENGENDERMENT

The central voluntaristic process by which structured gender inequality is maintained is engenderment. Engenderment entails the internalization of gender social definitions, so that they become basic components of people's personalities, self-concepts, and perceptions and evaluations of reality and result in gender-differentiated adults. Acceptance of gender ideology as

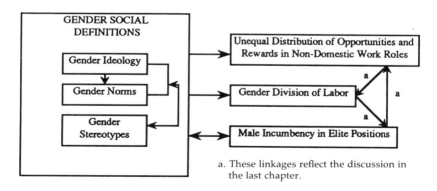

a. These linkages reflect the discussion in the last chapter.

Figure 3.1. A Process Model of Stability in Gender Social Definitions and Macro-Structural Gender Phenomena

the one true or correct model of maleness and femaleness, commitment to behaving in gender-normative ways as the only proper modes of behavior, and belief in the reality expressed by gender stereotypes constitute engenderment for people in a stable system of gender stratification. In other words, gender social definitions provide the specific content of gender differentiation in a given time and place. It is through gender social definitions that religion(s) and other general cultural beliefs and values, whose contents are specific to given times, places, and even to subpopulations within a society, have their major impact on gender system maintenance. Their impact is thus indirect, as mediated both by gender social definitions and by the variable level of engenderment in conformity to those definitions.

In this section several possible ways by which engenderment occurs, that is, by which gender differentiation emerges, will be reviewed. I leave to systematic empirical testing a more complete understanding of the relative contributions of each. It suffices to note that, in stable gender-stratified societies, each of the processes to be discussed functions to produce essentially the same results as the others.

The Socialization Perspective

The theoretical approaches that constitute the Socialization Perspective focus on variables that function to teach gender-"appropriate" characteristics, especially to children (see Chapter 1). Children are usually viewed as relatively active agents who are involved in seeking information about who they are and, given that, what forms of behavior are appropriate for them to exhibit. They are seen as immersed in a linguistic, behavioral, and symbolic gender sea from the moment of their birth on, as people in their environment constantly both emit gender and react to children on the basis of their gender. Children gradually develop the capacity to sort the world according to gender, to identify self as belonging to one category, and to take on the attributes socially assigned to that gender. Their identity thus becomes thoroughly gendered.

Three phenomena create this process: modeling, positive sanctions (rewards), and negative sanctions (punishments). Further, sanctions can be experienced directly, or they can be experienced vicariously as children observe responses—positive and negative—to the behavior of others. To the extent that children are surrounded by adults who are strongly gender differentiated, modeling and both positive and negative sanctions are likely to induce substantial engenderment in the younger generation. They will have an ample supply of potential models from which to choose, all exhibiting the same gender-specific traits. In contemporary nations, mass media often heavily expose children to further examples of models whose behavior is sharply gender differentiated. Moreover, especially parents, but also other relatives, neighbors, teachers, clergy, and so on, are likely to react in a consistent manner by defining and responding to behavior on the basis of children's gender. Room decor, clothing, hair styles, gifts, books, forms of play, and so on are likely to convey a constant and consistent gender content. Explicit rewards and punishments in response to children's behaviors and utterances will do likewise. Reactions to others that can be observed by children will further reinforce this process.

Analytically separate from, but obviously related to, the extent to which the adult generation is gender differentiated is the extent of the gender division of labor. When men and women perform sharply different work roles, they provide models that suggest to children the kinds of work they can and cannot do as adults, given their gender. Research has shown that at an early age children gender-type a wide range of work tasks—within and outside the home—and express preference for those associated with their own gender (e.g., see Beuf, 1974; Siegel, 1973; Tremaine, Schau, and Busch, 1982; Schlossberg and Goodman, 1971–72).

Finally, to the extent that gender social definitions are strong on both dimensions, the sanctioning aspect of the socialization process is likely to be strong. Where there is widespread agreement that the genders are and ought to be very different, adults and other children will ridicule, ostracize, and otherwise punish those defined as behaving in a gender-deviant fashion. They are also likely to admire and otherwise honor and reward those behaving in a gender-normative fashion. However, because gender normative behavior is perceived as "natural," "normal," and/or god-given, negative sanctions for transgression are more likely than the active rewarding of conformity.

Three propositions express this discussion of the socialization process:

Proposition 3.6. The greater the gender differentiation of the adult generation, the greater the gender differentiation of the subsequent generation, based on modeling and positive and negative sanctions.

Proposition 3.7. The greater the gender division of labor, the greater the gender differentiation based on modeling.

Proposition 3.8. The stronger the gender social definitions on both dimensions, the greater the gender differentiation based primarily on negative sanctions and, secondarily, on positive ones.

Other Engenderment Processes

Recall from both Chapters 1 and 2 the discussion of mezo-structural theory, and especially Kanter's work (1977; see also Miller et al., 1983). From this perspective, engenderment is an adult rather than a childhood process. It results from the fact that men and women do not play the same roles; they do not perform work that is equal in power, autonomy, opportunity, rewards, or other attributes. The result of that initial inequity is the development of traits that come to be differentiated along gender lines but are caused by the nature of the work each gender characteristically performs. This approach, like Proposition 3.7, links the gender division of labor to gender differentiation. Unlike Proposition 3.7, however, the mechanism is the unequal distribution of opportunities and rewards, not modeling.

Proposition 3.9. The greater the gender division of labor, the greater the gender differentiation based on the unequal distribution of opportunities and rewards.

Recall also the earlier discussion of Chodorow's theory (1978). She argues that the micro-level gender division of labor, by which women constitute the primary caretakers and love objects of infants and toddlers, produces radically different personality structures and work preferences for males and females (an argument cast in substantial question by the recent work of Jackson, 1989). Unlike the socialization processes, these are the automatic, not necessarily intended, and unconscious results of the gender division of labor. This theory suggests yet another variant of Proposition 3.7:

Proposition 3.10. The greater the micro-level gender division of labor, the greater the gender differentiation based on psychodynamics.

Figure 3.2 depicts Propositions 3.6–3.10 in a process model.

GENDER DIFFERENTIATION
AND GENDER SYSTEM MAINTENANCE

The topic for this chapter is the voluntaristic component of gender system maintenance. The final issue, then, concerns the relationship between gender differentiation and the choices women make that ultimately serve to perpetuate their disadvantaged status. Again, the focus is on women because there is little that is problematic about most men making choices that reproduce their advantaged status, especially when those choices are also socially normative. The various theories concerning childhood engenderment agree that a major component—conscious or not—of the feminine personality and self-identity is an orientation toward nurturant and caretaking roles; a caring for and sense of connnectedness with other individuals (in addition to already cited sources, see especially Gilligan, 1982). From this perspective, women, therefore, choose to place priority on family responsibilities, and, where financially possible, this priority often includes the choice to forgo other forms of work altogether.

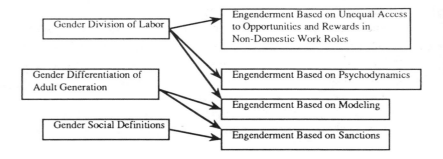

Figure 3.2. A Process Model of the Relationship Between Macro Variables and Engenderment

Indeed, Berk (1985) concludes from her study of the household division of labor that women choose to do various gender-traditional tasks as a means of expressing and reinforcing their feminine self-identity. When women assume nondomestic work roles, this perspective suggests that, when possible, they disproportionately choose those most involved with nurturance and helping others (e.g., teaching, nursing, social work, clerical jobs that involve personal services and emotional support for bosses). At a minimum, given the opportunity, women select jobs in the service sector, dealing with people, rather than in manufacturing, dealing with things. These kinds of work roles are indeed female dominated, at least in contemporary industrialized societies, and the overwhelming majority of women employed outside the home in industrial societies work in service jobs. Moreover, even if one ignores the presumably deep-seated, people orientation of women, they would choose to reproduce the gender division of labor on the basis of modeling other women during the engenderment process. A feminine self-concept expresses itself through the selection of roles socially defined as feminine, which designation, in turn, accrues to roles played primarily by women. Recall the earlier argument that female-dominated work roles are devalued and underrewarded, relative to other apparently equal work roles, simply because of their gender composition. Conformity to those traits and behaviors defined as specifically feminine encourages women to make choices that allow them to express their gendered self-concept through their work. In turn, these choices reproduce the gender division of labor and, therefore, women's resource disadvantage relative to men.

The choices women make on the basis of gender-differentiated feminine characteristics are not confined to work roles. Gender-differentiated femininity entails a variety of other attributes of cognitive style, emotional expression, language usage, behavior especially toward men, bodily comportment, and so on. The specific content of femininity reflects gender social definitions, which define it (and masculinity as well) in a given time and place and also for specific subpopulations of heterogeneous societies (e.g., class, race). As the Everyday Life Theory discussed in Chapter 1 suggests, people actively seek opportunities to display gender in their interactions with members of the other gender. They do so in order to confirm and reinforce their gendered self-concept. In displaying gender, that is, in behaving in gender-normative ways, people are constantly re-creating those very social definitions (West and Zimmerman, 1987) as well as gender differentiation. For women—at least in the United States until recently—the display of gender has entailed the display of vulnerability, weakness, and ineptitude to men. Women not only work to display traits that disadvantage themselves vis-à-vis men with whom they interact, they work to support men's performances of those very traits of masculinity that disadvantage women, such as demonstrations of strength and dominance (Goffman, 1977).

Recently, England and Kilbourne (forthcoming; see also England, forthcoming) cogently argued that gender differentiation is reflected in different orientations that men and women bring to an exchange relationship, which affects the distribution of power between them. Following Chodorow, Gilligan, and others, they claim that men tend to enter relationships with a "separative" ("S") orientation, which defines self-interested behavior as natural and de-emphasizes empathy. When in a bargaining situation, they will attempt to win. Women typically enter relationships with a "connective" ("C") orientation that emphasizes emotional relatedness. In bargaining situations, they take their partner's utility into equal account with their own. People (who are primarily women) who use a "C" orientation will be more altruistic than those (primarily men) who employ an "S" orientation; the latter will seek to win; the former, to compromise or defer in order to maintain harmony within the relationship. The result of exchanges between "S"- and "C"-oriented people is that the former will achieve their desires most often, regardless of power resources.

In the last chapter and the introduction to this one, I suggested that men frequently find that they need not use their power to enforce the gender system status quo. To the extent that engenderment results in substantial gender differentiation that is deepseated and lifelong (an as yet empirically undemonstrated phenomenon; see Epstein, 1988), feminine women make a variety of choices in their everyday life that make male use of power superfluous: to do the work they are "supposed" to do; to defer to and comply with the requests and demands of men; in short, to act in conformity with gender social definitions, as established primarily by elite men, which nonetheless serve the interests of virtually all men. In so doing, women further legitimate the entire system. Moreover, largely unused, the extent of male power remains unknown, possibly exaggerated, and certainly unchallenged. If it is exaggerated, women may comply with men's demands when they do not choose to and need not have done so. The exercise of power typically requires the expenditure of power resources, which may be less available for future use (Chafetz, 1980). If women permit men to "save" their power resources by voluntarily complying, even when they do not want to, men's potential power may actually increase. At the very least, it will not decrease. Unchallenged, power is in fact authority. Women come to legitimate the very system that disadvantages and devalues them.

Proposition 3.11. The greater the gender differentiation, the greater the micro- and macro-level gender division of labor.

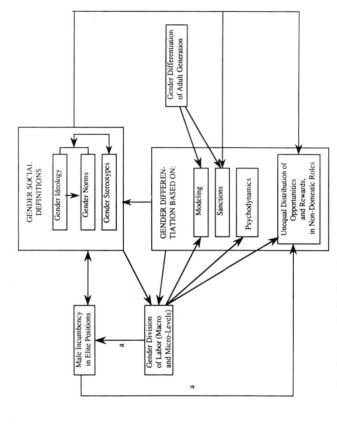

Figure 3.3. Summary Process Model of the Voluntaristic Aspects of Gender System Maintenance

a. These linkages are taken from Chapter 2

Proposition 3.12. The greater the gender differentiation, the stronger the gender social definitions on both dimensions.

CONCLUSION

Figure 3.3 incorporates all 12 propositions developed in this chapter, including those in the two previous figures, into a general process model of the voluntaristic aspects of gender system maintenance. The circular logic depicted in this chart can be summarized as follows. Elite roles are filled overwhelmingly by men because of the gender division of labor at both levels. Given that men occupy elite roles, gender social definitions tend to devalue femaleness and what women do, and value male attributes and work. The gender division of labor is also the single most important factor in producing gender differentiation, through its several effects on the engenderment process. Gender social definitions play an important role in producing gender differentiation as well, and provide much, if not all, of the concrete content of such differentiation in specific times and places. In turn, gender differentiation supports the gender division of labor at both levels and reinforces gender social definitions. Finally, we come full circle by noting that the gender division of labor (as discussed in the last chapter) and gender social definitions reinforce male elite incumbency.

The main point of this chapter should *not* be interpreted as victim blaming. Rather, the same macro resource power that men can potentially use coercively for gender system maintenance spawns a set of processes that mitigate their need to overtly employ resource power. These processes function to legitimate the gender system, to obscure its inequities, and to encourage women to make choices that inadvertently strengthen the very system that disadvantages and devalues them. Under these circumstances, women may perceive no more constraints than their male counterparts in a given society. However, were the voluntaristic components of the system to break down, the logic of the theory as presented in the last chapter suggests that men possess sufficient power resources—at the macro and micro levels—to maintain their advantaged position in the face of resistance by women. Given these considerations, the term "voluntaristic" should not be taken too literally. As Epstein (1988, p. 99) notes, "Individuals make choices, but institutional patterns shape the alternatives and make one choice more likely than another."

CHAPTER FOUR

An Integrated Theory of Stability in Systems of Gender Stratification

The theoretical constructs and their interrelationships that together explain how systems of gender inequality perpetuate themselves over time have now been presented. What remains to complete Part I is to systematically tie together the coercive and voluntaristic arguments into one integrated model of gender system stability. Figure 4.1 depicts that model. In this chart the main components of Figures 2.5 and 3.3 have been integrated but simplified by omitting and combining some elements. Also, some new linkages are presented in Figure 4.1, which became apparent only after the full logic of the model was simultaneously depicted.

Recall that the model presupposes a system of gender inequality rather than incorporating this as a theoretical construct. Nonetheless, several of the constructs used do represent aspects of the broader construct "gender stratification." Male micro resource power and incumbency in elite roles (i.e., macro-level resource power), along with the unequal distribution of opportunities and rewards in nondomestic roles, are in fact partial indicators of a general system of gender inequality. They are all crucial mechanisms for understanding the process by which gender systems maintain themselves. In a sense, by separating them a tautology results: male advantage produces male advantage. However, because my goal is to understand *how* that occurs, these parts of the more general phenomenon of gender inequity must be specified separately.

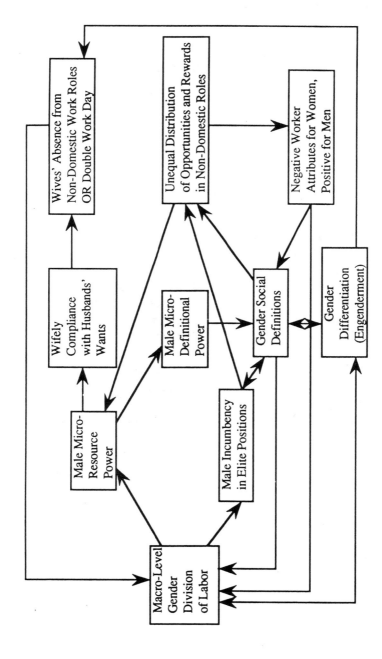

Figure 4.1. An Integrated Process Model of the Major Factors That Maintain and Reproduce Systems of Gender Stratification

Likewise, the construct "wives' absence from nondomestic work roles or double workday" is only an aspect of the more general construct "gender division of labor." It is, therefore, tautological to say that the former contributes to the latter, as I did in Chapter 2 and do again in Figure 4.1. Nonetheless, understanding the processes by which the gender division of labor within and outside the household is maintained requires that this aspect be separated from the more general construct.

In Chapter 2 discussions of micro and mezo/macro processes were separated. The result was that the unequal distribution of opportunities and rewards in nondomestic work roles was explained in one section (the mezo/macro) and male superiority in micro power resources in another. It is apparent that unequal distribution in the nondomestic arena is, in fact, a major reason why males possess superior micro power resources (the other reason being a gender division of labor that keeps women within the household altogether). Therefore, in Figure 4.1 a new link has been added, one between the unequal distribution of opportunities and rewards in nondomestic work and male micro resource power.

When Figures 2.5 and 3.3 are combined, two new linkages become obvious that were not possible before. To the extent that gender differentiation supports the gender division of labor, as argued in Chapter 3, it supports that aspect of the division of labor separated out as "wives' absence from nondomestic work or double workday." Also, to the extent that women (but not men) develop negative worker attributes in response to poor opportunities and rewards, the gender social definitional system that favors males is bolstered, especially the gender stereotypes concerning work-relevant traits. This linkage has been added to Figure 4.1 and can be stated as a new proposition:

Proposition 4.1. The more negative the worker attributes developed by women in response to poor opportunities and rewards, the stronger the gender social definitions on both dimensions, and especially the stronger the gender stereotypes.

In Chart 2.5 three specific aspects of the more general types of social definitional variables were depicted: devaluation of women's work; legitimation of unequal opportunities and rewards;

and higher value placed on traits of maleness compared to femaleness. In Figure 4.1 these are subsumed by the more general construct "gender social definitions." Likewise, the details within the constructs "gender social definitions" and "gender differentiation" presented in Figure 3.3 are omitted from Figure 4.1, along with the construct "gender differentiation of adult generation." For a summary model, the level of detail provided by such specifics is more confusing than helpful.

Finally, in Chapter 2 the argument was made that men use micro-definitional power to convince women of the appropriateness of the household division of labor. I noted in that context that this linkage introduces a voluntaristic element into the discussion of otherwise coercive phenomena. When combined with the material from Chapter 3, this linkage can be reconceptualized in a manner more consistent with the rest of the model. Men use their micro-definitional power to encourage women to accept gender social definitions, which include, but are not confined to, issues of the household division of labor. This is the linkage shown in Figure 4.1, while the earlier linkage is omitted. The effect on the gender division of labor of male micro-definitional power is now more indirect, but it nonetheless exists.

The central logic of Figure 4.1 can be summarized as follows. The macro-level gender division of labor is the fundamental phenomenon, out of which emerges superior male resource power at both the micro level of especially the family, and at the macro level through the virtual monopoly of elite roles by men. At the micro level, men use their superior resource power to maintain the gender division of labor and their definitional power to reinforce and legitimate gender social definitions, which in turn are created and disseminated by male elites at the mezo and macro levels. At all levels, men may use power for these purposes rather unconsciously or they may do so with substantial understanding of the ramifications of their behavior. The effects are the same regardless. Male elites also distribute concrete opportunities and rewards in nondomestic contexts, thereby setting in motion processes that function to sustain the gender division of labor at both levels. The gender division of labor and gender social definitions induce gender differentiation. In turn, gender-differentiated femininity encourages women to behave in ways that mitigate the need for men to use resource power to sustain the gender system status quo. Most women choose to be and do what they would otherwise be coerced by men into being and doing. In this way, the gender division of labor and superior male power are perpetuated and legitimated. The inequities involved at all levels of the system are largely hidden and unquestioned.

In granting primacy to the construct "gender division of labor," and arguing that women's economic dependency on men constitutes the major bulwark of systems of gender inequality, I am following the lead of a variety of structural theories developed by feminist scholars in recent years. Marxist-feminists such as Sacks (1974), Eisenstein (1979), and especially Vogel (1983) and Hartmann (1984) are quite explicit in arguing this. Other structural theories assert this position, although sometimes only implicitly (e.g., Lipman-Blumen, 1976; Holter, 1970; Blumberg, 1984; Curtis, 1986; Chafetz, 1984). Nor is a focus on the gender division of labor confined to macro/mezo-level theories that emphasize the coercive nature of gender system maintenance. Micro theories that focus on engenderment likewise emphasize the centrality of the gender division of labor, both for the engenderment process (e.g., Chodorow, 1978) and for providing a fundamental aspect of the specific content of the gender social definitions whose internalization constitute engenderment (see especially Coser, 1975, 1986).

A DIGRESSION ON PHYSICAL COERCION AND ON SEXUAL PREFERENCE

It may seem strange that, in a theory that incorporates a strong element of coercion, there is no mention of physical coercion. Clearly, men are, on the average, stronger and bigger than women. Mate-selection norms often reinforce this difference by specifying that, at the couple level, husbands should be larger than their wives (Goffman, 1977). Moreover, there is no paucity of evidence to demonstrate that men use their physical advantage by engaging in violence against women, especially rape and wife-beating. Nor is this evidence confined to the United States. Male violence against women has been widespread cross-culturally and historically. In addition, many scholars have viewed this as an important variable for explaining gender inequality (e.g., Collins, 1972, 1975; Brownmiller, 1975; Bullough, 1974). Why, then, has it been omitted?

As I suggested in an earlier work (Chafetz, 1984, p. 118), no one argues that other forms of social inequality are based on size or strength differences. Even slave systems, not to mention social class, status, and caste systems, are not said to be maintained because superordinates are bigger and stronger than subordinates. Why, then, should this argument be made for only one type of stratification, that based on gender? Superordinates do often use physical coercion and its threat to maintain a stratification system, as, for instance, owners over slaves. However, such coercion can often be committed without regard to physical strength, given modern weaponry.

Male *use* of their size and strength advantage, that is, the extent to which they physically abuse women, is highly variable across time and space. It is used most extensively under two conditions. First, where gender stratification is most extreme, men are most likely to be able to get away with abusing women without suffering serious—or any—penalty (see Blumberg, 1979, p. 132). The reasons for such abuse may or may not have anything to do with the behavior of women. Abuse may simply be cathartic—much as some people take out their frustrations by kicking the family dog. In this case, abuse is another indicator (but not a fundamental causal or maintenance mechanism) of gender inequality. Men can impose their physical will on women because political and legal elites do nothing to prevent it. In turn, that failure to act stems from women's disadvantaged and devalued status, as perpetuated precisely by elites.

Second, it is likely that some men resort to physical violence when they no longer possess authority or superior resource power at the micro level. That is, when systems of gender change in the direction of increased equality, a number of men will resist the loss of their advantages with the one type of power they have not lost: their greater physical strength (Blumberg, 1988). In this case, the abuse of women is an indicator of gender system change. Its potential to retard systemic change is limited, however, in modern nation-states where the *legitimate* use of physical coercion is monopolized by the state (Collins, 1975). Where women's status is increasing, the state is likely to more actively constrain and punish male violence against women. Imagine a society in which the physical abuse of women magically ceased but all other aspects of the gender system remained constant. Clearly, the level of gender inequality would not change. Now imagine a case in which the gender division of labor changed so that men and women received equal resources and shared elite roles equally. Women would quickly abandon abusive men and elites would consistently punish them. In light of these considerations, I do not think that physical coercion plays an important theoretical role in explaining gender system stability, which is not to deny its painful and widespread reality or its role in constraining some individual women.

Some feminist activists and scholars focus on compulsive heterosexuality, specifically for women, as a fundamental component of gender inequality. This, too, has largely been ignored, except for brief mention in the discussion of gender ideology. In many (but not all) gender-stratified societies, including the contemporary United States, extensive devaluation of, hostility toward, and discrimination against people whose sexual preference is directed to members of their own gender is only too obvious. However, where this is the case, male homosexuality is almost always the focus of greater antipathy than lesbianism. In fact, differential reaction to the two constitutes one of the relatively few instances in which social control of male behavior, and especially sexual behavior, is more extensive than the control of analogous female behavior. That male homosexuals are treated more harshly than lesbians is precisely the result of the greater value placed on maleness. Failure to conform to normative definitions of masculinity, which include heterosexuality every bit as much as, if not more than, do definitions of femininity, is especially threatening to the status quo because it comes from those whose gender status is privileged. For the same reason, "feminine" boys ("sissies") are typically treated far more harshly than "masculine" girls ("tomboys").

Lesbians and lesbian behavior are often largely ignored, if the women otherwise conform to gender social norms (see Faderman, 1989; Adam, 1987, pp. 4–5, 9–10). Where married women are romantically and sensually tied to other women, as may have been fairly widespread in the Victorian era, no significant attention is paid to their behavior or relationships (Faderman, 1989; Smith-Rosenberg, 1989). Where single women live together quietly as "closeted" lesbians, they also attract relatively little social attention or condemnation. Unlike women, after a certain age the very act of living alone with another man is taken as evidence of male homosexuality and condemned. It is when lesbians choose to live openly as competent women, independent of male support and control (as most do today), that their sexual preference becomes a major social issue. It is less their sexuality, and more their blatant disregard for gender norms prescribing dependence on, service to, and deference toward men, that causes the hostile reaction (Adam, 1987, pp. 9–10). This nonconformity they share with other independent women who, centuries ago were branded as witches, decades ago as mentally ill, and, more recently, regardless of sexual preference, as lesbian (see Chafetz and Dworkin, 1986, chap. 1).

The maintenance of a system of gender stratification probably requires that most people live in heterosexually based families in order to sustain the gender division of labor upon which the system rests. However, this requirement does not require compulsive heterosexuality of all members or exclusive heterosexuality of any. Societies have certainly varied in their reactions toward those who are sexually oriented to members of their own gender, in part or whole. In ancient Athens nonexclusive male homosexuality was not only accepted but praised. It was a highly gender-stratified society. I conclude that while issues pertaining to sexual orientation are not irrelevant to gender system maintenance, compulsive and exclusive heterosexuality, especially for women, are not fundamental bulwarks of such systems. When lesbianism is tied to rebellion against the gender system it is harshly sanctioned, especially when such rebellion is collective and political rather than simply a relatively rare, individual phenomenon. But it is against the rebellion, not the sexual preference per se, that societal reaction is most strongly directed, and such rebellion can take many forms other than lesbianism.

SOME THEORETICAL QUESTIONS ANSWERED

In the conclusion of Chapter 1, 15 theoretical questions were listed that would be addressed in the process of developing a general theory of stability and change in systems of gender stratification. Based on the theory of stability formulated in this part of the book, it is possible to provide answers for many of those questions.

Question 1 asked how engenderment occurs and what role gender inequality plays in the process by which gender differentiation results. First and foremost, gender differentiation results from the gender division of labor, which in turn is strengthened by gender differentiation. Gender social definitions also contribute to, and are in turn strengthened by, gender differentiation. Recall that gender inequality is presupposed in this model. Two variables that directly reflect it are those that pertain to resource power, at the micro level as it accrues primarily to husbands, and at the macro level as it accrues to elites who are overwhelmingly male. Both of these are indirectly linked to gender differentiation, primarily through their effects on gender social definitions. Also, because both forms of resource power are crucially, although indirectly, important for maintaining the gender division of labor, they are further linked to gender differentiation.

Question two asked how gender-differentiated traits come to be unequally valued on the basis of gender. Question 5 was the same except that it referred to work tasks. The answer to both of these is to be found in the linkage between gender differentiation and gender social definitions, which are produced, disseminated, and even imposed on societal members primarily by elites who are male. I argued that elites tend to foster social definitions that value male traits and work more highly than female as one way of maintaining their own privileged status. Women's work is devalued, at least in part because women do it. In part also, elites are able to reserve more valued tasks for men, whom they trust and value more highly than women. Finally, gender social definitions, which evaluate the genders unequally, are both directly involved in the engenderment process and provide the concrete content that is transmitted during that process.

Part of question 3 asked what the major ramifications are of gender differentiation for gender system maintenance. In the last chapter three major ramifications were discussed. First, gender differentiation defines femininity in ways that prompt women to choose those tasks traditional for their gender, thereby supporting the gender division of labor that underpins their disadvantages. Second, gender-differentiated traits and behaviors result in women choosing to behave deferentially toward men, and in men displaying dominance behaviors toward women, thereby bolstering power inequities. Such choices result from an apparently lifelong need to constantly reaffirm their self-concepts, which are thoroughly gendered. Finally, because women make choices to conform to gender social definitions and the gender division of labor, the entire gender system is legitimated and further strengthened. Men need rarely exercise their power in order to maintain the status quo. If male power is more apparent than real, women are unlikely to recognize that fact.

The fourth question asked how the gender division of labor is related to gender stratification. The two are related in a number of ways. One aspect of the gender division of labor is male incumbency in elite positions. This, in itself, is a major component of gender inequality. Moreover, male elites tend to favor males over females in the distribution of opportunities and rewards outside the household, another form of inequality. In

turn, distributional inequality results indirectly in further support for the gender division of labor. The gender division of labor
provides for men as individuals resource power superior to that of
women, in particular their wives, which constitutes yet another
aspect of gender inequality. Men are then able to use that power
to reinforce the gender division of labor by ensuring that their
wives continue to perform most domestic and familial tasks.

Question 7 asked how males acquire greater resource power
than females at the micro level. I suggested that their power
advantage emerges primarily from the fact that men supply substantially more (if not all) of those material resources needed
(and wanted) by family members than do their wives. Moreover,
those resources are less readily replaceable than the services
provided by wives. To balance the exchange with their husbands,
wives comply with and defer to their requests/demands. The
underpinning of male micro resource power is, therefore, the
macro-level gender division of labor and the inequitable distribution of opportunities and rewards that accrue to work roles outside the family on the basis of gender.

Question 8 asked how men use their resource power, at both
levels, to maintain the gender system. At the micro level, they use
it chiefly in two ways. First, they maintain the household division
of labor, which disadvantages women who seek work roles outside the household and reconfirms the gender division of labor
generally. Second, they convert their resource power into micro-
definitional power. In turn, this kind of power is used to reinforce gender social definitions and to encourage women to
choose to perform gender-traditional work. In this way, question
15 is also answered. It asked how male micro-definitional power
affects the gender division of labor within the family. In supporting the gender division of labor, men support the inequitable distribution of resources that gives them greater micro-level
resource power in the first place. At the mezo and macro levels,
male elites use their resource power as gatekeepers to distribute
opportunities and rewards preferentially to other men. They also
use their power to create and disseminate social definitions that
favor men. Such definitions indirectly serve to support the gen-

der system by legitimating unequal opportunities and rewards, and by affecting the engenderment process.

Question 10 asked how male power becomes authority. The answer is to be found primarily in social definitional phenomena and their relationship to gender differentiation. Gender ideology "explains" why the genders should be treated differently and, in fact, unequally. These explanations find concrete form in gender norms and stereotypes. To a considerable degree, engenderment entails the internalization of gender social definitions. Women, therefore, choose to behave in ways that support a system that demands deference and compliance from them toward men. Those choices legitimate male power, rendering it into authority.

Question 12 addressed the contribution of gender social definitions to gender system maintenance. They do so by legitimating unequal opportunities and rewards on the basis of gender for work done outside the home and family; by affecting the engenderment process and, therefore, the choices women make to behave in ways that bolster the system; and by directly supporting the gender division of labor.

The last question concerned the relationship between male micro-definitional power and women's acceptance of gender social definitions. In Chapter 2 the argument was made that, to the extent that women are relatively isolated from other adults, as homemakers often are, the definitions of reality offered by their husbands (and in some instances by male bosses) go unchallenged. Gender social definitions advantage men. Therefore, it is likely that most men accept them rather fully. As a result, the micro-definitional power that accrues to men will most likely be used in a manner that is congruent with gender social definitions, thereby further reinforcing the propriety of those definitions for women.

CONCLUSION

At the conclusion of Chapter 2 a caveat was introduced. I pointed out that the process models exaggerate male power and system stability in order to clearly identify the central processes that explain gender system stability. This caveat remains important for putting into proper perspective the arguments in this (and the last) chapter. But regardless of that caveat, systems of gender stratification are highly resistant to substantial change toward greater equality. In fact, systems of gender inequality are probably more resistant to change than other types of inequitable distribution systems (e.g., class, racial, ethnic, and religious stratification systems), both because they are deeply embedded in the personality and self-concept of almost all societal members and because fully half the population derives substantial, tangible benefits from them. Gender systems are structured so as to automatically reproduce themselves. The processes by which this reproduction occurs operate at all levels of analysis, from the intrapsychic to the interactional to the organizational and societal. Moreover, these processes occur in all institutional arenas of social life: within the family, the economy, polity, educational and religious institutions, and other culture-producing and disseminating ones. None of this should be interpreted as denying that there are individuals even in the most stable systems of gender who refuse to conform to the dictates of the system. However, as long as they remain isolated individuals, they are defined, treated, and controlled as "deviants" and their rebellion will lack system-level ramifications (see Schur, 1984; Chafetz and Dworkin, 1986, chap. 1).

Anyone who has lived through the last three decades as an adult, especially in a highly industrialized nation such as the United States, has experienced what at least appears to be substantial change in the gender system. To some observers the proverbial glass is half empty, to others half full. That is, some see gender system change as more apparent than real, while other observers perceive substantial change. In large measure, what people perceive is a question of the yardstick they use to assess change. I am inclined to see both substantial change in the gender systems of at least advanced industrial societies and much that presents an old system in a somewhat new guise. What has and has not changed, why some things have and others have not changed, and how whatever change has occurred has happened are central issues for Part II. They will be addressed in the process of explicating a general theory of change in systems of gender inequality: its targets, processes, and limits.

PART II

Gender System Change

CHAPTER FIVE

Decreasing Gender Inequality: Central Targets

In Chapter 1 I suggested that a theory that explains stability in systems of gender stratification *is* a theory of change targets, and vice versa. If those processes and structures that constitute the most fundamental supports of the status quo change, then the entire system should change. This logic emanates from the fact that all parts of the system are interrelated, although many are related to one another only indirectly. However, some aspects of the system are more likely than others to be capable of initiating a fundamental change process, that is, to serve as triggering mechanisms.

In the last chapter, and specifically in Figure 4.1, an integrated model was presented that specifies the major theoretical constructs, and their relationships to one another, required to explain how systems of gender inequality perpetuate themselves. That model of stability suggests four potential key targets, whose change (in the "right" direction) would presumably serve to reduce the level of gender stratification: the gender division of labor, superior male resource power, gender social definitions, and gender differentiation as it emerges from the engenderment process. In this chapter each of these will be examined in terms of their *theoretical* suitability to serve as a key change target.

In the world of social movement activism, targets are often chosen because they appear to be more amenable to change in *practical* terms than alternative targets, given the resources and opportunities available to movement organizations and activists. That is, it may be more feasible—or at least appear so—to attack certain practices and structures than others. However, practical targets are not necessarily theoretically important ones. It may be that less important supports to the status quo are more vulnerable to change, but their change would at best have a minor impact on the larger system of gender inequality. Nonetheless, because success is more likely, activists may indeed focus their energies on attacking the more vulnerable, if less important, targets.

For both intellectual and practical reasons, it is important to understand which targets are theoretically most central, even if they are difficult to change in practical terms. In strictly intellectual terms, such understanding is necessary for the development of a theory of the change process. In practical terms, a better understanding of how change occurs, which necessitates an understanding of key change targets, could contribute to the development by activists of better strategies to produce change. In the remainder of this chapter the four potential change targets identified above will be assessed in the reverse order specified, beginning with the engenderment process and ending with the gender division of labor.

THE ENGENDERMENT PROCESS

Since the late 1960s, when feminism reemerged as a major social movement in a number of nations, many activists and scholars have focused attention on the process by which children are taught to conform to gender norms and to become gender-differentiated adults. Two very different theoretical approaches have been discussed that, at least implicitly, suggest that childhood engenderment constitutes the chief barrier to change and, therefore, the fundamental change target: the Neo-Freudian, best represented by Chodorow's work, and the Socialization Approach, which includes scholars working on the basis of Symbolic Interactionist, Social Learning, Cognitive Developmental, and Social Role theories. Activists have focused on "sexism" in children's movies, advertisements, TV programs, texts, and other books; on the gender-related practices of schoolteachers, counselors, and administrators; on gender-specific toys, games, clothing, and room decor; and, of course, on gender-related parental behaviors.

Regardless of specific theoretical orientation or activist goal, these various approaches share a fundamental assumption. They assume that the engenderment that occurs chiefly during childhood has strong, lifelong effects on most people. As discussed in Chapter 3, the engenderment process presumably results in a thoroughly gendered self-identity, which actively seeks reconfirmation, and strongly affects the behaviors and choices males and females make, throughout their lives.

There is a fundamental logical flaw in focusing on childhood engenderment as a key change target. If it is as powerful as often suggested, gender system change is impossible to explain or produce. How could a significant number of adults—the chief agents of childhood socialization—emerge who could challenge, reject, or change gender norms? In other words, who would change the child socializers? To change such deeply rooted, engendered self-concepts and personality structures as implied by this approach would appear to require substantial, individual-level therapy. Why and how would the therapists change? How could a large proportion of an adult generation receive such therapy and why would they seek it? Clearly, in the past three decades change has occurred in many gender norms, in aspects of gender-relevant behaviors, and probably in the self-concepts of millions of people, especially younger women in advanced industrial societies. These changes will be discussed further in a later chapter. In this context it suffices to note that such change is inexplicable if one assumes that childhood engenderment casts the personalities and self-concepts of males and females in steel for life. In addition, there is no empirical evidence that demonstrates a direct linkage between childhood engenderment and adult behavior (see Epstein, 1988, chap. 4).

The mezo-structural approach, discussed in several places in Part I, suggests that behavior is best understood in terms of the opportunities, requirements, and rewards of the concrete roles and situations in which people find themselves (see also Stockard, Van De Kragt, and Dodge, 1988). The psychological and social psychological attributes that people bring to situations set the *outer boundaries* of their behavioral repertoire. Engenderment undoubtedly contributes to setting those outer boundaries. But to say that does not imply that people simply emit attributes of personality and personal psychology in each context in which they may find themselves. Men placed in primary parental roles will usually act in a nurturant fashion, as the role requires, although perhaps somewhat differently than will most women (e.g., Risman, 1987). Women placed in roles requiring dominance or displays of authority will usually act appropriately, although perhaps in a manner somewhat different than that of most men in the same roles (see, for instance, Zimmer's study of women prison guards, 1987; Martin's study of women police officers, 1980; Martin et al., concerning physicians in training, 1988).

Rebecca, Hefner, and Oleshansky (1976; see also Katz, 1979) suggest yet another reason to question an approach that places too much emphasis on childhood engenderment. Because human beings are capable of learning vicariously by observing others, they learn many things that are socially defined as inappropriate for them to express. Children observe how members of the other gender are taught to behave. Their *potential* behavioral repertoire, therefore, includes behaviors deemed inappropriate to their own gender, in a stable gender system. Given changes in the types of behaviors permitted or required on the basis of gender, people already possess the wherewithal to express the new behaviors. In other words, in a stable gender system, much of our potential behavioral repertoire is never expressed because it is socially deviant for our gender. Those repressed behaviors can be readily called up if social conditions and definitions change, however.

I conclude that childhood engenderment is not a theoretically meaningful, fundamental change target. In stable gender systems it probably does function to substantially bolster the system, as discussed in Chapter 3. However, if childhood engenderment is granted too much explanatory power, gender system change is impossible to produce or explain. Adults in large numbers can and have behaved in ways that in their youth were defined as gender inappropriate or deviant. As adults change, the engenderment process of subsequent generations undoubtedly changes. But an approach that emphasizes childhood engenderment cannot inform us about how systemic change might or does begin (for similar critiques, see also Lorber et al., 1981; Risman, 1987).

GENDER SOCIAL DEFINITIONS

Many anthropologists and sociologists have implicitly, if not explicitly, focused attention primarily on gender social definitions, and especially gender ideology, as the key change target (e.g., Sanday, 1981; Ortner, 1974; Giele, 1978; Kessler and McKenna, 1978; Schur, 1984). From its very inception, the modern feminist movement emphasized "consciousness-raising" as a major movement goal. Consciousness-raising can be seen as another term for the process by which traditional gender social definitions are rejected and replaced by a new gender consciousness. The creation of women's studies programs and mass circulation feminist media also reflect this activist orientation. So too does the feminist rejection of sexist language usage and religious ideas. Underlying this choice of target is the assumption that a set of social definitions that devalues women and feminine attributes, and positively values masculine attributes and men, constitutes the primary structure out of which other gender inequities grow. It is fundamentally a Weberian or philosophically idealistic approach to understanding gender systems.

There is no question that gender social definitions play an important role in the maintenance of systems of gender stratification. They provide the specific content learned during the process of engenderment, contribute directly to that process, and legitimate the entire structure of differentiation and inequality. Nonetheless, I do not think that they constitute a fundamental change target. Rather, the argument will be made in a later chapter that the development of gender consciousness (i.e., the rejection of gender social definitions) among a substantial number of people—especially women—constitutes a critically important *means* for the achievement of intentional gender system change toward greater equality.

My model of gender system stability includes both coercive and voluntaristic elements. The importance of social definitional phenomena is largely confined to the voluntaristic part of the model; *even in the absence of the voluntaristic components, in gender-stratified societies men collectively and individually possess sufficiently greater resource power than women to ensure gender system maintenance.* Women may cease to legitimate men's authority, but if men continue to possess superior resource power, they can coerce heretofore voluntary behavior from women. Women may seek nontraditional work roles, but if male elites refuse to make opportunities available, women will probably not acquire them. In short, gender consciousness cannot serve as a trigger to broad-scale gender system change.

In fact, I suggest that gender social definitions change largely *in response* to change in the gender division of labor and male power advantage. The Theory of Cognitive Dissonance posits that, confronted with a reality that contradicts their attitudes or beliefs, people are inclined to reduce the uncomfortable feeling of dissonance caused by the contradiction by altering their perceptions, attitudes, and beliefs. From this perspective, as well as that of the Italian social theorist Vilfredo Pareto, belief systems are largely developed ex post facto to justify and "explain" our behavior rather than constituting the a priori explanation of that behavior. Research by Hertz (1986) on marital partners, both of whom have demanding corporate careers, supports this contention. She found that they developed an ideology of equality within the family and household as a result of the fact that both had equally demanding careers. Hertz explicitly documents the absence of a preexisting "feminist ideology" (i.e., gender consciousness in my terminology). Conversely, Kandiyoti (1988, pp. 282–83) demonstrates how Third World women often fight social definitional changes that are ostensibly to their advantage, because the old system at least provided security and stability while the new one provides few if any "empowering alternatives."

I conclude that, to the extent that women and/or men in substantial numbers begin to behave in ways that traditional gender definitions define as inappropriate, those definitions will begin to change to justify the new reality. Therefore, definitional change cannot serve as a theoretically central target that is capable of triggering broader system change.

MALE POWER ADVANTAGE AND THE GENDER DIVISION OF LABOR

Superior male resource power and the gender division of labor are inextricably intertwined. Given resource power advantages, men shape the division of labor—within and outside the family—to their advantage. Given the gender division of labor, men acquire superior resource power—within and outside the family. Analytically, superior male power is a component, in fact, the most fundamental component, of systems of gender stratification. It is ultimately because males possess superior power that the gender division of labor, *which conceptually does not imply inequality,* empirically produces female disadvantage. Power permits men to devalue women's work and assign devalued work to women. The ultimate target of change is, therefore, the demise of male superiority in resource power. However, in saying this I am simply using other words to say that the ultimate target is the demise of gender stratification. Therefore, it would be tautological to focus on superior male power as the target to trigger change in the gender stratification system. Logically, the appropriate theoretical target that could serve as a trigger to produce such a broad systemic change must thus be the gender division of labor.

At least three components of the gender division of labor would have to change substantially to trigger broad systemic change. While all three are closely interconnected, two are especially intertwined, and it is impossible to assign priority to either of these two on theoretical grounds. The two are those most stressed by Marxist-feminist scholars (as well as many others), although they use a different vocabulary than mine: (1) the gender division of labor within the household and family and (2) gender inequality in the level of rewards attached to extradomestic work roles. Within the household husbands and wives must bear equal responsibility for, and expend about the same amount of time and effort on, all duties if women are to be able to compete equally with men for other work roles that generate resources. Spousal equality of domestic work does not preclude the overall reduction in the quantity of such work by having others, including children, paid workers, or purchased services provide more of it. Whatever amount remains to be done or supervised by the adults must be divided equally. Also, equality does not necessitate that both share all tasks. It merely requires that both devote the same amount of work time, attention, and energy to domestic work. In extradomestic work roles, it is also not the case that men and women must do the same work. Rather, they must perform work that is equally rewarded and provides equal opportunity for future rewards. It is the resources that flow from work roles, not the nature of the tasks per se, that provide access to other valued social resources, including power. The most basic resource that work roles can generate is money or exchangeable material goods. But this is not the only type of resource. Skills and knowledge, prestige, and alliances with nonkin are also resources that can accrue to a work role. In many technologically and socially simple foraging and horticultural societies, men and women do different work but are not substantially unequal in the resources gained from their work (see Chafetz, 1984, chap. 3; Bourguignon, 1980; Martin and Voorhies, 1975). Nonetheless, in more complex, including almost all contemporary, societies, it is likely that as long as men and women perform gender-specific work outside the household, their labor will not be rewarded equally. In practical terms, therefore, the gender segregation of extradomestic work will probably have to be largely eliminated in order to equalize access to resources and end gender stratification.

Public policy can potentially address issues of equity in extradomestic work roles. It is very unlikely, however, that legislation will have much impact on the household division of labor. Therefore, while there is no theoretical reason to grant priority to one of these two types of change in the gender division of labor, there is a practical one. In the United States and many other nations, legislation during the past two to three decades has rendered illegal gender discrimination in hiring, pay, and promotion (see Michel, 1985, concerning comparable legislation in France; Steinberg and Cook, 1988, pp. 316–18 for a review of it in nine Western, industrial nations). The active seeking of qualified women to fill jobs traditionally held by men has also been mandated by a policy of affirmative action in the United States. In some states in the United States a policy of equal pay for comparable worth has been enacted for state employees and is being sought by activists as a general employment policy to eliminate inequities based solely on the gender composition of occupations. These policies have certainly not (yet) resulted in gender equality in extradomestic work roles. It is arguable, however, that, at least for younger cohorts of women, they have contributed to a reduction of unequal opportunity and pay (a contention to be documented in the next chapter). It is likely that women will be able to increase their resources earned from extradomestic work before it is possible for them to exercise enough power to substantially reduce inequities in the household division of labor. One result of this disparity is probably the relatively high divorce rate experienced by dual-earner couples (see Spitze and South, 1985; Wilkie, 1988, p. 155). Whether divorced or married, however, women experience a double workday, which is, at best, a necessary way station to equality. But even equality in the provision of familial resources does not gain for wives equal micro-level power with their husbands (although such wives are substantially more equal than wives who do not share in provision). Blumberg (1984) argues that male macro power functions to "discount" the ability of wives to convert economic resources into micro-level power. Gender social definitions, and often political, legal, and other macro-structural gender inequities, produce this discounting. Therefore, in the absence of macro-level changes produced by elites, even equality in extradomestic work roles is unlikely to result in full equality in the domestic division of labor.

The third component of the gender division of labor is precisely male incumbency in elite roles. In Part I this construct was treated as separate from the gender division of labor. In fact, elite incumbency incorporates both male macro power advantages and the gender division of labor. By definition, elites control macro-level power resources. They also perform work that, in gender-stratified societies, is largely or totally male segregated. Although they constitute only a small fraction of a society's population — even of its male population — elites play a key role in sustaining gender inequality, as discussed in Part I. Women could theoretically gain equality with men on the basis of the other two aspects of the gender division of labor without gaining significant access to elite roles (although my theory of stability suggests that this is unlikely). Even if they did, as long as men constitute most of a society's law- and policymakers, gatekeepers, distributors of rewards and opportunities, and creators of social definitions, they are in a position to rather readily reverse gains made by women. It is conceivable that in a specific situation male elites could perceive that improving women's opportunities and resources would benefit their organizations or the nation, and hence their interests. However, if conditions changed, they could just as easily change their policies toward women. This process has often happened during wartime when, given shortages of male workers, employers and governments provide opportunities and resources heretofore unavailable to women, only to take them away after the hostilities cease (see Trey, 1972). Therefore, increased gender equality as a stable system, rather than a transitory phenomenon, cannot be achieved in the absence of substantially equal gender incumbency in elite roles, especially in the most central social institutions (see Friedl, 1975, epilogue). Substantial and lasting change must flow "downward" from the macro to the micro levels. This target will probably be the most difficult of all to achieve, as will be discussed more fully in the last chapter.

Ironically, the public policy relevant to paid employment most vigorously pursued by activists in the contemporary United States is potentially antithetical to the achievement of equality in elite incumbency. If pay equity or comparable worth were to become the law governing all employers, women might be encouraged to remain in traditionally female jobs, which would come to reward them equally with comparable men's jobs. However, those jobs that are traditional for women are rarely found at the heart of the most central social institutions. They are typically not part of the career ladders that lead to elite positions. In fact, Holter (1972) suggests in passing that women achieve access to traditionally male roles precisely when those roles are becoming "obsolete," that is, losing skill, prestige, pay, responsibility, autonomy, and/or general social importance. For instance, women replaced men as secretaries and bookkeepers as such work became mechanized, routinized, and ceased to function as a training position for managers and entrepreneurs. More recently, women have entered pharmacy as drugstores became chains dispensing premanufactured pharmaceuticals rather than individually owned stores where druggists mixed their own prescriptions (Reskin and Phipps, 1988, pp. 198–200). Women (and blacks) have gained access to mayoral mansions and school boards as local governments have lost autonomy to state and federal ones. While it is of fundamental importance that women earn rewards (resources) equal to men from their work, if they remain excluded from that minority of work roles that constitutes the elite, any improvement in their relative status is at best tenuous. If comparable worth diverts attention from the need to integrate work roles at the highest levels, it could prove counterproductive to the achievement of a stable system of gender equality.

CONCLUSION

I have argued that the theoretically critical change target that is potentially capable of triggering broad-scale change in the system of gender stratification is the gender division of labor. In turn, this construct has been reconceptualized as comprising three, rather than two, elements. Gender equality requires that men and women share equally household and familial labor; fill extradomestic roles that are equal in the material and nonmaterial resources they generate; and are equally represented among incumbents of elite roles. To the extent that the gender division of labor changes in these directions, the engenderment process would produce less differentiated adults in subsequent generations, and social definitions that invidiously distinguish between the genders would decline. Given more equal access to resources, the male power advantage over females would be reduced. It would be yet further reduced as gender differentiation and gender social definitions declined.

Having identified the critical target of gender system change, the next issue is *how* the gender division of labor changes or can be changed. The *process* by which change in the gender division of labor triggers other changes in the gender system must also be examined in more detail. Recall that in Chapter 1 I suggested that change toward greater equality may have both unintentional and intentional roots. In the next three chapters gender system change will be examined first as it results from unintentional processes, then as it results from intentional efforts, and finally as the two relate to one another. In the introductory chapter I also suggested that change can and has occurred that increases gender stratification, but that such change is best explained as the unintended result of other social changes. Therefore, the next chapter will include a discussion of change in both directions as it emanates from unintentional processes.

CHAPTER SIX

Unintentional Change Processes

The discussion in the last chapter suggests that the reasonable place to begin a search for the unintentional processes that trigger change in the degree of gender stratification is to examine those processes that affect the gender division of labor. I begin with the assumption that the same *general* types of processes can, in a lagged fashion, trigger an increase or decrease in gender stratification, depending on how they affect the gender division of labor. In other words, the same theory can explain change in both directions, the difference in direction being primarily a function of whether the broader systemic change reduces or exacerbates the gender division of labor.

SOME EXAMPLES OF UNINTENTIONAL CHANGE

Before the explication of a theory of change begins, some descriptions of gender system changes that have actually occurred are warranted, including recent changes in advanced industrial societies as well as selected other types of cases.

The Transition to Agrarian Technology

Recent anthropological and sociological accounts suggest that, in technologically simple, non-surplus-producing societies, there is usually minimal stratification of any kind, including gender (e.g., Chafetz, 1984; Blumberg, 1978; Nielsen, 1978; Martin and Voorhies, 1975; Sanday, 1981; Leacock, 1978; Huber, 1988). Women in foraging and the most technologically simple horticultural societies, in all but a few cases (e.g., the Eskimos who rely very heavily on hunting and fishing), provide half or more of the food and control their own means of production and the fruits of their labor. Sharing is the general principle of distribution. The genders are closer to equal than in any other form of society. Until about 10,000 years ago, all humans lived in such societies.

Gender stratification, as well as other forms of structured inequality, apparently became the norm as technological development in some societies resulted in the production of surplus, exchangeable commodities. This form of technological change began in a small way in advanced horticultural societies and was dramatically expanded with the development of agrarian technology (specifically the plow and irrigation). Many workers ceased to control the means and products of their labor. Rather, elites appropriated land and a variety of perquisites, and extracted from the vast majority of the population much of what they produced—as taxes, tithes, rents, and so on. Agrarian societies are typically the most highly stratified of any type (Lenski, 1966).

In an earlier work (1984) I argued that, with the agrarian revolution, women lost most of their opportunity to regularly engage in the surplus-producing work of growing food. Before people cultivated food and maintained domestic animals, in most cases men hunted game—especially large animals—and women gathered food and sometimes hunted small game. As foragers, women probably developed food cultivation and originally constituted the cultivators. Likewise, herding probably arose from hunting and was, therefore, a male task. Horticulture, which is still practiced in some parts of the world, is done on small plots, located near the dwelling unit, with a hoe or digging stick constituting the main implement. Women can readily combine horticulture with infant and child care. Where agriculture replaced horticulture, a far heavier implement, the plow, often drawn by a domesticated animal, has replaced the hoe. Agrarian technology typically requires larger fields, which are, therefore, often substantially removed from the homesite. This combination of attributes has usually resulted in the replacement of women by men as the primary growers of food where an agrarian technology has replaced a horticultural one. In agrarian societies women help in the fields as needed during the harvest or at other times of especially heavy work demands and process agricultural products into food consumable by the family. But with the exception of wetland rice cultivation, agrarian production relies on women primarily to produce children, whose job it is to help their fathers with the work of producing food, both for the family and as surplus for nobility, clergy, government, and/or exchange or sale. Where agrarian women grow food, it is usually in a garden plot next to their home, primarily for family consumption. They remain, at best, subsistence horticulturists in an exchange economy based on agrarian production. Their status, relative to men in such societies, is quite low, as it always is where women produce subsistence in an economy based on exchange (Huber, 1988; Blumberg, 1988). It is equally low or more so in those cases where production is entirely focused on herding—an overwhelmingly male occupation (Martin and Voorhies, 1975, chap. 10).

Industrialization

If the agrarian revolution served to decrease women's role in extradomestic, resource-generating work, the long-run impact of the industrial revolution has been the opposite. Because women's labor is often underutilized in agrarian economies, at least in the United States and Great Britain, it was the daughters of farmers who were the very first workers in the newly developing textile industry, which was the earliest form of factory-based production (Berch, 1982; Easton, 1976, p. 393; Oakley, 1974, p. 37). Elsewhere in Europe, general rural overpopulation meant that there were enough unemployed men to staff the new factories. Even where women entered the early factories, that phenomenon was short-lived and they were soon replaced by men. Nonetheless, by the last decades of the nineteenth century many poor (especially immigrant) married, as well as single, women were working in the sweatshops and factories of the industrial nations, although for extremely poor wages and in settings lacking adequate sanitation, safety, and job security. As the new century dawned, jobs for unmarried, middle-class women began to open up in stores, offices, libraries, and public schools. Jobs in these settings became increasingly female segregated, were relatively poorly paid, and were inevitably lost or given up upon marriage. Most women married, and, at least for the now burgeoning middle class, by common consensus married women's main sphere of activity was home and family.

At the same time, with industrialization came new opportunities for middle-class women exclusive of paid employment. In all industrialized nations, the general level of education rose, including women's. By the end of the nineteenth century women in such nations had gained entrance into colleges and universities. Unable to use their education for paid employment, married middle-class women increasingly turned to philanthropic and unpaid social welfare work, to public activism on behalf of a variety of causes (e.g., abolition, temperance, socialistic and nationalistic movements), and to religious activism. In an era when "nice" women did not open their mouths publicly, middle-class women forged new public roles for themselves—roles heretofore monopolized by men—throughout the waning decades of the nineteenth and opening decades of the twentieth centuries. By the 1920s, women in a number of nations capped this expansion of their public roles by gaining suffrage (see Chafetz and Dworkin, 1986, for a further discussion of these changes).

Early industrialization resulted in only highly exploitative new work opportunities for poor women. Their status, relative to their male class peers, was probably a little higher than that of their agrarian sisters, in that they brought some much-needed economic resources into their families. But they did so at the high cost of a paid workday of 12 or more hours, six days a week, plus heavy domestic work responsibilities in the absence of helpful household technological developments (not to mention the domestic servants available to middle-class wives). For middle-class women, the basic gender division of labor remained unchanged, but women added new extradomestic roles that gained for them confidence, a level of knowledge and influence, and a set of organizational skills heretofore lacking (i.e., non-material resources). This process occurred in Anglo-Saxon and Western European nations first, but by the mid-twentieth century had spread through most nations of the world in varying degrees.

The decades since World War II have witnessed further change in the gender division of labor in some of the most highly industrialized nations of the world. Sustained, high levels of economic expansion, in part contingent upon major technological innovations in electronics, communication, and information processing, have substantially expanded the absolute number of labor-force jobs. Expansion of the relative proportion and absolute number of jobs in the service (tertiary) sector of advanced industrial nations has accounted for almost all of the growth of such labor forces (Oppenheimer, 1970; Gershuny and Miles, 1983, chap. 3). Female-segregated jobs—filled primarily by unmarried women—were among those that expanded most dramatically, from shortly after the war to the present. They were overwhelmingly within the tertiary sector (King, 1978; Oppenheimer, 1970; Huet, 1982; Condon, 1985). Over three-quarters of all employed women work in the tertiary sector in the United States (Blau, 1978). Most unemployed men lacked the education and skills to fill these jobs in offices, schools, and hospitals.

By the 1950s, most unmarried women were already employed. This meant that jobs could be filled only by recruiting married women. Initially, married women with older children sufficed. Eventually, further economic expansion necessitated the employment of large numbers of women with young—even preschool—children. In France, 70% of the growth of the labor force between 1975 and 1980 was accounted for by women (Huet, 1982), and by 1983 nearly 60% of French women with children were in the labor force (Michel, 1985). In the United States, by the mid-1980s more married women held labor-force jobs than did not (O'Kelly and Carney, 1986) and nearly half of all mothers of preschool children were in the paid labor force (Ritzer and Walczak, 1986). However, throughout the industrialized world, a large proportion of married women employed outside the home fill part-time jobs. In turn, part-time work is almost entirely a female phenomenon (Steinberg and Cook, 1988, p. 313). Nonetheless, the more women entered the labor force, the more they created a demand for services to replace or supplement their domestic work, especially child caretakers, restaurant workers, and other personal service workers, and the more resources they had to purchase such services. This demand provided increased employment opportunities for poor and poorly educated women, albeit at minimum wages (or below).

During this massive transition that has moved married women's work outside the home, their deployment within the labor force has changed relatively little. Women are still largely segregated in the work they do, still paid about two-thirds of the wages men employed the same amount of hours per week or year earn, and remain overwhelmingly responsible for domestic/familial work (for detailed information concerning this for France, Japan, and the United States, see Lorenzen, 1986; for the United States alone, Fox and Hesse-Biber, 1984). There is evidence of increasing income equity among the youngest cohorts of men and women (O'Neill, 1985, Table 3), and decreasing gender segregation of paid work for that age group (Beller, 1982, as cited in O'Neill, 1985). In the United States, women under 25 earn 86.5% of men's pay, compared to only 66% for older women (Ritzer and Walczak, 1986). Younger, college-educated women have moved into male-dominated managerial and professional occupations in substantial numbers, in the United States at least. In a mere 20 years, the proportion of female MDs increased from 6% to 15%, and of lawyers and judges, from 3% to 15% (Ritzer and Walczak, 1986). Similar increases occurred in managerial and executive occupations (O'Kelly and Carney, 1986). Moreover, a substantial decline in the number and real wages of many male-dominated, unionized, manufacturing (secondary sector) jobs has apparently also increased gender equality. Some of these men have moved into tertiary sector jobs—usually at lower wages. Others who have maintained manufacturing jobs have sustained a decline in real income. In either case, gender equality has increased because working-class men's advantages have decreased, not because women's opportunities and rewards have increased (Lorence, 1988).

The Worldwide Expansion of Capitalism

Many contemporary scholars concerned with political economy focus on the rapidly increasing integration of the world economy. World Systems theorists talk about core, semiperipheral, and peripheral nations, in terms of their status within the world capitalist economy. The discussion above concerning recent changes wrought by industrial expansion was based on the experiences of core nations, such as the United States, Japan, and much of Western Europe. The expansion of industrial capitalism has had very different effects on the position of women in peripheral nations (see especially Ward, 1984; Blumberg, 1988, forthcoming-a; articles in D'Onofrio-Flores and Pfafflin, 1982). Core nations are defined as those having the most advanced, diversified, active, and wealthy economies in a given era. They also have strong, stable governments. Peripheral nations are at the opposite extreme. They are less wealthy—often very poor— have labor-intensive, technologically less sophisticated economies, and are typically specialized around one or a few commodities. They often have weak and unstable governments, and many are former or current colonies of other nations. This category includes many Latin American, Asian, Caribbean, and African nations. Semiperipheral nations, such as Israel, Argentina, and South Africa, are in the middle. In seeking to maximize profits, transnational corporations headquartered in core nations seek cheap, exploitable labor and raw materials. These, along with new markets, are provided by peripheral nations.

In peripheral nations, the policies of core-nation corporations, along with those of international aid organizations (e.g., Agency for International Development, World Bank), have all too often functioned to decrease the relative status of women (Ward, 1984; Boserup, 1970; Blumberg, forthcoming-a; Martin and Voorhies, 1975, pp. 298 ff.; Sanday, 1981, chap. 7; Etienne and Leacock, 1980). Saffioti (1978) and Vasquez de Miranda (1977) demonstrated the decline in women's participation in the Brazilian labor force that has accompanied economic development. Arizpe (1977, p. 31) documented the increasing unemployment rate of women, relative to men, in Mexico. Similar conclusions have been reached concerning African nations (Niethammer, 1981). Core-nation men, and indigenous male elites educated in core nations, work on the basis of gender social definitions from the core nations. They, therefore, focus development efforts on men, all but ignoring the indigenous gender division of labor. Societies where women grow the major crop(s) become transformed into cash-crop economies, utilizing a technology associated with men (e.g., tractors). Control of the land and technology, or at least employment in producing the cash crop, is given to men. Women are reduced to subsistence horticulturists within an exchange economy. The introduction of factory-produced goods often destroys women's native handicrafts industries. Large-scale commerce drives small traders—often women—out of business (see Ellovich, 1980, pp. 94–96). New jobs for women are often created on the "global assembly line," that is, factories exported from high-labor-cost core nations. However, these jobs are extremely poorly paid, insecure, nonunionized, heavily supervised, and in many cases confined to very young, unmarried women. Other new jobs in the more modernized part of the economy—those requiring education and skill—are reserved almost entirely for men (Papanek, 1977, p. 16). Ward concludes from her study that the stronger the peripheral nation's dependence on a core nation, and the higher the core nation's level of investment in the peripheral one, the greater the level of gender stratification will become (1984, pp. 40–43; see also Bennholdt-Tomsen, 1984).

Whether integration into the world capitalist economy serves to reduce, increase, or stabilize gender stratification in a specific peripheral nation depends ultimately on the nature of the preexisting system in that nation. Where women's status is relatively high, such integration typically functions to reduce their position relative to male class peers. It may have no change ramifications in cases where women were extremely disadvantaged earlier. But above all, it is facile and inaccurate to presuppose that "modernization" of a poor nation automatically works to the long-term advantage of its women, as many Western male scholars and policymakers have assumed for several decades.

Warfare and Political Conflict

To this point several concrete conditions have been discussed under which the gender division of labor and women's relative status have been affected specifically by technological and economic changes. Another literature exists—theoretical and empirical—that suggests that, when a community or society experiences profound stress, especially that produced by long-term or chronic war, or by sustained political conflict between subcultures within a society, women's relative status is also affected.

When warfare removes a large number of men from the home community for extended periods of time, such as occurred during the world wars in Japan, Europe, and the United States, women often gain access to work roles that were previously monopolized by men (Chafe, 1972; Koyama, 1961). In Harris's terminology, "external warfare" provides opportunities for women to modify the "sexist hierarchy"—even if only temporarily—until the men return (1978, pp. 61–63). Sanday described precisely this process among the Abipon and Seneca (1981, pp. 117, 121; see also White, 1987, p. 129). "Internal warfare," that is, conflict between neighboring communities or subpopulations of one nation, however, has the opposite effect, strengthening a system of gender inequality. Men are not absent for long enough periods of time to necessitate that women assume their tasks or gain autonomy from their daily control. However, as defenders of their communities, the prestige and perquisites of those involved in the struggle are enhanced. During times of conflict, those roles most central to winning the conflict become most highly valued, and by extension the people who play those roles likewise experience enhanced social evaluation. It is likely that this process constitutes the incentive and/or reward necessary to induce large numbers of people to jeopardize their lives (Harris, 1978).

Although women have often been involved in wars, revolutions, and other violent political contests in which their nation, political party, or subcultural group (racial, religious, ethnic) was engaged, by and large they have never constituted more than a handful of the actual fighters (see Sanday, 1981, p. 177, for a discussion of the maleness of warriors in technologically simple societies). Even in Israel, where women have been drafted ever since independence, they have not been allowed into combat roles since the 1948 war. Women have certainly participated in the struggles for national liberation that shook most colonies in the aftermath of World War II, but, again, in most cases only a few were actively engaged in direct fighting (see Chafetz and Dworkin, 1986, chap. 1). Ridd and Callaway (1987) present a series of case studies of women's recent involvement in political struggles in Cyprus, Iran, Northern Ireland, Lebanon, Turkey, and elsewhere, finding the same thing. In situations of armed or violent conflict, men do almost all of the fighting; at most, women serve as support personnel in a variety of ways.

Regardless of whether warfare is internal or external, it tends to produce or exacerbate gender social definitions. The Nazi regime reversed a growing gender consciousness in interwar Germany by glorifying men as warriors and proclaiming "kitchen, children and church" as the proper roles of women (Rupp, 1977). Sanday describes how, as conflict between Native American tribes on the Great Plains increased, the status of Cheyenne and Comanche women decreased (1981, pp. 147, 157). In her conclusion of the book of papers concerning women and political conflict, Callaway states that "in times of political conflict . . . masculine values become heightened and enhanced." Meanwhile, "the roles of 'mother' and 'housewife' may be enlarged and praised . . . yet . . . the value given to female roles emphasizes gender polarity, thus strengthening male roles as the dominant structure" (1987, p. 228). Indeed, conflict brings about an emphasis on returning to tradition, such as the reveiling of women in Iran, as "cultural images of women are called forth to represent the timeless world of the past" (p. 229).

In summary, at best warfare and political conflict sometimes permit women access to new, resource-generating work roles, usually temporarily. They appear always to exacerbate gender social definitions that devalue women and women's roles, relative to those of warrior men. Finally, in some cases, conflict serves to reverse earlier gains made by women by returning them to traditional work roles and gender-norm restrictions.

THE EFFECTS OF DEMOGRAPHIC, TECHNOLOGICAL, AND ECONOMIC CHANGE ON THE GENDER DIVISION OF LABOR

In the last section I described several types of cases where broad-scale technological and economic changes have affected the macro-level gender division of labor and, by implication, the level of gender stratification. In this section several general theoretical propositions that convey these relationships, as well as several pertaining to demographic variables, will be developed. The focus is primarily upon nondomestic/familial work roles, because these appear to be the ones most centrally affected by macro-level changes in demography, technology, and the economy.

Supply and Demand Factors

Before a theory of unintentional change in the gender division of labor is explicated, a commonplace error in much of the contemporary literature concerning women and work must be addressed. In trying to understand the dramatic rise in the labor-force participation rates of married women, especially in the United States, scholars all too frequently concentrate on changes in the attributes of women. A catalogue of traits is typically cited that differentiate women in recent decades from their mothers and grandmothers. Women today are much better educated, including college education. They have far fewer children and are relatively young when their youngest no longer need close supervision. They are far more likely to be divorced or to remain single. Those who marry are more likely to remain childfree until a later age. Their life expectancy is longer. Household technology has somewhat eased the burden of domestic labor, along with the growing availability of fast foods, frozen dinners, and so on. Finally, inflation, especially in housing costs, requires that wives earn money if couples are to create a middle-class life-style, including home ownership. For any or all of these types of reasons, married women are presumed to have entered or remained in the labor force in increasingly greater numbers since the mid-1950s, relative to earlier decades.

This is "supply-side logic." It helps us to understand why more women may want to participate in extradomestic work roles today than a generation or two ago. It is also largely irrelevant if opportunities for women outside the household are not available. It does not, in other words, explain why more women *are* in the paid labor force. This is not to deny the importance of supply variables for understanding *individual-level* variation in women's extra-domestic work. Supply variables do not determine the rate of women's participation, but they do influence which particular women do and do not participate, given available opportunities. The "demand side" refers to the availability of opportunities, without which desire could only be met by frustration in a gender-stratified society. In fact, given demand for women's labor, employers, governments, and other elites are usually able to provide sufficient incentives to substantially increase the supply of women workers. This was obvious during World War II, when day-care centers and all manner of other inducements resulted in an ample supply of women workers to replace the men who went off to fight. Moreover, when the men returned and the women were no longer "needed," the inducements evaporated, to be replaced by widespread firings, despite the expressed desire of many women to remain in the labor force (Trey, 1972).

I suggest that supply factors are more responsive to demand than vice versa (see also Ward and Weiss, 1982; Semyonov and Scott, 1983; Jones and Rosenfeld, 1989). For instance, it has long been known that, the fewer children a woman has, the more likely she will participate in the labor force, even among those with the largest amount of employment-related skills (Stewart, Lykes, and LaFrance, 1982). It has typically been assumed that this constitutes a major supply variable. However, it appears that women choose to have fewer children when they are employed outside the home (Cramer, 1980; Stolzenberg and Waite, 1977). Even in technologically simple societies, where women play important extradomestic work roles, birth rates tend to be low and children widely spaced, at least relative to other societies with the same type of economy and technology but with fewer extradomestic opportunities for women (Howell, 1976; Murray and Alvarez, 1975; Friedl, 1975, p. 137). Furthermore, in low-birthrate societies, where the demand for women's labor outside the home is low, social definitions of, and norms pertaining to, proper child rearing expand this task to a full-time job, as happened during the 1950s and early 1960s in the United States and is currently the case in Japan (White, 1987). When demand increased in the United States, quality replaced quantity of time as the measure of maternal commitment.

Demand factors not only affect decisions about the number, spacing, and maternal care of children, they may also affect the quantity and quality of domestic work. Although employed wives receive little more help from their husbands than full-time homemakers, the former put in far fewer hours than the latter on housework. Moore and Sawhill (1978) report that employed married women spend only about half the number of hours as full-time homemakers on housework in the United States. Apparently, wives employed outside the home are more willing to reduce their standards of what constitutes an appropriate level of domestic/familial work performance and/or to more efficiently utilize a labor-saving technology than their counterparts who do not have a double work load. The availability of labor-saving household goods (e.g., microwave ovens, convenience foods, washers and dryers, dishwashers) does not mean that they will be used to reduce work. They can and often are used to increase the frequency of task performance (e.g., clean laundry daily) or its quality (e.g., fancier meals). How they are used depends substantially on what other demands are placed on women's time and energy. To paraphrase an old cliché, domestic and familial work will expand to fill the ·time available. Likewise, they can retract considerably (see Chafetz and Dworkin, 1984; England and Farkas, 1986).

The above comments presuppose that women have sufficient autonomy to substantially control their fertility and set their own level of performance of domestic/familial tasks. In many societies they do not. However, where women largely lack such autonomy, it is precisely because they live in relatively stable, highly gender-stratified societies and lack any degree of resource power. If unintentional changes occurred that resulted in a substantial increase in the demand for their labor in resource-generating work roles, the result would be increased autonomy at the micro level of the household (Blumberg, 1988; Ward, 1984). Given such demand, elites would also probably shape policies and social definitions that would enhance women's ability to control their fertility—if not their domestic work load.

The Demand for Women's Nondomestic Labor

The theoretical issue central to this section concerns how macro-structural change unintentionally affects the nondomestic gender division of labor. Under what circumstances do women experience an increase in their access to resource-producing work roles? Under what circumstances do they experience a decrease? Given the previous discussion, factors that affect demand for their labor rather than their willingness to supply it will constitute the focus of attention. The primary structural factors whose change can affect the gender division of labor are technological, economic, and demographic. I will begin with the demographic because the probability that the other two will affect the gender division of labor is always contingent upon the demographic profile of a society.

Demographic Factors

Assuming a system of gender inequality, including a gender division of labor by which men enjoy greater access than women to resources as rewards for their work: *As long as there are a sufficient number of working-age men available to meet the demand for the work they traditionally perform, no change in the gender division of labor will occur.* Moreover, if new types of resource-generating work roles evolve, as long as there is a sufficient number of men available to meet the new demand, women will not gain access to these work roles. The question, then, is under what circumstances will there be too few men to fill the demand, holding constant for now the number of resource-generating work roles (i.e., in the absence of an expansion in the number of such roles relative to the number of working-age men).

Change in the gender division of labor may occur as a response to substantial change in the size of the total working-age population relative to available resource-generating work roles. If, in the absence of sufficient expansion in the availability of such roles, the size of the working-age population expands significantly, many people will be under- or unemployed. This situation characterizes much of the contemporary Third World. Given differences in cohort size, it has periodically affected wealthier nations as well. However, the surplus male population is often differentially distributed by social class and educational/skill level. In some Western nations today and in the recent past, there has been a surplus of relatively well-educated people. In poor nations the surplus is more typically of the poor and poorly educated. Under conditions of overpopulation, and, therefore, of significant numbers of under- or unemployed *men*, there will tend to be an invasion by men into those relatively few female-segregated work roles that offer reasonably high rewards for the particular segment of the under- or unemployed male population. College-educated men will not usually invade low-skill, poorly rewarded female jobs (e.g., domestic servant, low-level clerical work), just as poorly educated men cannot invade high-skill, better rewarded jobs (e.g., teacher). However, men will tend to invade female-segregated jobs at the commensurate level. For instance, there has been a small decline in the gender segregation of jobs in the U.S. labor force over the past three decades. Despite public attention to the influx of women into traditionally male jobs, more of the change has resulted from the invasion of men into the few preserves traditionally reserved for women (e.g., public school teaching, social work, medical careers other than physician, telephone operators, retail sales, librarians) (Jusenius, 1976; Berch, 1982). Moreover, as men have entered these fields, they have substantially taken over the higher-level, supervisory and administrative roles, traditionally the only avenues of career mobility open to women. That invasion resulted in substantial measure from the fact that the very large baby boom generation received college educations in unprecedented numbers. The traditionally male fields that provide jobs commensurate with that level of education could not absorb the huge cohort of educated men. Many, therefore, turned to those female-dominated fields that were both expanding and offering rewards that, although not the equivalent of their male-dominated counterpart occupations, were better in a variety of ways than either no job or jobs requiring substantially less education. In this instance, the female-dominated jobs were expanding rapidly enough that women were not generally displaced. However, were overpopulation and underutilization of *man*power to occur in a steady-state economy, the result would be the displacement of women from resource-generating work roles.

Proposition 6.1. Holding constant the number of available work roles that generate resources, the greater the growth in the working-age population, the more likely that females will be displaced by males from those work roles they traditionally fill.

If overpopulation can function to displace women, it is reasonable to assume that underpopulation, relative to available work opportunities, would produce the opposite effect. As a very small birth cohort, such as the "baby bust," which began in the 1960s in the United States, reaches working age, there may not be enough men to fill the available jobs (holding demand constant). In such a circumstance, women may gain increased access to traditionally male jobs. Indeed, the small cohort born during the depression of the 1930s provided too few young men to meet the expanding demand for labor after World War II, thus providing a substantial increase in labor-force jobs for older married women in the 1950s (Michael, 1985; Easterlin, 1987, chap. 4).

Proposition 6.2. Holding constant the number of available work roles that generate resources, the greater the decline in the working-age population, the more likely women will gain access to traditionally male jobs.

Proposition 6.2 requires a proviso, however. It is altogether possible that a shortage of workers will be met not by recruiting women but by recruiting men from another society. Slaves captured from elsewhere, guest workers, or immigrants can be used to meet the demand. This is especially the case for relatively low-skill jobs. In a world filled with overpopulated nations, this response is at least as likely as that of opening new opportunities to women in a highly gender-stratified society. In the contemporary world, slavery is not generally an option. Whether a nation turns to foreign labor or to its own women substantially depends both on the match between the educational, skill, and class levels of its nonemployed women and the kinds of work roles that need to be filled. In part, too, it probably reflects the degree of ethnic, racial, and religious homogeneity of the nation. Highly homogeneous nations may be more reluctant to admit people from culturally different backgrounds than nations with an already diversified population. Finally, other aspects of the nation where demand for workers is high may affect the willingness of foreign workers to migrate there. Lack of political or religious freedom, for example, may dissuade immigration even when economic opportunities are extensive.

To this point, discussion has centered on the size of the total working-age population, ignoring its sex ratio. Independent of total population size, a sex ratio that becomes substantially skewed can also affect the gender division of labor, again holding constant the demand for workers. Substantial change in the sex ratio of adults is likely to result primarily from two phenomena: war and migration.

Warfare in the contemporary era removes a large number of men from their normal work. During the period of hostilities, this removal often results in the recruitment of women into those roles (assuming no surplus, under- or unemployed male population not absorbed by the military). However, the longer-term impact of war depends on the male casualty rate. Where it is relatively low (e.g., the United States in World War II), the status quo ante follows hard on the heels of peace (Trey, 1972; Chafe, 1972). Where male casualties are very high, resulting in a low sex ratio (i.e., a shortage of males) for an entire generation, as occurred in Eastern Europe and the Soviet Union during and after World War II, expanded opportunities for women survive long after the war is over (Scott, 1979, pp. 180–81).

Sex ratios may also be substantially skewed by differential migration by gender. In particular, rural-to-urban and international migration are often highly gender specific (see Smith, Khoo, and Go, 1984, Table 2.1). Where males constitute the bulk of migrants, the sending community (community of origin) will experience a low sex ratio of working-age people. This could open new work opportunities to women. However, where there is large-scale male immigration, they usually migrate as single individuals (that is, not as a part of a family) precisely because of the absence of economic opportunities at home. It is a surplus, usually young male population that departs, presumably leaving behind enough men to meet local demand (Massey et al., 1986). If the male migrants share one or a few common destinations, they will raise the sex ratio of the receiving communities. Because their motivation is largely economic, they will tend to be willing to take whatever work is available (Piore, 1979). Depending on the kinds of work women do in the receiving community, male migrants might either displace them or prevent them from acquiring new work opportunities. For instance, although women constituted the first factory workers in New England, they were rapidly displaced by males migrating both from rural areas and from abroad (Huber, 1976).

Where females constitute the migrants, as they do in many Third World nations, they will typically be young, single, and seeking work that is not available in their home communities (Thadani and Todaro, 1984). They usually end up in low-skill, traditionally female jobs in the "informal" labor market (Shah and Smith, 1984). This market includes such work as private domestic employment (e.g., the Irish in Great Britain and the United States in the nineteenth century; Hispanics in many parts of the United States today), bar girls, street-vending, and prostitution (Arizpe, 1977; Chincilla, 1977). Increasingly, they also end up working on the "global assembly line" producing goods for transnational corporations at heavily exploitative wages (Berch, 1982, reports the following 1976 hourly wages for female industrial workers: Hong Kong, 55 cents; South Korea, 52 cents; the Philippines, 32 cents; Indonesia, 17 cents). In wealthier nations, female migrants typically head for major cities that provide a large number of especially clerical and low-level white-collar jobs, such as New York and Washington, D.C. In both kinds of cases, they do not compete in any sizable numbers for the same kinds of work men traditionally perform. However, the influx of women may create competition between the newcomers and the indigenous female population for scarce jobs, depriving some of the old-timers of extradomestic work and driving (or keeping) the wages of all down. Usually, the sending community loses women's unpaid domestic work, often their subsistence horticultural work in Third World nations, and their availability as wives for local men. Ironically, the effect of scarcity of women (a high sex ratio) in the sending community may be further restriction on the autonomy of those who remain behind. Guttentag and Secord (1983) argue that, given gender inequality, a high sex ratio (shortage of women) results in substantial "dyadic power" for women vis-à-vis their husbands, because of their value as a scarce commodity. But that very value means that they will be jealously guarded and heavily restricted from engaging in extradomestic roles that might bring them into contact with other men. Conversely, if the sex ratio of the receiving community becomes excessively low (a surplus of women), the value placed on women declines, to be replaced by misogyny and sexual exploitation. The modicum of independence gained by migrating women who acquire some kind of employment is, therefore, at least partially offset by their excessively negative treatment by men.

Proposition 6.3. A long-term reduction in the sex ratio (below parity) of the working-age population, resulting primarily from war or migration, will tend to increase women's access to resource-generating work roles, in the absence of a surplus male population.

Proposition 6.4. A long-term increase in the sex ratio of the working-age population (above parity) will tend to increase restrictions on women's extradomestic work, as men compete for available work and attempt to guard access to their wives.

Economic and Technological Factors

In discussing demographic factors whose change may alter the gender division of labor, the demand for labor was held constant. In this section that approach is reversed and total population size and sex ratio are held constant. I will assume that there are enough males, but not a large surplus, to meet the demand for the kind of work they traditionally perform, and that the sex ratio is about 100 (parity).

There are two biologically rooted aspects of sex that can, and often have, seriously affected the gender division of labor: superior male physical strength and the fact that pregnancy and lactation are confined to women. Sociocultural arrangements typically elaborate on and exaggerate the importance of these basic sex differences, especially women's reproductive function.

Where sufficient male labor power exists, women's basic reproductive functions are socially elaborated into much more extensive responsibility for infant and child care than the biological facts require. Nonetheless, in technologically simple societies, pregnancy and lactation—hence the need to maintain proximity to infants and toddlers—render it inefficient for women to participate extensively in work roles that require prolonged and rapid mobility or long stretches of concentrated attention. Likewise, the greater average strength of males makes it more efficient—although not absolutely necessary—for them to specialize in tasks that require substantial strength (see Chafetz, 1984, especially chap. 3). Any technological change that seriously alters work roles in terms of strength requirements, the need for prolonged and rapid mobility, and/or the attention span required has the potential of changing the gender composition of those work roles.

In the case of the agrarian revolution, the strength and attention-span aspects of food growing changed in the direction of favoring male participation over female. It is substantially more efficient for men to employ an agrarian technology than for women (assuming sufficient numbers of men to accomplish the work). The result was the replacement of female horticulture by male agriculture as the central economic arrangement. In the case of the industrial revolution, strength requirements of nondomestic work roles diminish substantially over time. Women gradually gain greater access to such work roles, but there is also a countervailing tendency. With industrialization, work and home sites are spatially separated more than under previous forms of technology, making it perhaps more difficult for women to combine motherhood with extradomestic work roles. Moreover, attention-span requirements of most nondomestic work roles in industrial societies preclude the simultaneous care of young children. Therefore, before women in large numbers are able to take advantage of the fact that industrialized work roles no longer favor men on the basis of strength and mobility considerations, a reduction in family size and alternative modes of child care are required to supplement the technological change. Nonetheless, I suggest the following:

Proposition 6.5. The more technological change enhances the strength, mobility, and/or attention-span requirements of nondomestic work roles, the more likely those roles will come to be filled by men.

Proposition 6.6. Conversely, the more technological change reduces the strength, mobility, and/or attention-span requirements of nondomestic work roles, the more likely that women will gain entrance to such roles.

In a gender-stratified society it is unlikely that women will displace men from resource-generating work roles. Proposition 6.6 really means that women will be more able to enter them, not that they will necessarily be given the opportunity to do so. In short, technological changes that enhance the importance of the biologically rooted advantages possessed by men will result directly in their assumption of the new or altered nondomestic work roles. Those new technologies that reduce men's inherent advantages produce no such automatic change in the gender division of labor. Technological change has an asymmetric effect on the gender division of labor.

Major technological changes typically result in one or more of the following: (1) expanded level of production; (2) reduced time and effort to produce the same amount of goods or services, and, therefore, a lower price per unit; and (3) enhanced quality of goods or services. Each of these changes can potentially affect the gender division of labor.

Where a new technology enhances quality and/or reduces prices, those who used the old technology will be increasingly unable to exchange or sell their product or service and will be driven from that form of work. Where the old technology belonged to one gender and the new is associated with the other, the gender composition of the affected work roles changes. This has been the case in many Third World nations where women produced traditional handicrafts for sale. The introduction of industrial production, usually by transnational corporations, and/or the increase in imports from industrial nations, have rendered obsolete women's handicrafts. Control of industrial production and the import business, and work within these sectors, are overwhelmingly in the hands of men—foreign and indigenous. Unlike women, men as a collectivity (although not necessarily as individuals) do not tend to lose work opportunities when technology renders their old skills obsolete because they gain access to the new technology (see Saffioti, 1986).

Proposition 6.7. When a new technology renders obsolete the work done by members of one gender, regardless of which gender is affected, women are more likely than men to lose access to resource-generating work roles.

When a new technology reduces the time and effort required to produce goods or services, typically the same time and effort is still expended, resulting in the expansion of production. Each major technological change has produced an expansion in total productivity and the amount of surplus generated by workers (Lenski, 1966). The development of cultivation and the hoe produced the first, although very small, surpluses. Agrarian technology enhanced the size of the surplus. The industrial revolution expanded surplus production enormously. Finally, late-stage industrial development, as brought about by the "electronics revolution," experienced by some nations since World War II, has expanded surplus production yet further.

Although technological change ostensibly allows the same number of workers to produce more, its long-term effects have often been to utilize more workers, each producing more than their counterparts utilizing a simpler technology. The more surplus generated, the more elites apparently have often been motivated to further expand the economy by employing yet more people outside of subsistence and household maintenance work. Some part of the surplus produced by workers has always been used by elites for personal aggrandizement and pleasure. Economic elites, who control the means and products of production, skim part of the surplus as profits or extremely high salaries. Political elites take their share as taxes; religious elites, as tithes. For the past several centuries, beginning in Western Europe and gradually spreading throughout much of the world, elites have devoted a significant (although highly variable) proportion of surplus production to expanding productive capacity. Especially, but not only, under capitalism, continuous economic growth has been a major goal of political as well as economic elites. In the process, the total nondomestic work forces of many societies have expanded over time, although not without periodic retractions during depressions and recessions.

From the onset of industrialization until World War II, the economies of industrialized nations were generally able to provide resource-generating work roles for most men, some wives of poor, working-class men, and many unmarried women. These categories supplied enough labor to meet, and often exceed, demand. When the economy experienced a downturn, labor supply exceeded demand. Under these circumstances, women in the past, and still today, usually experience greater job loss than men (Berch, 1982, pp. 17–18). In a comparison of eight industrial nations at two times each (1976 and 1981), Steinberg and Cook (1988, p. 312) found higher rates of unemployment for females than males in all but two instances. Since World War II, the economies of the most highly industrialized nations have expanded substantially, in part as a result of major technological changes in electronics, communication, and transportation. As noted earlier, job expansion specifically in service-sector industries and occupations has been the result to date, more than offsetting any job contraction in manufacturing experienced by these nations (Urquhart, 1984). Because most men and single women were already employed, married women's labor has been increasingly sought.

Proposition 6.8. The greater the technological change, the more likely an economy is to expand, in many cases gradually employing more people in resource-generating work roles.

Proposition 6.9. Given essentially full employment for men, the greater the economic expansion, the more opportunities for resource-generating work roles are made available to women— first single and impoverished married women and subsequently other married women.

Proposition 6.10. Conversely, the more an economy retracts, the more likely that women will disproportionately lose access to resource-generating work roles.

Technological change and both economic expansion and retraction do not usually affect all types of work roles in the same way, in a given time and place. Technological developments may function simultaneously to create new kinds of work, eliminate other types, deskill some work roles, and enhance the skill level of yet others. Economic expansion may be confined to certain types of industries and occupations, as may economic downturn. Indeed, expansion and downturn may coexist in different parts of the same economy, as may skill degradation and enhancement.

Given gender stratification, it is likely that deskilling will occur more often in those jobs held by women than by men and that, when a male-dominated job is deskilled, women will often come to replace men in it, if alternative, more highly skilled work opportunities exist into which men can move (Reskin and Roos, 1987, p. 13; Saffioti, 1986; Game and Pringle, 1983). Conversely, skill-enhanced jobs and new positions that offer substantial rewards will go chiefly to men, if they are available to meet the demand. Likewise, in gender-stratified societies, where opportunities in industries and occupations staffed by men decline, they are likely to move to other sectors of the economy, possibly displacing women. Where decline occurs in industries and occupations staffed primarily by women, they are more likely to be removed from extradomestic work roles altogether—at least until their segment of the economy experiences an upturn. In short, the costs of technological change and economic retraction will be borne most heavily by women. The benefits of technological change and economic expansion will accrue first to men. Only if the new opportunities exceed men's ability to meet the demand will women benefit substantially from them.

Proposition 6.11. Given uneven effects of technological change, women will more often than men end up in deskilled positions, while men will more often than women end up in enhanced skill work roles.

Proposition 6.12. Given the uneven effects of economic change, men in declining sectors of the economy will tend to move into expanding sectors, if need be displacing women, while women in declining sectors will tend to lose resource-generating work roles entirely, unless the total demand for workers continues to outstrip the capacity of men to meet it.

The process described above is always uneven in time. For a short time, men may be displaced from certain work and lack the skills necessary to enter resource-generating work roles traditionally filled by women. Many older men may never gain such skills and will remain permanently under- or unemployed. Nonetheless, over the course of a decade or two, many younger men will acquire the skills necessary to enter expanding occupations and industries, possibly displacing women already there, and almost definitely winning the competition with female age peers who would previously have entered those positions (see Oakley, 1974, pp. 43–44, for a description of this process in nineteenth-century Great Britain).

The computer revolution exemplifies the argument concerning technological change and the gender composition of nondomestic work. Many low-level, white-collar and clerical jobs, traditionally done by women, remain female-dominated and have undergone deskilling. New jobs have been created at both extremes of skill level. Low-level, data entry, and routinized computer assembly jobs have gone to women. High-skill-level, computer design and programming jobs have become primarily male occupations (see Reskin and Roos, 1987, p. 15; Bergom-Larsson, 1982, pp. 53–55). Needless to say, pay rates and prestige are closely related to skill level. The argument concerning economic change is exemplified by the movement of men into the expanding tertiary sector as manufacturing positions have declined (Lorence, 1988). That they have not (yet) displaced women is due to the very rapid growth of service jobs during the last three decades.

In summary of this section, when technological and economic changes occur that enlarge the demand for workers in resource-generating work roles, women will tend to gain new opportunities. However, their gains are primarily at the lower levels of skill and reward. When such changes adversely affect the entire economy or a part of it, disproportionately to men, women experience the negative effects of unemployment or deskilling. Just as the effects of demographic change are asymmetric with reference to gender, so too are they for technological and economic change. This asymmetry is reflected in Blumberg's assertion that "women's relative economic power (generally) . . . falls more rapidly than it rises" (1988, p. 55).

Summary

Figure 6.1 depicts a summary model of the processes by which demographic, technological, and economic changes affect the gender division of labor. It incorporates the logic of all propositions presented so far in this chapter. Depending on the type of macro-structural change, women's opportunities to gain access to resource-generating work roles are enhanced or reduced, or the work they do may be deskilled. The demographic variables have been kept separate from the technological and economic variables. The two sets may in some concrete instances vary in ways that counteract one another, thereby reducing the probability of any change in the gender division of labor. For instance, technological change and economic expansion may be offset by population expansion, so that there are ample men available to meet expanded demand. In other instances, the two sets of variables may enhance one another, producing profound change in the gender division of labor. For instance, a decline in the working-age population or the sex ratio, combined with technological change and economic expansion, could dramatically increase women's opportunities. Conversely, rising population numbers and economic retraction could dramatically reduce women's opportunities. Generally, however, economic variables are probably more important than demographic. In their analysis of the impact of sex ratio on a variety of dependent variables in a sample of 117 nations, South and Trent (1988) found that the level of economic development explained more of the variance than did sex ratio, especially for the dependent variable "female labor-force participation rate."

In general, major technological changes that produce long-term alterations in the economy are the most important for understanding changes in the gender division of labor and gender stratification systems. Short-term economic fluctuations are likely to have short-term ramifications for women's opportunities. War directly enhances women's access to new work roles only temporarily. Even where it reduces the sex ratio through very high male casualties, the effects will gradually decrease as the generation that fought the war ages. The demographic variable most likely to strongly affect the gender division of labor is long-term overpopulation, as experienced by many contemporary Third World nations. In these nations, economic expansion has not been able to outstrip—or even keep up with—population growth. Women's opportunities have remained poor or have shrunk. The lack of extradomestic work roles in such cases may prompt women to high levels of fertility, which maintain or exacerbate overpopulation and, therefore, their lack of access to extradomestic work. Once a cycle of overpopulation and declining extradomestic work opportunities for women begins, it may, therefore, be exacerbated by women choosing to expand their fertility, as depicted by the double arrow in Figure 6.1. In the contemporary world, economic expansion has been experienced most notably by wealthy, low-population-growth nations. In these cases, women's opportunities to acquire resource-generating work roles have been enhanced, although generally at relatively low skill and reward levels compared to the work available to comparably educated men. Expanding opportunities for women can become self-enhancing, as women employed outside the home opt to have fewer children, thereby expanding future demand for women's labor. This is also depicted by a double arrow in Figure 6.1.

THE EFFECTS OF POLITICAL CONFLICT ON GENDER SOCIAL DEFINITIONS AND THE GENDER DIVISION OF LABOR

In the last chapter I argued that gender social definitions cannot serve as a key change target, whose change could serve to

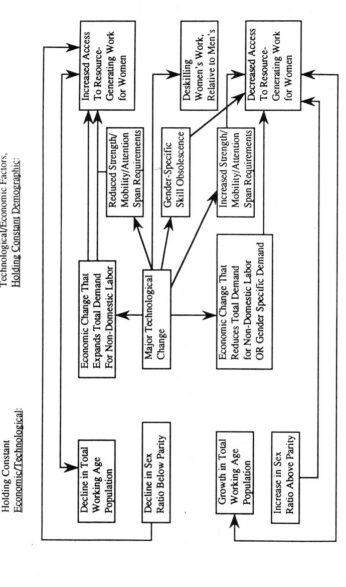

Demographic Factors,
Holding Constant
Economic/Technological:

Technological/Economic Factors,
Holding Constant Demographic:

Figure 6.1. Summary Process Model of Unintentional Change in the Gender Division of Labor

139

trigger change in the gender stratification system. In that discussion the focus of attention was specifically on change that *reduces* female disadvantage. In the first part of this chapter some cases were discussed that suggest that, during episodes of profound and sustained political conflict, including but not confined to warfare, traditional values are often reinforced or resurrected. The strengthening of gender social definitions occurs as the parties to the conflict attempt to develop internal cohesion and solidarity and to strengthen boundaries between contending groups (see Coser, 1956, on the theoretical relationship between external group conflict and internal cohesiveness).

In the process of reaffirming traditional values, beliefs, and customs, traditional gender social definitions are bound to be included. This is not to say that those, usually male, elites who lead their collectivity's fight self-consciously set about to devalue women, return them to traditional roles, or reduce their status in some conspiratorial fashion. Rather, these types of results often occur as "fallout" from a general, elite-sponsored effort to resurrect or reinforce traditional social and cultural arrangements that are ostensibly under threat from an opposing force. In short, sociopolitical conflict tends to produce enhanced group conservatism, one aspect of which concerns gender social definitions.

Whether or not this process entails change depends on the conditions immediately preceding the emergence of the conflict. If the gender system were one of stability, the reinforcement of traditional gender social definitions constitutes no real change. If, however, the kinds of changes described in the preceding section had been occurring in the direction of enhancing women's access to resource-generating work roles, then the onset of political conflict is likely to rescind, or at least reduce, those changes. Elites will look back to an earlier era of gender system stability and stress that the gender social definitions and arrangements characteristic of that era constitute an important part of the heritage for which the collectivity is fighting.

Proposition 6.13. The more intense and prolonged a political struggle or war, the greater the likelihood that traditional gender social definitions will be strengthened.

Whether or not women actually lose access to resource-generating work roles under these conditions depends primarily on the extent to which the ongoing conflict creates a shortage of male workers. If, as discussed earlier, conflict results in too few men to meet the demand for their labor, despite neoconservative gender social definitions, women will maintain—even increase—their access to nondomestic work roles. The reality of women's lives will be in sharp contradiction with social definitions in such cases. They may experience a simultaneous increase in resources and decrease in general social evaluation. This contradiction is most likely to occur in international warfare.

Where the conflict is internal and pits subpopulations against one another (e.g., ethnic, racial, religious), men may continue their normal work most days. Under these circumstances, the strengthening of traditional gender social definitions may contribute to women's loss of newly gained roles and their return to the domestic sphere of work. Women will be especially strongly exhorted to produce children—really sons—to continue the "cause" into the future. A pronatalist policy may also occur in situations of international warfare. A heavily pronatalist emphasis will make it more difficult for women to work outside the home. Women may experience enhanced social evaluation, but this will be confined to their role as mothers and may come at the expense of access to resource-generating roles.

Proposition 6.14. The more prolonged the political conflict, especially internal conflict, the greater the emphasis on women's role as mother, regardless of other work women may do.

Proposition 6.15. If women's access to resource-generating work had begun to improve, the more intense and prolonged the political conflict, especially internal conflict, and the more traditional gender social definitions are strengthened, the greater the likelihood that women will lose newly gained access to resource-generating work roles, barring insufficient males to meet the labor demand.

The fact that conflict enhances conservative gender social definitions creates a longer-term and often ironic aftermath to the cessation of hostilities. Women may achieve access to new roles especially during periods of external conflict. However, regardless of type of conflict and whether or not women do achieve such access, the strengthening of conservative social definitions tends to outlast the conflict by a considerable period of time. Attitudes and beliefs tend to change more slowly than behavior—especially behavior that is an immediate response to an emergency. Therefore, women will be removed from newly acquired work roles with impunity to "make room for the men," as soon as the situation permits. Therefore, also, a decade after the end of hostilities gender social definitions are likely to be more conservative than just prior to the onset of conflict—as exemplified by the "feminine mystique" of the 1950s in the United States (Friedan, 1963). The fact that gender social definitions become more conservative during periods of intense conflict, regardless of the reality of women's work, also explains why women's movements do not arise during such periods, and, if they are already ongoing, tend to cease activism during the conflict (see Chafetz and Dworkin, 1986, especially chaps. 3–4). As will be described in the next chapter, many of the main factors that produce such movements are often present during wartime. That they do not result in women's movements should be understood in light of

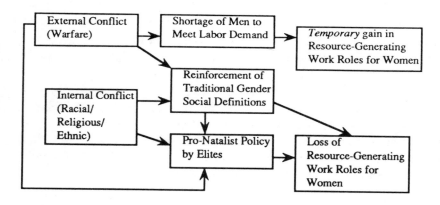

Figure 6.2. A Process Model of Socio-Political Conflict, Gender Social Definitions, and the Gender Division of Labor

the conservative and even reactionary definitional forces produced by prolonged and intense conflict.

In summary of this section, Figure 6.2 depicts the mostly adverse effects of political conflict on gender social definitions and women's status.

THE IMPACT OF DECREASING WOMEN'S RESOURCES ON OTHER ASPECTS OF THE GENDER SYSTEM

The primary focus of this chapter has been upon changes, primarily of a demographic, technological, and economic nature, that unintentionally produce change in women's access to resource-generating work roles. Secondarily, I have examined the unintended effects of political conflict on gender social definitions as they affect women in mostly adverse ways. Throughout this book the systemic nature of gender arrangements has been stressed, which means that change in one major variable should trigger change in the others. For instance, when women's access to resource-generating roles changes (in either direction), assuming that the change is not short-lived, then gender social definitions, gender differentiation, the division of domestic and familial work, and women's access to other scarce values, including power and authority, should change. Is there any evidence to support this theoretical logic? How, precisely, does one form of change trigger others?

When change entails an increase in gender stratification, I argued in Chapter 1 that its sources should be considered only as unintentional. To posit intentionality is to propound a conspiracy theory, a largely discredited sociological approach. However, when change entails a decrease in gender inequality, intentionality is possible. Indeed, the next chapter will demonstrate that it is likely. Because in this case there are two, often contemporaneous forces working to produce gender system change, it is impossible to attribute most aspects of change specifically to one or the other. An error commonly made in the mass media, and sometimes by scholars as well, is to attribute causal agency to a social movement, ignoring the broader social currents that may have led or contributed to the change in question. For instance, as already described, unintentional factors have enhanced women's access to resource-generating work roles for the past three decades in the United States and other highly industrialized nations. For much of that time there have also been women's movements committed to achieving gender equality in those same nations. If one were also to find a decrease in gender social definitions and differentiation, or a decrease in the gender division of domestic labor, is that attributable to movement pressure? To the ramifications of women's expanded access to work roles outside the home? To both? Given the impossibility of sorting that out, I leave to Chapter 8 (after I discuss intentional change efforts) a discussion of what other aspects of the gender system have (and have not) changed in the direction of greater equality beyond women's increased access to resource-generating work roles. In this section some instances of change that have exacerbated women's disadvantaged status will be further explored. The literature describing the *sequential process* of such change is not substantial, but a few examples should suffice to illustrate the systemic impact of change in the gender division of labor.

In her examination of trends in women's work and status on Israeli kibbutzim, Blumberg (forthcoming-b; see also Spiro, 1979, chap. 2) found the following sequence. Although women never shared equally with men the prestigious agricultural labor, many pioneer kibbutz women did perform such work. As they began to have children, women completely left the fields for service jobs in the communal laundries, kitchens, and nurseries. As this work became more mechanized, more and more women staffed the nurseries, where adult/child ratios steadily increased. Requirements were subsequently instituted by which adolescent girls work part-time in the nurseries, regardless of their preference, while boys are sent for part-time work to the fields and factories. A social ideology then developed that makes this gender division of labor seem "natural." One major result is that "80 percent of kibbutz boys and girls, vs. only 20 percent of a control sample of upper middle class Israeli city children chose extreme sex-stereotyped types of occupations" (p. 21). Blumberg found especially striking the low level of occupational aspiration and expectation among young kibbutz girls compared with kibbutz boys. By high school, the girls show decreasing scholastic achievement over their earlier performance. As adults, 80% of kibbutz residents seeking psychological therapy are women, and their complaints are largely depression and alienation, for which "they tend to blame themselves" (p. 23). Women of the kibbutz are criticized as gossips, whiners, petty, prematurely aged, and preoccupied with appearance.

Even though their personal income has remained identical to that of men over the entire history of kibbutz existence, the vastly unequal prestige that attaches to service versus "productive" work (agrarian and industrial) profoundly affected the gender system as the division of labor became increasingly gender segregated. In the terminology of this book, an increasing gender division of labor has produced stronger gender social definitions and greater gender differentiation. In turn, these changes strengthened and legitimated the gender division of labor (Blumberg, forthcoming-b, p. 24). Finally, fertility rates are relatively high on kibbutzim (3–4 or more children per woman), higher than elsewhere in Israel (pp. 19 and 25). High fertility is the result of both a strong pronatalist policy by the kibbutzim and the fact that women know that they will be child caretakers regardless of their personal fertility.

In discussing her research, and that of others from a variety of African, Latin American, and Asian communities, Blumberg (1988, forthcoming-a) demonstrates that, where a change in the gender division of labor occurs such that women's relative economic contribution to the family declines, their input into familial decision making does as well. In particular, women come to have far less say in how money is spent within the family. In addition, husbands get to decide their wives' fertility on the basis of their own interests, indicating an increase in male micro resource power. The reduction of women's power and autonomy within the family is especially evident when women's work comes to be confined to the domestic sphere (Blumberg, 1988, pp. 66–67). Moreover, this decline follows very rapidly upon a reduction in their "economic power" (that is, women's personal income).

Sanday (1981, pp. 141–43) describes how the matriarchal Iroquois became increasingly gender stratified around the turn of the nineteenth century. During the eighteenth century, wild game became increasingly scarce, making the male work of hunting decreasingly tenable. At the urging of Quaker missionaries, and in the absence of alternative work activities, men experimented with keeping domestic animals and with plow cultivation. Women had been the traditional cultivators, employing the hoe of a characteristically horticultural technology. The greater yield produced by the men's experiment "challenged the ancient belief that only women could make crops grow" (1981, p. 143). Shortly after, a prophet by the name of Handsome Lake began to preach a new religion that provided new rights and duties for each gender. He taught "that men were to practice agriculture in the white man's style and that . . . women were to conceive and obey" (1981, p. 157). Women were turned into homemakers, men into cultivators (p. 157). Women who failed to follow this new way were accused of witchcraft and a few were actually executed. "Many women adopted the new way quickly" (p. 142). The result, during both Handsome Lake's life and thereafter, was that "Iroquoian women held power in name only"; their "world diminished in scope and power" (pp. 141, 157).

In recent years the Chinese government has introduced substantial changes in the organization of rural work in an attempt to enhance agricultural productivity. Prior to the changes, women and men worked as individual, wage-earning employees of agricultural communes. Now, as in prerevolutionary China, the household has again become the primary unit of production, turning over a fixed quota of produce to the state and dispensing with the rest as small-scale, private entrepreneurs. Citing Elizabeth Croll, Hartmann (1987, p. 151) reports that, by strengthening the individual household as the unit of production, women reassumed their traditional roles, with the result that their movement, visibility, and independence have been reduced. Moreover, traditional values have witnessed a resurgence, "including the view that women's main purpose in life is to bear and raise children."

On the basis of these descriptions, I suggest that the following process results from a change in the gender division of labor by which women's access to resource-generating (including as resources prestige as well as income) work decreases. When the loss is economic, the first, almost immediate result is an increase in their husbands' micro-level power. The rest of the process occurs regardless of whether the loss is economic or in terms of the relative prestige of women's work. Another relatively rapid result is the loss of self-confidence, work commitment, and aspiration by women. They thereby become increasingly unfit for "better" work. More slowly, gender social definitions arise, or are strengthened, that "explain" and justify the new division of labor and increased gender inequality. Finally, over the course of a generation or two, childhood engenderment is affected, and gender differentiation increases. With the strengthening of gender social definitions and differentiation, we come full circle as they reinforce the new gender division of labor and women's increased disadvantages. Barring rapid intervention to reverse women's initial loss of resources, a stable gender system will emerge in which gender stratification has been heightened.

CONCLUSION

In Figure 6.3 a model is presented of how, given a decline in women's access to resource-generating work roles, other aspects of the gender system are affected over time. In Figure 6.4, the earlier sections of this chapter are summarized as they pertain to the question: What produces a decline in women's access to resource-generating work roles? This figure depicts how economic, technological, demographic, and political conflict factors can reduce women's opportunities. In Chapter 8 summary process models will be presented that delineate the factors that pro-

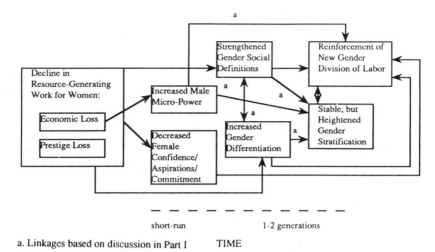

Figure 6.3. A Process Model of the Effects Over Time of Women's Decline in Access to Resource-Generating Work Roles

duce an increase in women's access to resource-generating work roles, along with their effects on other aspects of the gender system. The reasons for leaving those figures until a later chapter were explained at the beginning of the last section. Combining the last two charts, the clear conclusion is that, when macro-level forces having nothing to do with gender set in motion processes that reduce women's access to resource-generating work, all aspects of an inequitable gender system are exacerbated. The loss of opportunity by women quickly begins to affect other aspects of the gender system, especially increasing male micro-level power. Women may also increase their fertility as they lose access to nondomestic work roles, which can result in rising population numbers and yet fewer opportunities for women over time. More slowly, gender social definitions and differentiation are strengthened. Ultimately, a new, stable system of gender stratification emerges in which women are more disadvantaged than in earlier generations.

The macro-structural changes that produce the processes that

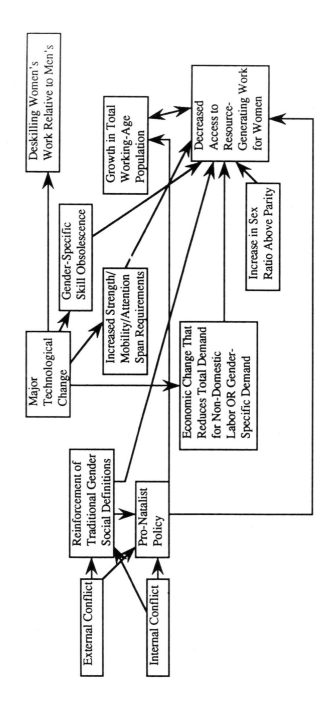

Figure 6.4. A Summary Model of the Unintentional Processes That Decrease Women's Access to Resource-Generating Work Roles

exacerbate female disadvantage have been set in motion by endogenous developments—especially technological—in many times and places. In the past few centuries, such changes were often the result of exogenous pressure from colonial powers. Today, Third World nations often experience them as the result of exogenous pressure from the expanding economies of core nations. Where exogenous forces have precipitated change, many if not most men have been victimized as well. Nonetheless, the resulting political, economic, and/or demographic stresses usually affect women in a doubly negative way: as members of the indigenous population along with men, and as women who become further subordinated to men. Even wealthy core nations are not immune from macro-structural changes that could set in motion the processes described as serving to increase gender stratification, a prospect to be discussed in the final chapter.

CHAPTER SEVEN

Toward Gender Equality: Intentional Change Processes

Although some degree of gender inequality is to be found in the vast majority of societies, for reasons discussed in Chapter 3, it is actually fairly rare for that reality to be perceived by a large number of societal members. Moreover, women in societies where they are maximally disadvantaged are not more likely to perceive inequality than their sisters in less gender-stratified societies. In fact, there is good reason to believe that the opposite is typically the case. In order to *intentionally* set about reducing gender stratification, change agents and activists must first come to perceive inequality. But perception is not enough. Actors must also be motivated to do something to change the situation and must believe that their actions have at least some likelihood of succeeding. Finally, material and nonmaterial resources will have to be devoted to any effort (Gale, 1986; Jenkins, 1983; Zald and McCarthy, 1979). Such resources must be available to those people who perceive inequality, are motivated to change it, and are convinced that their actions can matter. There are two categories of people who sometimes come to combine these attributes in an intentional effort to reduce or eliminate gender stratification: elites and women's movement activists. In this chapter the processes that sometimes impel these two categories to such an effort are explored. In the next chapter the material from this and the last chapters will be integrated, and the extent to which, and ways in which, gender system change toward greater equality is likely to result from combined intentional and unintentional processes will be explored.

FROM THE TOP:
ELITE-SPONSORED CHANGE EFFORTS

I have assumed two things about elites throughout this book: (1) that they are overwhelmingly male and (2) that they typically act to preserve or enhance their privileged positions, or at least in a manner that does not jeopardize them. Why, then, would they institute a conscious, active effort to reduce gender inequality? There are two circumstances, which are not mutually exclusive, under which elite members might do so. First, they may perceive that basic problems faced by their society, which negatively affect large numbers of people and may possibly jeopardize their incumbency in elite roles, are exacerbated by a gender system that devalues and disadvantages women. Second, until now elites have been treated as a unified collectivity. In fact, quite often there exist contending elite factions, or a group of would-be elites engaged in a struggle for power with de facto elites. Where such competition exists, one faction may actively recruit women's support for its cause by promising to ameliorate their disadvantaged status. Once motivated to seek change, it can be assumed that de facto elites have access to sufficient resources and possess a sense of political efficacy that together enable at least partial success.

In both of these cases, gender equality does not constitute the first or primary priority of real or would-be elite members. Their commitment to ameliorating women's disadvantages is strategic. It constitutes a means that they perceive as enhancing the probability of achieving or maintaining power and perquisites or the other goals they seek. This fact strongly limits the extent to which gender system change is likely to result from their commitment, even if they are completely successful in their pursuit of power. Whenever issues of women's rights and opportunities are seen as jeopardizing the support of large numbers of male allies, or jeopardizing the achievement of their first priority (gaining or maintaining power for themselves, their faction, their party, and so on), elite commitment to gender equity will be downplayed, if not abandoned. Their first priority is typically depicted ideologically as a "larger" issue of worker, national, racial/ethnic/ religious, or political party power. In speaking of such groups, whose leaders ostensibly supported women's rights, Lipman-Blumen (1984, pp. 181–82) succinctly concluded:

> Abolitionists, Zionists, nationalists, civil rights workers all admonished women that they were selfish, elitist, or politically inept to press the women's question as an explicit component of social justice and power relationships.

Marxist parties have been especially inclined to recruit women with promises of gender equity and then reduce or abandon that commitment in response to the resistance of male members (for a summary of this history, see Chafetz and Dworkin, 1986, especially chap. 1; for Britain, Foreman, 1977, and Rowbotham, 1976; for Germany, Jancar, 1978, Heitlinger, 1979, and Boxer and Quataert, 1978; for Russia, Jancar, 1978, and Boxer and Quataert, 1978; for China, Croll, 1978, and Johnson, 1978).

Despite the fact that male elites are prone to give short shrift to issues of gender equity in the name of "larger" priorities, nonetheless limited gains have often been made by women as a result of elite-initiated actions. A few brief examples will suffice to demonstrate both types of circumstances enumerated above.

In the Interest of the Nation

In the late nineteenth century, many elite men in China, Japan, and India began efforts to "modernize" and Westernize their impoverished societies. They became convinced that their nations' "backwardness" was, in part, the result of women's extremely suppressed status. In China they worked to end foot-binding and open educational opportunities to females. Along with foreign women, Chinese intellectuals, gentry, and government officials (but rarely Chinese women) formed the Unbound Feet Society in 1892, which eventually numbered 10,000 members (Croll, 1978, chap. 3). Just after the turn of the century, they succeeded in opening schools for girls. In Japan, the period of 1868 to 1912 was a time of official government commitment to national modernization known as the Meiji Period. While the government was not inclined to permit any changes in the traditional role of women, many privileged men fought particularly for educational opportunities for women (Sievers, 1983, chap. 2; Robins-Mowry, 1983, p. 42). Likewise, in India it was a group of privileged men who first sought educational opportunities for women and the banning of child marriages, *sati* (widow suicide), and *purdah* (the seclusion of women). They argued that these changes would increase "women's efficiency," strengthen the family and social traditions, and thereby aid in the modernization of Indian society (Mazumdar, 1979, p. xi; Everett, 1979, chap. 4). Under the leadership of Gandhi, the Congress party was especially active in working for these types of reforms in the status of women in order to reform the entire society (Thomas, 1964, chap. 11; Everett, 1979, chap. 4).

In all three cases, men worked to organize women who would join in the fight for their own rights. Within a couple of decades, women's movements did emerge. Gradually, also, the basic reforms sought for women by the Westernized, privileged men were gained, mostly benefiting urban, middle- and upper-class women (i.e., their wives and daughters). In none of these cases, however, did men seek overall gender equality or to restructure the traditional gender division of labor. Rather, women's most severe disadvantages were to be ameliorated to make them better wives and mothers in a "modernized" society (Chafetz and Dworkin, 1986, chap. 4).

Proposition 7.1. Given an extremely high level of gender stratification and national poverty, the more committed a society's elites are to changing the nation to resemble wealthier ones, the more inclined they are to institute policies that ameliorate women's most extreme disadvantages.

The major focus of elite men is education for women. Because they assume that women will continue to function primarily as wives and mothers, their goal is to produce mothers who will raise nontraditional children—really sons—and wives who are properly supportive of "modern" husbands. In order for girls and young women to receive an education, traditional practices such as seclusion and child marriages must be abandoned as well. Such men undoubtedly assume that the change process should and will end with the granting of limited, mostly formal rights and opportunities to women. However, because they encourage women to organize in pursuit of these changes, the result eventually is likely to be a relatively autonomous women's movement—often small—that develops a fuller agenda of change targets and some degree of gender consciousness. I will return to this topic later in the chapter.

Contending Elite Factions

In the last section attention focused on cases where the primary motivation that induced male elites to work for an improvement in women's status was what they perceived as national interest. They identified women's extreme disadvantages as a partial cause of national problems that adversely affected most, if not all, societal members. They sought to ameliorate national disadvantage in part by reducing women's disadvantages. Probably more frequently, male elites are motivated to help women in order to gain their support in a struggle against a colonial power, an existing indigenous government, or one or more other political parties. The two forms of motivation are not, however, mutually exclusive. In a situation of competition, male elites may also perceive an improvement in women's status as important for the enhanced well-being of the entire collectivity. Indeed, they will typically claim this, even if only cynically in order to garner women's support.

In the late nineteenth century, Westernized Persian men began a movement to institute constitutional government. These men, like their Chinese, Japanese, and Indian counterparts, began to educate their daughters on the assumption that they would raise "better" children (Nashat, 1983, p. 15). After a failed attempt to institute constitutional government in 1906, these men saw the need to mobilize women for their struggle (Bámdád, 1977, pp. 25–26). They organized mostly secret women's groups and became outspoken supporters of education for females. Between 1906 and 1911 several thousand women were mobilized to support the men's movement (Bámdád, 1977, pp. 34–35). In 1925 the reformist Pahlavi Dynasty was founded. Between then and 1941 when he abdicated, the first Shah opened numerous state schools for girls, banned veils, and opened universities to women (Nashat, 1983). A conservative backlash followed the Shah's abdication in 1941, threatening the relatively few gains made by mostly urban, wealthy women. During the 1940s, the opposition Communist Tudah party "launched the most consistent campaign advocating women's rights" (Nashat, 1983, p. 29). In 1949 it organized the Society for Democratic Women, which campaigned for education for women, equal pay, and suffrage. It was suppressed by the government in 1953.

In pre-World War I Egypt, male reformers sought independence from British colonial rule. They too took up the cause of education for females, who would thus supposedly raise "enlightened children," as well as an end to polygyny and to child marriage (Philipp, 1978; Zwemer and Zwemer, 1926). They thereby won the active support of women, who participated in the 1919 nationalist revolution. Nevertheless, the new constitution offered no political rights or other reforms for women (Philipp, 1978, p. 278).

Immediately after the Bolshevik coup in Russia, the Communist party faced the need to mobilize the active support of women for its revolution (Heitlinger, 1979, p. 56). It created local women's groups (*zhenotdel*) throughout the country, whose purpose was to educate and "emancipate" women. Similar post-Communist revolution women's organizations have been established in Cuba, China, Yugoslavia, and Vietnam (Stites, 1980). They basically serve as vehicles for state and party mobilization (Lapidus, 1977), although they have undoubtedly helped to reduce women's disadvantages (Heitlinger, 1979; Stites, 1980). The Chinese Communist party was especially active in its attempts to mobilize women. From its inception in 1921, women's emancipation was a basic part of its party platform. In 1923 it established a Women's Section to recruit women, and by 1927 300,000 women were members (Croll, 1978, pp. 118–21). Johnson (1978), however, stresses that the emphasis on women's emancipation was a handy recruitment tactic that was fought by rank-and-file male members. Nonetheless, in the long years of bloody conflict with the Nationalist party after 1927, wherever the Communists gained control they improved the social, legal, and economic status of Chinese women. The result was that on the eve of party victory in 1948, 20 million women were members of its women's associations (Croll, 1978, p. 220).

When groups of men contend for, or seek to consolidate their power, they often seek women's support by promising to ameliorate some or many of their disadvantages. They are often very successful in recruiting women on that basis. When they succeed in their primary objective, such elite men may or may not even attempt to deliver on those promises. In no case has gender equality eventuated from this process. But in most cases some amelioration of women's disadvantages does occur when the elite faction seeking women's support gains or consolidates its power. At the very least, such regimes usually improve the formal, de jure legal and constitutional rights of women, even specifying complete legal and political equality in many cases. Faced with resistance from male supporters, and given the fact that gender equity never constitutes their first priority or goal, the de jure improvements in women's status are rarely enforced very actively, however. Decades later, women's real gains in status, power, and opportunities are, therefore, likely to be more apparent than real. Where a real decrease in gender stratification follows upon the empowerment of supportive male elites, I suggest that one or more of the processes discussed in the last chapter were occurring as well. Where unintentional processes encourage the reduction of female disadvantage, a male elite committed to that goal can substantially expedite change. In the absence of those processes, elites will do little to create substantially new opportunities for women that challenge the power and perquisites of men.

Proposition 7.2. The more severe the conflict between contending male elites, and/or the need to consolidate power by a nominally ruling elite, the more likely one or more groups of men will attempt to mobilize the support of women.

Proposition 7.3. The more strongly a group of men attempts to mobilize the support of women, the more improvements in women's opportunities, rights, and status they will promise.

Proposition 7.4. The more women are promised, the more likely they are to receive formal, de jure legal and political equality, given the success of the male elites who seek their support.

Proposition 7.5. The more unintentional processes are functioning to enhance women's opportunities and status, the more likely that the de jure improvements in women's status will be matched by a real decrease in gender stratification.

Conversely:

Proposition 7.6. In the absence of unintentional processes functioning to enhance women's opportunities, there is a low probability that women's newly gained de jure rights and opportunities will be enforced, and a high probability that they will be resisted by male rank-and-file supporters of de facto elites.

Conclusion

Figure 7.1 is a process model depicting how male elites sometimes come to work for—and partially achieve—greater gender equity. In it two linkages have been added that connect the previous sections. Competition between elite factions and threats to the power of de facto elites arise from myriad different causes. However, in the contemporary world at least, sustained national poverty is especially likely to cause recurrent political contention and turmoil. In the years since World War II, many societies have thrown off the yoke of colonialism, and poor nations have often

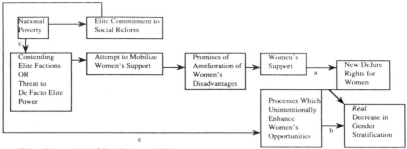

Figure 7.1. A Process Model of Intentional Male Elite Efforts to Enhance Gender Equality

thrown out governments that represent the interests of a tiny minority of rich, privileged families. In the process, constitutions have been written and rewritten, often specifying gender equality in many, if not all, arenas of political, legal, economic, and social life. In most of these cases, the daily lives and opportunities of the vast majority of mostly poor women have changed very little if at all for the better. In fact, I suggested in the last chapter that they have often changed for the worse.

In many so-called Communist nations, such as China, the Soviet Union, and Cuba, the average woman is undoubtedly better off than her prerevolutionary foremothers. In these cases, elite commitment to ameliorating women's disadvantages has been combined with one or both of two things: idiosyncratic demographic factors and economic expansion. In the case of the Soviet Union, casualty rates—especially male—in the aftermath of the revolution and during both world wars were so high that women's access to nondomestic work has remained very high for most of this century. China's severe overpopulation problem resulted in a strict antinatalist policy that has recently reduced women's familial obligations, at least in urban areas. In all three nations elites have engaged in efforts to expand national economies that were highly impoverished when their revolutions occurred. In the process, new opportunities have been developed over and above the capacity of men to fill them. Nonetheless, in all three cases women still perform nondomestic work that, on average, is well below that of equally educated men in pay and prestige. National elites are still overwhelmingly male. Women remain responsible for domestic and familial labor, with little if any help from their husbands. Moreover, their double workday is worse than that of their counterparts in wealthy capitalist nations, because Communist nations have not invested in consumer goods and services that can lighten domestic work (e.g., one-stop supermarkets, fast foods, dishwashers, and refrigerators). But the appropriate comparison for this book is not cross-national, it is historical. There can be no question that over time, gender stratification has decreased in most Communist nations, although none approach gender equality. This did not result *primarily* from elite commitment to gender equity. Rather, the demographic and economic realities faced by, and especially the policies pursued by, elites in these nations have constituted the primary impetus for the partial amelioration of women's disadvantages (see Croll, 1986). It has been their commitment to ameliorating poverty through economic change that has been most important to women. Nonetheless, the fact that Communist party elites have placed at least a secondary priority on gender equity has probably hastened and expanded the effects of demographic and economic phenomena on the gender stratification system. In short, elite commitment specifically to gender system change matters, but probably only marginally.

Before leaving a discussion of elite-inspired change efforts, it is interesting to note that occasionally women profit from a political "fluke," including conscious efforts to prevent change in women's status and opportunities. One example of this is Title VII of the U.S. Civil Rights Act, which included women in antidiscrimination legislation designed to protect blacks. Women were added by Southern senators attempting to defeat the act, on the assumption that this addition would demonstrate just how bad the legislation was and elicit more negative votes. Of course, they lost and women gained. A second example pertains to President Kennedy's 1961 National Commission on the Status of Women. According to Rupp and Taylor (1987), organized labor and several other interests sought to bury the Equal Rights Amendment that was gradually gaining support in Congress due to the active lobbying efforts of the small National Woman's Party. The foes of the ERA convinced Kennedy that such a commission would distract support from the amendment, thereby preventing threats to existing protective legislation for women (that functioned primarily to "protect" women out of many well-paying jobs). The outcome of the national commission was the establishment of women's commissions in a large number of states and the written documentation of women's substantial economic, social, and political disadvantages. Some observers suggest that, in collecting together a group of political and professionally employed women to discuss women's status, the Kennedy Commission constituted an important spark in the ignition of the Second Wave women's movement (e.g., Freeman, 1975; Carden, 1974). It is impossible to incorporate such "flukes" into a general theory, but they are important to remember inasmuch as they sometimes produce profound, unforeseen effects.

FROM THE GRASS ROOTS: WOMEN'S MOVEMENTS

Women's movements are organized attempts, mounted largely (but not necessarily exclusively) by women, to ameliorate socially rooted disadvantages that they confront on the basis of their gender. They are in opposition to the status quo and thus are considered change-oriented social movements. They have at their core one or more groups or organizations committed to this goal as their first priority, although they often include substantial numbers of nonorganizational members who share their commitment. They are independent of control by any male-dominated organization, political party, or government. Women's movements vary in how large they grow, from a relatively small group in one city to a mass movement represented throughout a nation. They also vary in the radicalness of the ideology and goals they develop. At one extreme, they challenge all aspects of the gender system and call for the restructuring of all social, cultural, economic, and political institutions to bring about gender equity. At the other extreme, they accept the fundamental gender system and seek amelioration of a limited number of specific disadvantages confronted by women (see Chafetz and Dworkin, 1986, for an elaboration of this definition).

The degree of radicalness of goals and ideology directly reflects the extent of gender consciousness developed by movement activists. The more aspects of the gender system activists define as illegitimate, and the more specific alternatives they propose to it (i.e., the greater their gender consciousness), the more radical their movement ideology is likely to be. It should be noted, however, that at least some movement leaders may have a significantly more radical gender consciousness than implied by the public ideology of the movement organizations they lead. The need to recruit followers, who for reasons to be discussed later are typically more conservative, sometimes functions to modify their publicly proclaimed ideology. Larger movements, comprising a number of groups and organizations, are typically characterized by ideological diversity. The groups will tend to share some specific goals and a general, often vague commitment to gender equality, but they differ on other goals, priorities among goals, strategies, and tactics. The importance of such diversity will become apparent later in this section.

Women's movements date only to the mid-nineteenth century. But since their first emergence in the United States and some Western European nations, they have appeared in nations spread across the globe, and on every continent. Historically, two waves of women's movements have emerged. The earlier, First Wave movements were overwhelmingly at the ideologically less radical end of the continuum, while the later, Second Wave has been at the most radical end. My colleague, A. G. Dworkin, and I documented First Wave movements in 31 nations, beginning as early as 1848 in the United States, and ending as late as the 1950s in India and Iran. Second Wave movements all began after about 1968. We found clear evidence for them in 16 nations (Chafetz and Dworkin, 1986, chaps. 4 and 5, 1989).

For a theory of change, two issues concerning women's movements must be addressed. First, under what conditions do they emerge and grow? Given the nearly universal existence of gender inequality, why does organized opposition arise in only some times and places? Second, once a women's movement does emerge and grow beyond a very small, incipient level, how does it contribute to the lessening of gender stratification? What does it do that contributes to gender system change?

Emergence and Growth

Dworkin and I (Chafetz and Dworkin, 1986, 1989) developed, and through a partial test were able to support, a theory that explains why women's movements emerge and grow (and by implication fail to do so). Its application is somewhat different for First and Second Wave movements. That difference will be discussed after the basic outline of the theory is presented (for more detail on the theory and test, see 1986, chaps. 3 and 6).

The impetus for the development and subsequent growth of women's movements is macro-structural change. The specific variables are increases in industrialization, urbanization, and the size of the middle class, all of which covary extensively with one another. Women's movements in virtually all nations and both waves are overwhelmingly constituted, and, especially, led by middle-class women. The three macro-structural changes, but most centrally industrialization, permit or induce the emergence of new, nondomestic, and nonfamilial role opportunities for middle-class women. In the terminology of this book, women experience expanded access to resource-generating roles. As some women assume public roles that are nontraditional for their gender, status/role dilemmas arise for them. These dilemmas consist of contradictions between traditionally ascribed gender norms and those associated with their newly emerging social roles. Women are typically treated according to traditional expectations that are inappropriate to their new roles. They may be expected to behave in what are increasingly inappropriate or contradictory ways. In addition, while playing their new roles they come into increasing contact with men other than family members and friends. These men, who often perform similar nondomestic roles, may be equally or less competent than women are, yet they receive substantially more rewards and opportunities. Prior to the assumption of their new roles, most women compared their lot with that of other women who shared similar domestic roles and social status. Their new experiences prompt a change of comparative reference group to men. In turn, they are likely to experience a sense of relative deprivation (see also Holter, 1970; Safilios-Rothschild, 1979; Zanna, Crosby, and Loewenstein, 1987).

Women's movements begin in large cities and, until they approach a mass level, do not penetrate rural areas and small towns. Because of the density of urban life, and the types of roles in which they are now involved, women who experience expanded roles, status/role dilemmas, and a sense of relative deprivation are likely to come into contact with one another. As they exchange experiences and perceptions, at least some members of this growing pool of women are likely to develop a perception that their problems are not individual but shared on the basis of gender, that those problems are created by an inequitable social system, that the reward and opportunity structure is unfair and illegitimate, and that social change in the gender system should be sought. In short, a cadre of women will develop gender consciousness. The larger the pool of women who experience expanded roles, the larger the number of women who will develop gender consciousness, although clearly many will not. Once such a gender-conscious cadre exists, it can serve as a new normative reference group for other women, who had traditionally looked primarily to men to define gender-appropriate behavior for them (as discussed in Part I).

Gender consciousness provides the motivation for women to organize in pursuit of gender system change. However, for any social movement to emerge, two further factors must exist: a sense of potential efficacy and resources. Efficacy, or the perception that organized efforts have the potential for bringing about the desired changes, results at least in part from the new roles women are entering. As pioneers, many are likely to experience enhanced self-confidence and an increasing sense that goal achievement is possible. Poole and Zeigler's data on American women show that, from 1952 to 1980, employed women had consistently higher political efficacy scores than homemakers (1985, p. 137). Their new roles also contribute to the accumulation of necessary resources. At least some of the women develop expanded connections with community members, even elites; organizational and public speaking skills; media, fund-raising, and lobbying experience; access to their own money; and other resources organizations require to pursue collective goals. As described in the last section, in some cases sympathetic men expedite this process, contributing their own material and non-material resources to the early organizational efforts. Even where women begin their movement, the same macro-structural changes that expand role opportunities for women may encourage some men to actively support gender system change and, therefore, the new women's movement. Such support is especially likely among men whose female loved ones are experiencing role expansion and its attendant problems. With the combination of gender consciousness, a sense of efficacy, and resources, a women's movement emerges. The larger the pool of women who experience expanded roles produced by macro-structural change, the larger the movement becomes.

The above process presupposes a national political situation that is conducive to movement formation and growth. Dworkin and I found that there are two extreme political situations that prevent or retard that development: repression and co-optation. Repression exists when governments prohibit grass-roots organizations generally (other than those sponsored by the government or ruling party) or when they specifically prohibit political activity or organization by women. Techniques of governmental repression have improved markedly during the course of this century. In the Second Wave era, repressive governments have been well able to prevent the emergence of independent women's movements. In the period of the First Wave, however, they were often only able to retard their development. At the outset of their First Wave movements, Germany, Russia, China, and Japan had laws specifically denying women the right to join political organizations, attend political meetings, or publicly discuss political issues. These movements remained small and covert until the restrictions were lifted, after which some expanded very rapidly. At some point in their histories, ongoing First Wave movements in France, Russia, China, Japan, Persia/Iran, Brazil, and Peru were temporarily repressed.

Co-optation exists when male political elites move quickly to grant some demands made by a newly emerging women's movement, thereby appearing to render moot the movement itself. New Zealand, Australia, Norway, and Finland effectively co-opted their First Wave women's movements by quickly enfranchising women before World War I. These movements never reached their maximum potential size, as estimated by the magnitude of industrialization, urbanization, and size of the middle class in each case.

The following propositions summarize the most fundamental aspects of Dworkin's and my partially verified theory of the emergence and growth of women's movements. Given a politically conducive situation:

Proposition 7.7. The more rapid the growth in industrialization, urbanization, and the size of the middle class, the more middle-class women experience expanded role opportunities outside the home and family.

Proposition 7.8. The greater the expansion of middle-class women's role opportunities, the more they will confront status/role dilemmas, acquire a sense of efficacy as well as material and nonmaterial resources, and change their reference groups.

Proposition 7.9. The more women change their reference

groups, the more likely they are to experience a sense of relative deprivation.

Proposition 7.10. The more women experiencing status/role dilemmas and relative deprivation are in contact with one another, the greater the number of women who will develop gender consciousness.

Proposition 7.11. The more women who develop gender consciousness and a sense of efficacy, and acquire resources, the more likely a women's movement is to emerge and grow.

The process of women's movement development can be depicted as a model, as in Figure 7.2.

The First and Second Waves were ideologically quite different, largely because the types of role expansion experienced by middle-class women were very different. During the early stages of industrialization, employment opportunities for married middle-class women were all but nonexistent. Single middle-class women were able to move into the paid labor force in many instances, however. The founders of First Wave movements experienced expanded educational opportunities and an expansion in

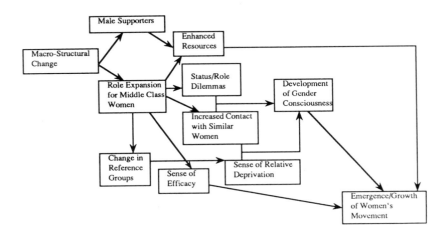

Figure 7.2. A Process Model of the Emergence and Growth of Women's Movements

nonpaid public roles. Middle-class women became active and outspoken philanthropists, religious revivalists, social welfare workers, club organizers and members, and activists in abolition, temperance, pacifist, nationalist, and socialist movements. Prior to the first generation of pioneers in these roles, women throughout most of the world—including the United States and Western Europe—were expected to remain silent in public. Activism on behalf of their ideals was confined to the family. For them, the assumption of publicly active roles on behalf of their ideals represented substantial role expansion. Their new roles may not have enhanced their material resources, but they did enhance their nonmaterial ones. Nonetheless, they as well as their husbands continued to assume that married women's first priority and commitment was to the home and family. The women's movements created by these pioneers largely reflected this assumption. Rather than seeking an end of "separate spheres" for men and women, they mostly sought to ameliorate women's most extreme educational, legal, and political disadvantages in the name of doing a better job as wives and mothers. It should be noted, however, that in many nations some of the leaders were far more ideologically radical than suggested by the publicly proclaimed organizational ideology. Indeed, almost every issue raised by the more radical Second Wave movements had its First Wave proponents. There was simply little potential followership for more radical ideas and goals (for more detail on First Wave ideology, see Chafetz and Dworkin, 1986, chap. 4).

The role expansion that produced the Second Wave was largely the dramatic expansion of labor-force participation by married women. As long as middle-class women were at most employed only temporarily while awaiting marriage and children, male coworkers would not constitute their comparative reference group. Rather, young, single, employed women compared themselves with each other and with their older married sisters who were full-time homemakers. They mostly assumed—and correctly so—that paid employment was a temporary occurrence in their lives. With the increasing employment of married middle-class women, it became ever more apparent that most women would spend a very large proportion of their lives in the labor force. Under that circumstance, it begins to make sense for women to compare themselves with the men they encounter at their jobs. The disadvantages women confront there, and the unequal burden of domestic labor they face at home, become more apparent as their reference group shifts. The resultant ideology has been predicated on the assumption that men and women inhabit basically the same spheres, but in a very unequal way.

Impact

Once a women's movement emerges and grows beyond a local, small group of socially privileged members, how does it come to realize some of its change goals? There are two avenues, which are interrelated, by which it can potentially effect change: through pressure on elites and by affecting public opinion.

In order to reduce gender inequality, women's movements pursue goals that entail policy change by elites. They may also pursue other goals (e.g., the establishment of women's self-help groups, shelters, cultural centers, or their own feminist media), but at a minimum women's movements seek concrete legal changes, usually political ones, and often policy changes in economic, educational, religious, and other cultural institutions. Movement organizations function as interest groups attempting to directly sway elite policy formation (Costain, 1982). Movements also function as change agents for public opinion, attempting to galvanize broad-based pressure on elites to change policy. In order to understand the relative importance of these two avenues in producing desired changes, it is important to note that, even in those few cases where women's movements have reached unambiguously mass proportions, only about 3% (or less) of the public are members of organizations and groups whose raison d'être is the reduction or elimination of gender inequality (Chafetz and Dworkin, 1986, chaps. 4, 5).

I begin with the assumption that elites will change laws and policies in the direction sought by a women's movement primarily because they perceive it to be rewarding to do so and/or costly not to. Given the relatively small proportion of societal members who involve themselves in organizations specifically part of the women's movement, their ability to *directly* reward or punish elites is limited. As discussed earlier in this chapter, where elite factions are contending for power, women's support may constitute the margin necessary for victory. Under such circumstances, some of the goals of women activists may be achieved. However, it was evident that substantial change in the gender system is not likely to eventuate from this.

What have been some of the tactics employed by women's movements to up the reward or cost ante for elites? I begin by noting one virtually unused tactic: violence, including property destruction. This tactic—which has probably on occasion netted at least token changes for collectivities such as workers, students, and black Americans (e.g., during the riots of the late 1960s)—was used only by a minority of (well-publicized) British suffrage activists, and they were disavowed by their fellow activists (for data substantiating the general efficacy of this strategy, see Gamson, 1975, chap. 6). Violence and property destruction appear to be particularly antithetical to a gender consciousness, for what reason I do not know.

Since suffrage was granted to women, women's movement groups have sometimes attempted to gain specific goals (e.g., the ERA, pay equity for state employees) by actively supporting or opposing specific candidates for election. In the main, however, candidates have infrequently won or lost an election specifically because of the efforts of a women's movement. The vaunted "gender gap" in the political preferences of American men and women in recent years has not involved issues explicitly focused on gender equity, but those of defense, welfare spending, environmental issues, and other social programs. Moreover, it has been relatively small, within gender differences by education, employment status, and so on being greater than between gender differences (Poole and Zeigler, 1985, chap. 2). Much more so than most disadvantaged groups, women constitute a highly het-

erogeneous collectivity. They differ extensively on all social variables except gender. Political parties and candidates support policies relevant to many different social categories. Women are,
therefore, more frequently confronted with cross-cutting loyal-
ties than other deprived groups. Is it reasonable to suppose that
a black, high school dropout, welfare mother and a white,
professionally employed, single woman will vote the same way
simply because they share a gender? Is it reasonable to suppose
that gender issues will be more salient for them than class or
racial ones? Also, unlike many other disadvantaged groups,
women do not live in segregated areas. They are geographically
dispersed throughout all electoral districts. This further reduces
their potential electoral clout.

Women's movements have occasionally employed the labor
strategy of boycott (e.g., of states that failed to ratify the ERA; of
Nestlé for dumping infant formula in Third World nations).
While ultimately successful in the case of Nestlé, the more
important ERA boycott failed to achieve its goal. As distinct from
labor unions primarily comprising women, women's movements
have not employed the labor tactic of striking, except occasionally
as symbolic, one-day events. The one cost tactic that women's
movement groups, at least in the United States, have used extensively and with a fair success rate has been the legal suit against
employment discrimination and harassment. This type of action,
however, presupposes the existence of antidiscrimination legislation, which already symbolizes elite action on behalf of women.
In short, women's movements have not been able to seriously
affect the reward or cost ante of elites and have, therefore, had
relatively little *direct* impact on elite policy formation.

Having said that, it must now be noted that, since their inception in the nineteenth century, many concrete goals propounded
and worked for by women's movements have been achieved. In
the First Wave, women in a large number of nations gained substantially improved access to educational opportunities; some
important legal changes in the rights especially of married
women, most notably in terms of property, control of their own
income, and child custody; the vote; and assorted other changes

specific to particular cases (e.g., the end of foot-binding in China, of widow suicide in India). In the case of Second Wave movements, women in several nations have achieved control over their reproduction through better access to contraception and abortion; legislation rendering illegal discrimination in employment and education; legal and policy changes pertaining to rape and other forms of male violence against women; and a variety of other policy, program, and legal changes specific to each nation. Nor have such changes been confined to what political elites can institute through legislation or judges through their decisions. Television networks and stations have made programming changes. Newspapers and magazines now largely avoid sexist language. Advertisers have changed their depictions of both genders to some degree. Universities have expanded their curricula to include courses on women and in many cases have established women's studies programs. Many hospitals have changed their policies pertaining to childbirth in directions originally propounded by women's movement activists (e.g., developing birthing centers, employing midwives for normal deliveries). Foundations and community agencies have funded new types of projects to meet women's needs (e.g., shelters for battered women). Many religions have changed wording and admitted women to heretofore exclusively male ritual and organizational roles. Police as well as courts have changed their treatment of rape victims. And this is but a partial list of the changes that have occurred in recent decades in a number of nations experiencing women's movements. In almost all cases, the initial suggestion and impetus for such changes came from organizations or groups that were part of a women's movement.

If women's movements are largely unable to directly achieve their goals, what has produced so much change in law, policy, and programs under the control of primarily male elites? *I suggest that the major importance of women's movements is to articulate a set of specific change goals and an ideology that legitimates gender system change.* In a situation where large numbers of women are experiencing role expansion, and, therefore, status/role dilemmas and some sense of relative deprivation, they will be prepared to "hear" the message delivered by the women's movement, as will some of the men to whom they are attached by emotional relationships. The pool of affected women will always be much larger than the relatively small number who become activist members of movement organizations. *The dissemination of a gender-conscious ideology and set of specific goals constitutes the major mechanism that allows nonactivists to reformulate into social and political terms their definitions of the origins of and solutions to personally experienced problems.* In Second Wave movements, this process has been called "consciousness-raising." It is crucial to understand that it occurs not only in self-conscious groups of activists, but in *varying degrees* among significant segments of the public (as will be discussed in the next chapter; see Poole and Zeigler, 1985). Gender consciousness spreads primarily through movement access to the media of mass communication (mostly magazines and newspapers in the First Wave, plus radio and especially TV in the Second). However, in the absence of a large number of women who are experiencing role expansion and its attendant problems, the message of what typically is a movement comprising a tiny fraction of the population falls on largely deaf ears. Holter (1970, pp. 33–34, 217) argues that many contemporary societies are particularly vulnerable to this kind of public opinion change. Especially Western nations stress achievement as the primary basis for stratification. Gender is an ascribed status and stands in contradiction to the underlying values of such societies. Gender inequality is, therefore, likely to be perceived as violating standards of justice, once a women's movement has raised the issue.

One of the resources that activists have usually developed (or expanded) before the women's movement arises is ties to community organizations. Especially important in this context are ties to potentially co-optable organizations mostly or entirely comprising women, such as business and professional groups, social service organizations, unions that mostly comprise women, other types of social movement organizations, even women's religious organizations. They are potentially co-optable to the extent that their members have also experienced expanded roles. Movement activists are often able to raise the gender consciousness of members, and especially leaders of organizations with which they have preexisting ties. Subsequently, such organizations become allies of the women's movement, at least for the pursuit of specific goals (Freeman, 1975, especially chap. 2). For instance, First Wave women's movements in a number of nations formed an alliance with the Woman's Christian Temperance Union in pursuit of women's suffrage (Chafetz and Dworkin, 1986, chaps. 1, 4; Epstein, 1981; Mitchinson, 1981; Grimshaw, 1972; Summers, 1975; Croll, 1978; Robins-Mowry, 1983). The Second Wave U.S. movement was able to develop alliances with such traditional and long-standing organizations as the YWCA, the Federation of Business and Professional Women's Clubs, the League of Women Voters, the American Civil Liberties Union, and the American Association of University Women, which collectively represent many millions of women (Banks, 1981, p. 247; Carden, 1974, pp. 3, 144 ff.; Freeman, 1975, pp. 214 ff.; Gelb and Palley, 1982, pp. 14, 27). By co-opting entire organizations, a women's movement dramatically increases support for the specific goals it seeks as well as resources that can be used to pursue them. In addition, often co-opted groups have long-term, established lobbying linkages to political elites that can be effectively exploited for some of the new issues raised by the movement.

Earlier I noted that, especially large women's movements are likely to be marked by considerable diversity in goals, ideology, priorities, tactics, and so on. Nonactivist members of the public will tend to support the least radical ideology and tactics (Giele, 1978). They will pick and choose among the many potential concrete goals those that appear most directly pertinent to the specific problems they face. It is the pressure of public opinion, including preexisting, now co-opted, organizations, that sways elite behavior. Most organizations and institutions, as well as governments, have constituents upon whose support and goodwill they rely. They will tend to respond to demands made by that constituency, if a large enough proportion supports them. Of course, there are many issues where, despite strong public consensus, political and other elites fail to respond (e.g., gun control legislation). I am not suggesting that elites will automatically accede to changes in public opinion. Rather, because they are also a part of the population and subject to the same processes as others, they will act on some of the demands of the women's movement that increasingly appear "reasonable" to them as well as to most of their constituents. In so doing, elites not only encounter a low risk of alienating their constituents, they are likely to be rewarded for their conformity to changed public opinion. As elites change their views, as well as laws and policies, they serve to further legitimate the ideology and goals of the women's movement. In this way, elite change further expedites public opinion change. Therefore, elites will tend to make changes that reduce women's disadvantages, but, like most of the public, they will be those that represent responses to the least radical goals of the movement. As Boneparth and Stoper (1988, p. 14) note, "If a policy has low visibility, fits with prevailing values, and involves narrow concerns, its chances are greater than if it [has the opposite characteristics]." The importance of intramovement diversity is that the very existence of highly radical demands, ideology, and tactics makes those of the moderates appear more reasonable and legitimate than would otherwise be the case (see Ferree and Hess, 1985). This legitimacy enhances the probability that at least some change in the desired direction will be achieved.

Proposition 7.12. The larger the proportion of women who experience role expansion, the greater the public acceptance of the goals and ideology of a women's movement.

Proposition 7.13. The more diverse the ideologies, concrete goals, priorities, and tactics of women's movement groups, the more legitimate and acceptable those of the more moderate group(s) will appear to the public.

Proposition 7.14. The greater the public support for concrete goals pursued by women's movement organizations, the more likely elites will introduce legal, policy, and programmatic changes that decrease women's disadvantages, but they will be those sought by the moderate wing of the movement.

Proposition 7.15. The greater the elite support for gender system change, the more legitimate such change will appear to members of the public.

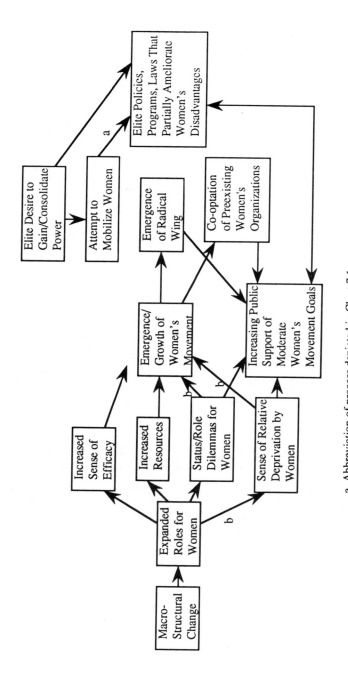

Figure 7.3. A Summary Model of the Main Intentional Processes that Reduce Gender Stratification

a. Abbreviation of process depicted in Chart 7.1

b. Abbreviation of process depicted in Chart 7.2

CONCLUSION

Figure 7.3 summarizes the main points developed in this chapter. When confronted with problems, male elites sometimes come to define the partial amelioration—or its promise—of women's disadvantages as necessary to a solution. The outcome is usually more de jure than real gender equity, however. Women organize to pursue gender equity when, given expanded opportunities resulting from macro-structural changes, they confront new problems, develop gender consciousness, and gain new resources. In this they are sometimes aided by sympathetic men. The primary role played by women's movements is to change public opinion, to replace gender social definitions with some degree of gender consciousness, and to legitimate the need for specific changes in laws, policies, and programs. They are successful in this to the extent that a sufficiently large proportion of women have experienced expanded roles. But public opinion tends to be more conservative than movement activists. The development of a radical branch of a women's movement, therefore, expedites public perception that the goals, ideology, priorities, and tactics of the moderate branch are legitimate. Finally, elites in all major institutional arenas tend to respond to opinion change by their constituents, and in so doing to legitimate and reinforce it. Political elites also respond to some of the lobbying efforts made by movement organizations and their co-opted organizational allies. The outcome is that changes instituted by elites will typically be quite moderate, at least relative to the agenda developed by radical activists. Radical activists are, therefore, likely to perceive change as more apparent than real—the glass more empty than full. However, other change advocates are equally likely to perceive real and meaningful change—a substantially more full glass than earlier.

CHAPTER EIGHT

Toward Gender Equality: An Integrated Theory

In order to understand how systems of gender stratification change in the direction of reducing female disadvantage, the theoretical points developed in the last chapter must be integrated with the relevant material from Chapter 6 concerning unintentional processes. In addition, a full understanding of the change process requires insight into how, over time, change in one aspect of the gender system gives rise to change in other parts. Preparatory to that, this chapter begins with a description of what has and has not changed during recent decades in advanced industrial societies, focusing on the United States, for which information is most readily available.

HALF FULL, HALF EMPTY: RECENT CHANGES IN HIGHLY INDUSTRIALIZED NATIONS

No one over the age of 40 in the United States and other highly industrialized nations can doubt that gender arrangements in 1990 are substantially different than they were in their childhood. Things have changed, but how much? To what extent and in what ways are the genders more equal now than before? In what ways are they not? Scattered throughout the earlier chapters of this book specific facts and trends concerning gender systems in the most highly industrialized nations of the world have been discussed. In this section these are brought together and supplemented in order to develop an overview of ongoing change and stability in the gender systems of such societies.

The most obvious change is the rapid and radical increase in the proportion of married women in the paid labor force, as repeatedly noted. Women *as a collectivity* now have more access to the material and other resources (e.g., prestige, knowledge, alliances, skills) that accrue to nondomestic work than they did in 1950, 1960, or even 1970. For the vast majority of women who now work outside the home, the nature of their work differs little or not at all from that done by women in the paid labor force 40 or 50 years ago. Gender segregation within the paid labor force remains the norm (Steinberg and Cook, 1988, p. 310). Moreover, much of the paid labor of women is part-time work. Recent research indicates that, on a scale comprising 13 nonmonetary job characteristics, jobs held predominantly by men are rated by workers as 1.38 times more desirable than predominantly female occupations. Moreover, employed men enjoy over twice the nonmonetary advantages as employed women (Jencks et al., 1988). Nonetheless, especially younger, college-educated women have, in fairly large numbers, successfully entered traditionally male professional, administrative, and managerial occupations since the early 1970s. They have been able to move up to midlevel, although rarely top-level, positions within these occupations. Their pay, relative to male peers, approaches equality. As older cohorts of women who overwhelmingly perform gender-traditional jobs retire, the *proportion* of female labor-force participants who do traditionally male work for nearly equal pay and other types of rewards should increase in the next century (see England and Farkas, 1986, chap. 8). In short, many more women today earn 60%-70% of their husband's income rather than 0%; in the 1950s, the opposite was the case. By 2020, more women will probably earn 75%-90% of their husband's income than those earning two-thirds or less today.

My theory predicts that, if women's access to resources increases, then their husbands' micro-level power should decrease. One major indicator of household power is the division of domestic and familial labor. However, research in a number of industrial nations, including the United States and the Soviet Union, shows that, on average, husbands of employed wives do little more such work than husbands of full-time homemakers. Unlike men, most married women work a double day. This is surely a form of substantial gender inequality, in fact, a new form for the middle class. Again, however, there is some indication that among younger, college-educated couples, where both spouses are heavily invested in their careers, substantially more equal sharing of domestic and child-rearing work is occurring (Hertz, 1986; Jump and Haas, 1987). Yet if Berk (1985) is correct in arguing that domestic labor provides the opportunity to display and reinforce engendered self-concepts, / then the household division of labor will not change substantially until women not only achieve equality in micro-level power, but engenderment processes change as well.

There is some evidence suggesting that, at least for girls, the childhood engenderment process has been changing. Research at the individual level has consistently demonstrated a relationship between maternal employment and/or nontraditional gender attitudes (which are themselves related) on the one hand, and nontraditional attitudes toward gender, work, and family by children—especially daughters—on the other (e.g., Thornton et al., 1983; Herzog and Bachman, 1982; Simmons and Turner, 1976; Wilkie, 1988, p. 162). To the extent that mothers are increasingly employed, and that public attitudes concerning gender have become less traditional in recent years (as will be discussed later in this section), children should be more androgynous or less gender differentiated today than in previous generations. To my knowledge, research specifically directed to the issue of *generational change* in engenderment (i.e., in the degree of gender differentiation among children in different cohorts) has not been conducted. Existing research compares the offspring of a cross-sectional sample of parents who differ on maternal employment, gender-related attitudes, and other variables. In the absence of intergenerational research on the degree of gender differentiation among children, I can only reiterate that cross-sectional studies suggest a moderate relationship between variables known to be changing extensively (maternal employment rates and gender-related attitudes) and child outcomes. The logical conclusion is that childhood engenderment is decreasing over time, with the result that gender differentiation is likewise decreasing (see also England and Farkas, 1986, chap. 8).

Returning to the gender division of domestic labor, it is likely that the very high divorce rates characteristic of most industrial societies, including not only the United States and a number of Western European nations, but Soviet-bloc nations as well, reflect a transitional state. Faced with a double workday, married women in the labor force are apt to develop feelings of anger toward their husbands who can relax after their paid work is done. This assertion flows from Social Exchange theory, which argues that, when actors' notions of "fair exchange" (Blau, 1964) or "distributive justice" (Homans, 1961) are violated, they react negatively toward the exchange partner who has failed to provide equitable rewards. Armed with greater resources than when married women were not employed outside the home, divorce is likely to appear both feasible and attractive to many such women (see Wilkie, 1988, pp. 155–56; England and Kilbourne, forthcoming). Until there is a new generation of men brought up in a substantially less gender-traditional manner (presumably by mothers employed outside the home), many men's self-concept may be threatened by heavy involvement in female-traditional household tasks. Facing pressure from their resource-enriched wives to do more of that work, or hostility because they do not, divorce is also likely to appear more attractive and feasible to many men. In other words, high divorce rates characterize a transitional state in which the domestic division of labor is incongruent with the division of resource-generating labor (see Spitze and South, 1985, especially p. 311; Huber and Spitze, 1980). For at least a generation or two, many men, and perhaps many women as well, may lack the psychic wherewithal to substantially alter the domestic division of labor through which they express their gendered self-concepts. Women's resource power is not sufficient in most cases to coerce such change, even if the women want to. The resulting double workday for women strains marriages, many of which buckle under that strain. In turn, the result of increasing marital dissolution is a new form of gender inequality: the feminization of poverty. Given women's substantially lower paychecks, divorce often ends in severe financial difficulty for them and their dependent children (Weitzman, 1987). Poverty and near-poverty become increasingly characteristic of, in particular, women and children.

The theory predicts that gender social definitions should change in response to a change in the gender division of labor. I argued in the last chapter that the gender consciousness that women's movement activists develop evolves out of the expansion of resource-generating roles for women. In turn, women's movements contribute substantially to public opinion change. However, public opinion change was not documented. Considerable data from public opinion polls in the United States suggest widespread change in gender-related attitudes in recent decades.

Harris (1987) reports changes in public opinion on a range of topics over the 15 years between 1970 and 1985. He notes that perceptions of antifemale discrimination in the labor force rose from between a third and 42% to nearly 60%, depending on the precise wording of the questions. More striking, while 42% "favored social efforts to strengthen women's status" in 1970, by 1985 71% did so (1987, pp. 189–90). Stereotypes about women's competence to perform nondomestic work apparently declined as well. One indicator of this decline is responses to a question the Gallup Poll has used for decades: "Would you vote for a woman presidential candidate if she were qualified for the job?" "Yes" answers have increased from 31% in 1937 to 52% in 1955, 66% in 1971, and 73% in 1976 (Dye, 1978, p. 68).

When Harris looks at attitudes toward marriage, he finds that in 1974 nearly half of all men and women considered best "a traditional marriage with the husband assuming responsibility for providing for the family and the wife running the home and taking care of the children." In 1985, over half defined the best form of marriage as one "where the husband and wife share responsibility more—both work, share the housekeeping and child responsibilities" (1987, p. 87).

Turning to motherhood, Harris found that, among those employed outside the home, 82% said they would prefer to continue employment, even "if family finances were not an issue," and 71% of mothers who were not in the labor force said they would prefer to be in it (1987, p. 92). A decade ago, only 52% of women wanted to "combine marriage, a career, and children," compared with 63% in the mid-1980s. Conversely, those who did not want a career after marriage and children declined from 38% to 26%. This change in attitude has been made possible by changing definitions of what constitutes good maternal behavior, from a focus on quantity to one on quality of time. By a three to one margin, mothers employed outside the home endorsed the statement: "I may spend less time with my children because I work, but I feel I give them as much as nonworking mothers because of the way I spend my time with them" (1987, pp. 94–95). Nonetheless, the strain of the double workday shows up in the endorsement by half of employed mothers of the statement: "When I'm home I try to make up to my family for being away at work, and as result I rarely have any time for myself" (1987, p. 95). It is interesting to note that analogous questions were not even posed about or to fathers. This reflects the fact that, to date, the substantial change in women's roles has not been matched by noticeable change in those of men. Attitudes are changing to come into congruence with a changing reality, but that changing reality is confined largely to women. Harris does, however, report responses to a largely hypothetical question concerning how much respect people would give to a man who stayed home. In 1970 63% said "less respect," compared to 1980 when only 41% did, and 1985 when the percentage dropped further to 25. Moreover, the younger and more affluent the respondent, the less likely she or he is to offer less respect to stay-at-home men (1987, pp. 99–100).

In the mid-1980s teenagers were noticeably inclined to define domestic and familial labor as joint spousal responsibilities, perhaps reflecting a decrease in gender differentiation (comparative data from earlier surveys were not reported). Half or fewer felt that the following household tasks, once done almost exclusively by women, should be done by the wife alone: vacuuming (40%), mopping (50%), cooking (39%), dish washing (26%). However, nearly two-thirds defined the traditionally male task of lawn mowing as still the man's responsibility, again reflecting the asymmetry of change between the genders. Teenagers' views concerning child care are an even more dramatic indicator that they accept equal responsibility within the home—at least at the verbal level: 91% felt that playing with children is equally the responsibility of fathers and mothers; 71% said that feeding babies is a joint duty; 64% believed that both should change diapers; 65% think that bathing a baby should be shared; and about 70% said that putting babies or toddlers to bed should be done by both parents (Harris, 1987, pp. 100–101). Moreover, in a study of high school seniors, Herzog and Bachman (1982) found an increase in just four years, between 1976 and 1980, in the acceptability of women working in nondomestic roles.

Using longitudinal data from 1,000 married women in the Detroit metropolitan area, Thornton, Alwin, and Camburn (1983) found extensive attitude shifts between 1962 and 1980. Disagreement with the assertion that "most important decisions in the life of the family should be made by the man of the house" rose from 32.5% in 1960 to 67.4% in 1977, and then to 71.3% in 1980. In 1960 56.4% disagreed with the statement "there is some work that is men's and some that is women's, and they should not be doing each other's"; in 1977 and 1980 the percentages were 77 and 66.6. Less than half (47.4%) of the respondents expected that husbands should help with housework in 1960, but by 1977 61.7%, and in 1980 over two-thirds (69.2%) did. Several questions were asked only in 1977 and 1980, but change is also evident in these few years. By 1977 65% already agreed with the assertion that employed women establish relationships with their children that are equal to those of full-time mothers and their children, a figure that increased by 13% in three additional years. Less dramatic changes, but always in the nontraditional direction, were noted concerning whether women are happier at home, whether everyone is better off if women stay home, and whether it is advisable for women to help their husband's career rather than to have one of their own.

Clearly, in the last 30 years Americans have substantially changed their attitudes toward the domestic division of labor and responsibility, women's roles and opportunities outside the home, and the obligations and rights of husbands and wives toward one another. In short, there has been a marked reduction in gender social definitions—especially as they pertain to women and their traditional roles—and an increase in gender consciousness among the public. By the mid-1980s, almost any nonextreme question dealing with gender was likely to receive a majority nontraditional response. What is not clear is the extent to which such massive definitional change is attributable directly to the efforts of the women's movement rather than being the outgrowth of the unintentional improvements in women's opportunities that were also occurring. It appears that some attitude shift in the nontraditional direction was already in progress before 1970, when the women's movement first achieved extensive public visibility. This early change reflects the impact of changing women's roles. It also appears that the rate of attitude change picked up markedly during the 1970s, a phenomenon that is undoubtedly attributable in large measure to the movement.

To conclude this section, there has indeed been real change in the gender systems of advanced industrial nations in recent decades. But many aspects of the system have not changed substantially. Moreover, in terms of the double workday and the feminization of poverty, in some ways gender inequality has been heightened. The glass is clearly both half full and half empty. Ogburn (1927) recognized well over half a century ago that "culture lag," or uneven change within a system, creates "maladjustments" or social problems. Earlier in this section high divorce rates were viewed as one indicator of such a lag. In Chapter 4 I also noted that men's *use* of their innate superiority in physical coercive power may be an indication that gender system change is occurring; increased rates of rape, wife abuse, and sexual harassment may be indicators of this lag. Indeed, increased abuse by husbands probably further exacerbates the divorce rate. Despite the fact that *aggregate* data concerning such things as employed women's income relative to men's, segregation of labor-force jobs, and the domestic division of labor show virtually no change, *cohort* data suggest a different picture. Compared with older cohorts, among the youngest and best educated segments of the population—those most likely to represent the "wave of the future"—occupations, income, and the division of domestic and familial labor appear substantially more egalitarian. It remains to be seen whether, as the younger cohort ages, inequality within it will increase to resemble the situation of older cohorts. Are we witnessing a short-term, life-cycle phenomenon or a long-term historical trend?

AN INTEGRATED THEORY OF INCREASING GENDER EQUALITY

In this section the material from the last two chapters and the previous section are integrated to depict the processes that induce a reduction in the system of gender stratification. The *extent* to which that result flows from intended versus unintentional factors is probably not specifiable, theoretically or empirically. The *sequential process* can, however, be suggested theoretically and eventually tested empirically.

Figure 8.1 is a process model summarizing that part of Chapter 6 that deals with unintentional changes that increase women's access to resource-generating work roles. The variables postulated to have that effect are primarily technological, economic, and demographic.

In comparison with Figure 6.4, which depicted the processes by which women's access to resource-generating work roles is unintentionally reduced, this figure shows fewer variables. As Blumberg (1988) suggests, it appears easier for women's status to fall than to rise. This conclusion also follows logically from the discussion in Part I of the myriad factors that reinforce any system of gender inequality.

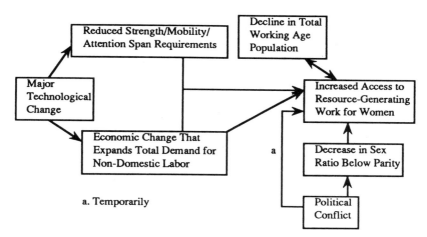

Figure 8.1. A Summary Model of the Unintentional Processes That Increase Women's Access to Resource-Generating Work Roles

The unintentional factors together function to increase women's access to resource-generating work roles. I argued in the last chapter that expanding role opportunities constitute the starting point for understanding organized, grass-roots opposition to the gender system. In general, the most important variables for triggering unintentional gender system change—technological change and economic expansion—are the same as that postulated as producing women's movements: industrialization (and the increased size of the middle class and the urbanization that result from it). Industrialization refers to a specific form of technological change accompanied by economic expansion. In short, the very processes that trigger an unintentional decrease in gender inequality also trigger the emergence and growth of women's movements in modern societies. *Women's movements should, therefore, be viewed as primarily reflecting and expediting a process already in motion rather than as a fundamental cause of increasing gender equality.*

Earlier in this chapter gender system changes were described that have occurred over the last three to four decades in advanced industrial societies, most notably our own. Figure 8.2 depicts the sequential process by which increased access by women to resource-generating work roles affects other aspects of the gender system. It is the counterpart of Figure 6.3, which concerned the sequence by which decreased access affects the rest of the gender system.

In the short run, the main effects of increased access for women are a set of social problems that may make the lives of many women harder than before. Physical abuse, double workdays, and high divorce rates resulting in increased female poverty may all emerge from women's increased access to resource-generating work roles. These social problems may prompt government reaction, in the form of policies directed at ameliorating them. In the process, such policies sometimes further contribute to the reduction of gender inequities. In the short run also, men lose at least some of their micro power advantage over women. While this loss is not manifested by rapid change in the division of household labor, Blumberg (1988) has shown that both female autonomy (e.g., control over their own fertility) and women's familial decision making (e.g., say in how family money is spent) increase considerably when they achieve access to resource-generating work (see also Wilkie, 1988, pp. 152-53). In the longer run, Propositions 3.7, 3.9, and 3.10 logically imply that, to the extent that there is a reduction in the gender division of labor, the engenderment process changes to decrease gender differentiation. Data reported in the last section on the attitudes of teenagers support this contention. Furthermore, as also demonstrated in the last section, gender social definitions change to come into increasing conformity with the new reality, thereby becoming less traditional. The logical implication of Proposition 3.8 is that a reduction in gender social definitions results in a further weakening of gender differentiation. With decreased male micro-level power and less gender differentiation, the division of domestic and familial work eventually begins to become more equal. In turn, this feeds back to further reduce gender differentiation and to enhance women's opportunities to com-

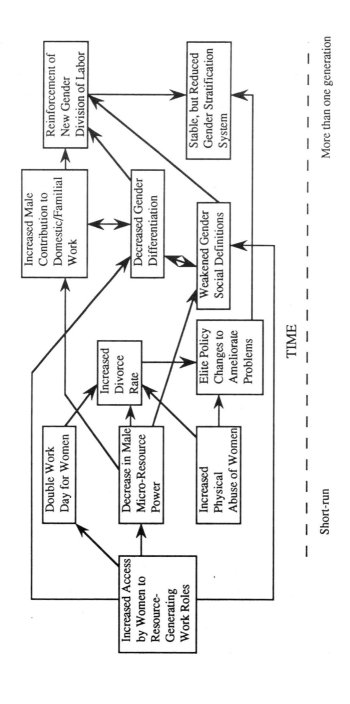

Figure 8.2. A Process Model of The Effects Over Time of Women's Increase in Access to Resource-Generating Work Roles

pete in extradomestic work roles. The end result, a few generations later, is a stable gender system at a reduced level of gender
stratification.

Figure 8.3 summarizes the main parts of the total argument
concerning how the level of gender stratification is reduced. This
figure summarizes and abbreviates the previous two, along with
Figures 7.1 and 7.2. Recall that "gender stratification" refers to the
extent to which men and women are equal in their access to
scarce and valued societal resources—material and nonmaterial.
When men contribute more to domestic labor, women's relative
access to leisure—a scarce and usually highly valued resource—
increases. By definition, when male micro-level power declines,
greater equality exists. Likewise by definition, increased access
by women to roles that generate resources implies greater gender
equality. Specific laws, policies, and programs can affect virtually
any form of gender inequity in access to scarce and valued resources, including resource-generating work (e.g., legislation
pertaining to promotion and hiring, affirmative action, and pay
equity), formal power (e.g., by granting political rights previously lacking to women), autonomy, access to skill enrichment
and educational opportunities, and so on. What this figure
underscores, yet again, is the critical role of expanding nondomestic opportunities for women in explaining gender system
change. In turn, such role expansion is triggered by broad-scale
systemic changes the nation is experiencing. As other aspects of
the gender system change, they feed back to reinforce and possibly further expand women's extradomestic opportunities. Wom-
en's movements emerge out of this transformation of women's
roles. They serve to expedite and reinforce the ongoing process of
gender system change, primarily through their effect on definitional phenomena (i.e., public opinion). While indirect, the
impact of women's movements can, nonetheless, be extensive, in
that elites in all major institutional arenas come to change their
practices, and everyday citizens, their gender social definitions.
These changes may then spread throughout the entire gender
system, propelling further changes. A direct linkage between
weakened gender social definitions and public support for

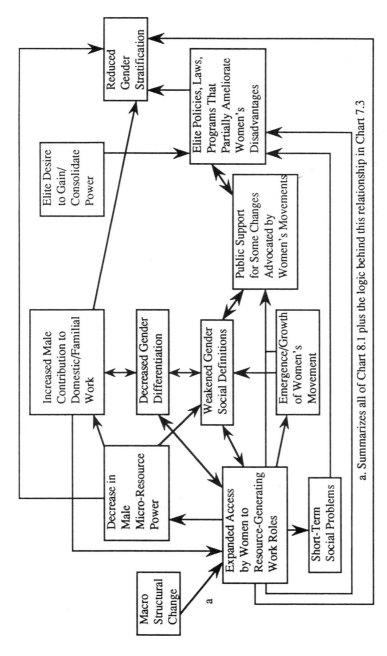

Figure 8.3. A Summary Process Model of the Main Factors Producing a Decrease in Gender Stratification

a. Summarizes all of Chart 8.1 plus the logic behind this relationship in Chart 7.3

191

change has been added to this figure. They are, in fact, part and parcel of the same phenomenon—increased gender consciousness. Finally, the changes won in this process will tend to be moderate and uneven, leaving substantial gender inequities for a future generation to fight.

A DIGRESSION ON TESTING
A THEORY OF CHANGE

Social change is inevitably uneven in its effects on different social structures, processes, practices, and beliefs. Standing in the midst of a system undergoing relatively rapid, extensive, yet uneven, change, observers (including sociologists) often develop one of two exaggerated perceptions: (1) that there has been more widespread change than in fact has occurred to date; or (2) that because many things have changed little if at all, change is more illusion than reality. This second view reflects a general lack of understanding of historical time. To postulate that change in one variable ultimately produces change in others does not necessarily mean that the latter change will be observed in 10 or 20 years. It is quite reasonable to suppose that complex and strongly entrenched social phenomena, such as gender systems, require at a minimum the passage of two or three generations for changes introduced in one part of the system to work their full effects on the other parts. We do not, therefore, disprove a theory concerning change with data confined to the last 10 or 20 years (not to mention data that are cross-sectional).

The prospect of waiting that long to adequately assess the effects of change—and theories about change—is not one that currently practicing sociologists are likely to find pleasant. Historians have long understood that the passage of several decades is necessary if one is to achieve a reasonable and balanced perspective on the importance and meaning of events or trends. Social scientists, especially in the United States, have been primarily concerned with understanding contemporary phenomena. This present and near-present focus has contributed substantially to the fact that social scientific predictions of the future are so frequently wrong.

The amount of time required before an adequate test of a theory of change can be conducted cannot be open-ended, or the theory can never be disconfirmed. One can always say: "The data do not support the theory yet, but the elapsed time has not been sufficient." In light of this, I propose a specific amount of elapsed time. The onset of the trend toward the nearly lifetime employment of the majority of women outside the home began about 1965–70 in the United States and several other advanced industrial societies. After that time, *young* women could assume that it was highly probable that they would be absent from the paid labor force for no more than a few years during the early childhood of their likely two children, spaced two to three years apart in age. By about the year 2020, and at the latest 2030, nearly all women in the paid labor force will have entered it after 1965. Moreover, a substantial majority of all labor-force participants—men and women—will have had mothers who were in the paid labor force for most, if not all, of their lives. Indeed, younger workers will have had grandmothers who were lifetime or near lifetime workers outside the home. If the postulated changes in gender social definitions, engenderment, the division of household and family labor, and gender power relations have not occurred by then, it will be clear that the theoretical perspective developed in this book is wrong—in whole or part.

One final caveat is in order. My theory of change toward greater gender equality hinges upon the widespread participation of women, regardless of social class or marital or parental status, in the paid labor force for most of their adult lives. If the economy and/or technology of advanced industrial societies changes in ways that substantially reduce the demand for women in the labor force, then obviously my predictions will not come to pass. Indeed, in all likelihood gender inequality will increase if women return to a more dependent position vis-à-vis their husbands.

SOME QUESTIONS ANSWERED

In the conclusion to Chapter 1 a variety of questions were listed whose answers would be provided during the course of explicating a theory of stability and change in gender systems. Those pertaining to stability were addressed in Chapter 4. Attention is now turned to the remaining questions that concern change.

Question 3 asked what the ramifications of engenderment are for gender system change. Two aspects of the theory pertain to this question. I suggested that engenderment may, in the short run, prevent change in the domestic division of labor that should follow upon an increase in women's access to resources. Despite the decline in male micro power, husbands especially, but many wives as well, may continue to see the traditional household division of labor as an expression of their gendered self-concepts. In the longer run, as the gender division of nondomestic labor changes in a more equalitarian direction, and as gender social definitions are weakened, gender differentiation as produced primarily by childhood engenderment should decline. In turn, a decline in gender differentiation should reinforce the new division of nondomestic labor and contribute to a more equalitarian division of domestic labor.

Question 6 inquired into the causes of change in the gender division of labor. I have consistently argued that nondomestic work changes in gender composition primarily as a result of macro-structural changes in technology, demography, and the economy. Women gain or lose access to resource-generating work roles, depending on the nature of the macro-structural changes. Furthermore, the idea that change in the nondomestic division of labor emanates from changes in the characteristics of women themselves (supply-side variables) was explicitly rejected. Change in the domestic division of labor is a long-run and indirect outcome of change in the nondomestic division of labor, as discussed in the previous paragraph.

The ninth question asked how male power advantages are reduced. I have not yet addressed the issue of reducing male macro power, which in practice means increasing women's representation among elites. This issue is the central focus of the final chapter. Men's micro-level power advantage is reduced to the extent that women gain increasingly better access to resource-generating work roles. Recall Blumberg's (1984) contention, however, that women's economic resource power at the micro level is "discounted" by the continuation of superior male macro-level power. The concept of discounting suggests that men maintain a small micro-power advantage even when their wives bring equal resources into the family. Nonetheless, substantially more equal spousal power results from substantially more equal access to especially material, but also nonmaterial, resources provided by extradomestic work roles.

Questions 11 and 13 are closely related to one another. They ask under what conditions women reject the legitimacy of male power and what causes the development of gender consciousness. Among other things, gender consciousness implies a rejection of the legitimacy of male power, so they are really the same question. In the last chapter the social psychological processes were discussed by which a cadre of women who have experienced expanded roles develop gender consciousness. The crux of that argument is that, once in contact with one another, women who experience role expansion share their experiences of status/role dilemmas and their feelings of relative deprivation that arise from a change in reference groups. Out of this sharing gradually emerges what might be called a system—rather than personal—blame view of their problems. They come to conclude that an unjust, inequitable, and illegitimate system of male privilege exists and should be changed. To the extent that a large pool of women has experienced role expansion, they will be led to the development of a partial gender consciousness by the organized activism of that cadre. In advocating change goals and new definitions that are counter to traditional gender social definitions, gender-conscious activists provide potential solutions to the problems personally experienced by many other women. Gender consciousness is a matter of degree, and those with the greatest amount function as teachers for much of the rest of the population.

The final question queried the relationship between male micro-definitional power and women's conversion to gender consciousness. I argued, in Part I, that this form of power is typically used by men to bolster gender social definitions. There is no direct relationship between it and gender consciousness. Gender consciousness emerges in response to processes that enhance women's resources. This means that the men—especially husbands—with whom they interact have experienced a reduction in their relative resource power. Given that definitional power emerges out of resource power, they have experienced a decline in it as well. While male micro-definitional power and female gender consciousness vary inversely, change in one will not directly cause change in the other. Rather, they are both reflections of women's expanding access to resource-generating work roles.

A DIGRESSION ON CLASS
AND MINORITY STRATIFICATION

The emphasis throughout this book has been on women as a category. In all but a few instances the enormous diversity among women in complex societies has been ignored. Women differ from one another in terms of social class in virtually all contemporary societies, and in many they differ according to ethnic, racial, or religious groupings. The processes discussed in this book will affect women differentially according to their other social statuses. For instance, within a given society, gender social definitions, especially stereotypes and norms, may be different for wealthy and poor women, for white women and those of color, for women from one ethnic or religious subculture compared with another. Within a socially disadvantaged category, spousal power may be more equal than that among more advantaged segments of the society, not because women fare well, but because men's access to resources is also very poor (Chafetz, 1980). Expanded opportunities for women are also likely to be differentially distributed along these other stratification lines.

Just as women typically experience new opportunities only after men "cream" the most rewarding ones, those women whose other statuses (class, race, ethnic, religious) are highest are likely to be better able to avail themselves of new and rewarding opportunities, relative to other women. In turn, the fact that women are characterized by positions in status hierarchies other than gender means that their sociopolitical consciousness will vary (e.g., see Dill, 1983). Women who enjoy high social status in all ways but gender may develop a consciousness focused exclusively on their gender-based disadvantages. The less fortunate may totally ignore gender issues and focus on other sources (class, racial, and so on) of deprivation, or they may develop a form of consciousness that combines awareness of several sources of disadvantage. I have argued that gender consciousness results in substantial measure from a change in comparative reference group from women to men, contingent upon expanded opportunities. Women who suffer low status in these other stratification hierarchies may respond to expanded opportunities by a change in reference group to other, more advantaged *women*, thereby developing a racial, ethnic, class, or religious consciousness rather than, or in conjunction with, a gender one.

   Clearly, to understand stability and change in the gender system of any given society necessitates the inclusion of these other forms of stratification among women (see Epstein, 1988, chap. 5). Because almost all contemporary societies are class stratified, future theoretical attention should be devoted to more *systematically* incorporating this dimension into our understanding of gender system change and stability. Many fine research accounts of the relationship between class and gender already exist in the literature, especially studies of Third World women, providing a good empirical basis for systematic theorizing. Other status hierarchies—racial, ethnic, religious—are nation-specific and more difficult to incorporate into a general theory. At the very least, it is likely that *how* change affects subpopulations of women in any given time and place is strongly contingent upon their positions within other stratification hierarchies, but that the effects of their various statuses may be quite complex and not simply additive. Likewise, the precise and detailed mechanisms that bolster the gender system status quo (e.g., the specific contents of gender social definitions and gender differentiation) may vary in complex ways according to women's positions on a multiplicity of status hierarchies.

The theoretical task is to discover cross-national and historical uniformities in the relationships between gender and other forms of stratification and social differentiation as they affect and are affected by the variables discussed in this book. As a start in that direction, a set of propositions could be developed that have as their independent construct "among women, the higher (lower) their social status . . ." Two simple examples suffice to demonstrate this idea: (1) Among women, the lower their social status the less likely that traditional gender social definitions will preclude extradomestic work obligations as a component of femininity; (2) As the demand for women's labor in nondomestic and familial roles increases, among women the higher their social status the more highly skilled and rewarded the work roles that will be made available to them.

CONCLUSION

In this chapter the discussions of the various processes that together explain how a reduction in gender stratification occurs have been integrated. Given the systemic nature of these processes, and the extensive feedback between the different constructs, it might appear that, once such a process begins, it would perpetuate itself until either complete gender equality was achieved or adverse macro-structural factors began to reverse it. Yet this is probably not the case. Certainly, economic downturns and technological and demographic factors may sometimes stop the process once begun. Clearly, nowhere has it eventuated in complete equality. In the next chapter some other factors that tend to eventually contribute to stalling, if not reversing, the process of change toward gender equality will be examined.

CHAPTER NINE

The Limits of Change: Reaction and Apathy

Improvement in the relative status of any disadvantaged group—workers, blacks in America, women—tends to occur in spurts. An era of declining inequality and increasing grass-roots activism in support of change is followed by one of stagnation, even regression, in the relative status of that group and low public visibility and influence of its movement organizations (e.g., in the case of U.S. women, see Rupp and Taylor's, 1987, analysis of the period between the two waves of women's movement activism). This chapter asks the question: why? Other than macrostructural factors that decrease women's opportunities, what contributes to slowing, halting, or reversing a process of decreasing gender stratification? I will argue that four types of phenomena contribute to it: (1) the emergence and growth of organized opposition to change; (2) dynamics internal to women's movements; (3) a decrease in public awareness of the need for, and in its support of, further change; and (4) political and economic factors, exclusive of those that affect the demand for women's labor outside the household.

ORGANIZED OPPOSITION: ANTIFEMINIST MOVEMENTS

In the process of conducting research on the emergence and growth of women's movements, Dworkin and I found scattered references to consciously organized efforts to block or reverse the changes sought by such movements (see Chafetz and Dworkin, 1987, 1989). We call such collective efforts "antifeminist movements" (although they should properly be termed "anti-women's-movement movements"). They arise when a change-oriented women's movement appears to be succeeding in achieving its goals, but they rarely arise in response to small, weak, or unsuccessful ones. We found evidence of such countermovements during the First Wave in the United States, Great Britain, France, Italy, New Zealand, Jewish Palestine, Germany, Canada, and Australia. In the Second Wave, antifeminist movements have been documented in the United States, Australia, Italy, France, Germany, and Great Britain. Regardless of wave or nation, we found remarkable similarity in these countermovements.

When fully developed, antifeminist movements are composed of two very different types of groups. The first are vested interest groups whose status is threatened by real and/or proposed gender system changes. Such groups predate the rise of a women's movement and have often benefited from women's relative disadvantages. They comprise those elites and groups against whose practices and composition the women's movement is battling. Their motive for supporting or organizing an antifeminist movement is to protect their dominant, advantaged position. Vested interest groups include political, economic, religious, higher educational, and other organizations and elites. Vested interest groups often employ people whose job it is to monitor proposed legislation, public opinion, trends, and current events in order to learn quickly of impending threats to their interests. Elite networks among themselves (formal and informal), along with their control of organizational resources, permit rapid mobilization when threat is perceived. Nonetheless, they often refrain from doing anything in response to perceived threat. Self-interest also entails the maintenance of good public relations with whatever their constituency may be (consumers, congregants, contributors, voters, and so on). Organizations and their elites may not be in a position to publicly oppose the changes proposed by a women's movement (see Gale, 1986, p. 210). Their perceptions of the magnitude of the threat and the opinions of their constituents will influence the extent of their action. Such perceptions will also affect their decision whether to act overtly or covertly, if they decide to take action.

The second type of antifeminist movement organization is grass-roots voluntary associations. Where vested interest groups are composed almost entirely of men, antifeminist voluntary associations include members of both genders. Members fear that the new or proposed changes in the gender system will disrupt their social and/or economic status. Unlike vested interest groups, those who eventually join antifeminist voluntary associations are usually slow to perceive a threat from gender system change or a women's movement. Therefore, such associations arise later in time than either a women's movement or antifeminist interest group activism. The voluntary association members must undergo a process of consciousness-raising analogous to that required for members of the women's movement against whom they battle. Antifeminist vested interest groups play a major role in mobilizing and organizing grass-roots voluntary associations.

The descriptions we found of antifeminist movements in both waves suggest that, shortly after a women's movement emerges and/or significant gender system change begins to occur, vested interest groups begin to use their ongoing channels of influence to resist change covertly. They are especially likely to use preexisting lobbying networks to influence political elites. For instance, Conover and Grey found that state-level legislation during the 1970s antithetical to the ERA and abortion were most likely to have passed in states that had the largest number of business lobbies. In fact, this variable constituted the best predictor in multivariate analysis used to explain the passage of abortion restrictions (1983, pp. 189–91). Further, they found that, the stronger and more numerous the business lobbies, the fewer the grass-roots antifeminist organizations. Apparently, the people who would normally mobilize such organizations felt that their interests were sufficiently well-represented by ongoing lobbies (1983, p. 189). Brewers' lobbies and organizations actively worked to prevent women's suffrage in New Zealand (Evans, 1977, p. 217; Grimshaw, 1972, p. 57), Canada (Grimshaw, 1972, pp. 57, 67, 90; Bacchi, 1983, pp. 47, 76), Great Britain (Harrison, 1978, p. 127; Banks, 1981, p. 131), and the United States (Flexner, 1975, pp. 306–7). Also during the First Wave, in Great Britain unions lobbied in support of legislation curtailing the number of hours women could work as a means of reducing increased competition for jobs from women (Evans, 1977, p. 14; Banks, 1981, p. 178; Harrison, 1978, pp. 40, 141). More recently, the U.S. Chamber of Commerce, the National Association of Manufacturers, the National Retail Federation, and a number of insurance companies lobbied against the Pregnancy Disability Act in the United States, which was designed to protect the rights of pregnant workers and to provide medical insurance for pregnancy and childbirth (Gelb and Palley, 1982, p. 160).

In addition to lobbying, vested interest groups have often been the primary vehicles for organizing antifeminist voluntary associations. They may do so overtly or more quietly by using such organizations as "fronts" into which they channel money and other resources. Unions and organizations of male clerical workers were often overt in their antifeminist activism during the First Wave. For instance, in 1912 German male teachers, fearful of the incursion of women into their profession, organized the League for the Prevention of the Emancipation of Women. This small group was strongly supported by the considerably larger German National Commercial Employee's Union, an organization of lower-middle-class men who also feared the incursion of female workers into their occupations (Evans, 1976, pp. 178–79). Liquor interests covertly financed grass-roots antisuffrage organizations in Toronto and Australia (Bacchi, 1983), in Great Britain (Harrison, 1978, p. 727; Banks, 1981, p. 131), and in the United States (Flexner, 1975, pp. 306–7). Additional, largely covert funds for grass-roots organizing and for lobbying against women's suffrage were provided in the United States by railroad, oil, meatpacking, cement, ranching, banking, and general manufacturing interest groups (Flexner, 1975, pp. 309–11).

One type of vested interest group has been strongly, overtly, and nearly universally involved in organized antifeminist activism: conservative, orthodox, or fundamentalist religions. They have publicly proclaimed an antifeminist ideology, provided funds for voluntary associations, and worked to establish such organizations during both waves in almost all nations that experienced an antifeminist movement. First Wave women's movements were publicly fought by Catholic leaders in France (Boxer, 1982, pp. 557–58; Evans, 1977, p. 239), Italy (Evans, 1977, p. 239), New Zealand (Grimshaw, 1972, p. 56), and the United States (Flexner, 1975, p. 309). Under the British mandate in Palestine during the first two decades of the twentieth century, Orthodox rabbis led the opposition to women's demands for equality within Jewish bodies of self-government (Izraeli, 1981, p. 106). The German Evangelical Women's League was organized by a clergyman to fight feminist demands, including suffrage, while another German religious leader established the Christian National Group Against the Emancipation of Women (Evans, 1976, pp. 195–98). Analogous activism by Catholic, Mormon, Fundamentalist Protestant, and Orthodox Jewish religious leaders has been amply demonstrated for the Second Wave case in the United States, especially but not exclusively around the issue of abortion (see Conover and Grey, 1983; Gelb and Palley, 1982). The 1970s witnessed the same type of behavior, especially but not only around the issue of abortion, in France (Sauter-Bailliet, 1981), Britain (Bouchier, 1984), and Germany (Jacobs, 1978).

Women's movements are composed overwhelmingly of women; in most cases men play a minor, supportive role. Antifeminist movements are more equally composed of both genders, and men typically constitute the leaders and public spokespersons as well as the primary organizers and providers of resources. Male members of antifeminist voluntary associations are frequently characterized by the same traits as the vested interest groups that work to oppose gender system change. They are men whose occupations are threatened by the incursion of female workers, and elite men whose organizations are threatened. For instance, wealthy, influential, and aristocratic men in the professions, arts, sciences, military, business, and government were the members of antisuffrage groups in Germany (Evans, 1976), New Zealand (Harrison, 1978), and the United States (Flexner, 1975) during the First Wave. Some antifeminist voluntary associations have comprised only men, especially during the First Wave. Others have comprised both genders, but the women's real role has been to enlarge the membership while men actually run the organizations (Harrison, 1978, p. 128; Marshall, 1985).

Female members of antifeminist voluntary associations are often the wives of male organizers and vested interest group members. Especially in the First Wave, women antifeminist activists were often members of elite families (see Harrison, 1978, concerning Britain; Flexner, 1975, for the United States). In the Second Wave, these women tend to be middle to upper-middle class, middle-aged housewives, dependent upon the income of their husbands. In both waves such women have typically been "tenaciously clinging to traditional roles" that they perceive as "increasingly threatened" (Howard, 1982, p. 465; see also Ehrenreich, 1982; Luker, 1984). They are especially threatened by newly emerging gender social definitions that award prestige to women on the basis of their individual, extradomestic achievements, thereby implicitly reducing the status of women who remain encapsulated in traditional household and familial roles. Given economic dependence on their husbands, such women may also experience insecurity on the basis of threats to their husbands' economic interests.

Antifeminist vested interest groups, especially religions, help to shape these perceptions of threat through the media of mass communication and from the pulpit. Equally important, the very rhetoric of the change-oriented women's movement helps more traditional women to perceive that movement as a source of threat. The antifeminist ideology that emerges to legitimate countermovement activism takes on a characteristic flavor, regardless of time, nation, or the particular demands of the women's movement against which it fights. Gender system change, and the women's movement that supports and furthers it, are accused of endangering the family. In turn, the family is defined as the mainstay of the nation. A division of labor by which women care for the home and family members, and men provide economic support for the family, is defined as necessary for the well-being of the family, hence the nation. Finally, religious and patriotic symbolism is used to further legitimate the ideology. This is often supplemented by notions concerning innate or biologically rooted sex differences that require this particular division of labor. In the First Wave, this argument was heard in France (Boxer, 1982), Germany (Evans, 1976), New Zealand (Grimshaw, 1972), Canada (Bacchi, 1983), Great Britain (Harrison, 1978), and the United States (Marshall, 1985; Howard, 1982). Its echo has been heard in recent years in Italy (Dodds, 1982), Australia (Webley, 1980), and the United States (Pohli, 1983).

The process by which a fully developed antifeminist movement emerges (i.e., one comprising one or more voluntary associations as well as vested interest groups) can be depicted using a set of constructs that closely parallels those used in Chapter 7 to explain the emergence of women's movements. Indeed, the two types of movements arise dialectically, each influencing the other (see Chafetz and Dworkin, 1989). Figure 9.1 depicts that process, which begins with the fact that macro-structural change is always uneven in its impact on subpopulations within a society. Changes that expand the role opportunities of many women leave others unaffected. Many women are unable or unwilling to take advantage of the new opportunities because of insufficient human capital, family obligations, religious or other normative constraints, and/or insufficient opportunity. They remain encapsulated in roles that had been traditional for their gender.

Recall that role expansion produces status/role dilemmas for women. Role encapsulation (i.e., confinement within gender-traditional roles) during an era of rapid role expansion does so as well. As more and more women assume new roles, those who do not increasingly find that they are asked to explain and justify their "failure" to do so. For instance, married women in the United States today—especially if their children are school-

206

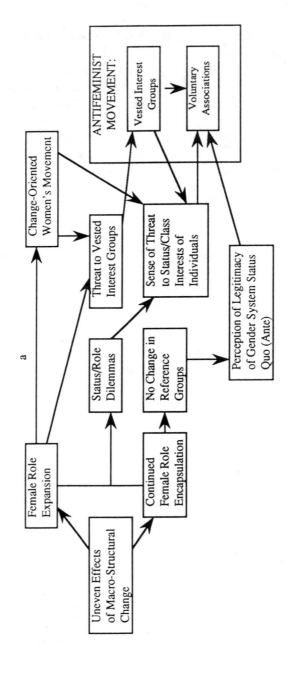

a. For details of this process see Chart 7.2

Figure 9.1. A Process Model of the Emergence of Antifeminist Movements

aged—are increasingly defined by societal members as anomalies who need to explain their labor-force absence. It is precisely such dilemmas that create for role-encapsulated women a sense of status threat. That perception is encouraged by the rhetoric and activity of antifeminist vested interest groups and enhanced by the rhetoric of the women's movement.

Women who continue to perform traditional roles have little impetus to change their reference groups. Other women like themselves function as a comparative reference group, and men continue to constitute their normative reference group. Therefore, unlike women who experience expanded roles and a change in reference groups, role-encapsulated women have no reason to question or challenge the traditional gender system. They maintain a perception that the status quo—or, more likely, the system as it was before recent changes—is legitimate. When their personal sense of status threat and the sense that their husbands' economic interests are threatened combine with an awareness of gender system legitimacy, such women become mobilizable for countermovement activism.

The actual expansion of women's roles and the changes proposed by a women's movement together create a sense of threat to many vested interest groups. They both act on their own to attempt to thwart change and provide the resources required to mount a grass-roots countermovement. As individuals, men who perceive that their interests are threatened organize or join antifeminist voluntary associations, recruit members—especially their wives—and develop or disseminate an ideology justifying their stance.

Organized antifeminism emerges only if real or imminent gender system change is of sufficient magnitude to produce a sense of threat to vested interests. They are the first to act to thwart such change. It is only when their mostly covert efforts appear to be insufficient that antifeminist voluntary associations are likely to arise. When they arise, they constitute a good indicator of substantial change and/or the existence of a powerful women's movement. Dworkin and I (1987) concluded from our research that the emergence and growth of antifeminist movements do not represent a shift in public opinion. Nor do they create such a shift. Such movements tend to organize, give public voice to, and make apparent the size of that part of the population that has opposed gender system change all along. In fact, to some extent, the emergence of a countermovement helps the recruitment efforts of a women's movement by sharpening the focus of debate (see Harrison, 1978, chap. 6). In their systematic review of U.S. public opinion research during the 1970s, Conover and Grey found that, despite the increasing visibility of organized antifeminism, very little attitude change occurred concerning abortion and the ERA. However, emotional intensity on both sides of both issues did increase (1983, p. 167; see also Burris, 1983).

Despite the fact that antifeminist movements do not affect the distribution of public opinion, they do contribute to stalling the momentum for gender system change. They make apparent to elites the fact that there is considerable—even if minority—opposition to change. Furthermore, they divert a women's movement from pursuing its objectives. It must expend considerable time, effort, and resources simply combating its opposition's attempts to thwart the changes it supports. Finally, antifeminist movements tend to enjoy more political clout than their numbers and public support warrant. This advantage results from the active involvement of vested interest groups. These groups typically have far more extensive resources than those allied with a women's movement. Further, they have ongoing, long-standing relationships of influence and mutual exchange of favors with political elites. Moreover, their membership includes socioeconomic, political, and cultural elites.

In summary of the main points of this section:

Proposition 9.1. The greater the gender system change and/or the stronger and more successful a women's movement becomes, the more likely that powerful vested interest groups will perceive threat.

Proposition 9.2. The more widespread women's role expansion, the more role-encapsulated women will come to experience status/role dilemmas and to perceive threat to their status and to the economic interests of the husbands upon whom they are dependent.

Proposition 9.3. The greater the sense of threat perceived by vested interest groups, the more likely they are to lobby against gender system change and to organize antifeminist voluntary associations.

Proposition 9.4. The greater the sense of threat perceived by role-encapsulated women, the more likely they are to join antifeminist voluntary associations.

Proposition 9.5. The more organized an antifeminist movement becomes, the more likely it will successfully persuade political elites to slow, halt, or reverse policies, programs, and laws supporting gender system change and gender equality.

INTERNAL DYNAMICS
OF WOMEN'S MOVEMENTS

In Chapter 7 I argued that ideological, programmatic, and strategic differences within women's movements are helpful for the achievement of at least some of the more moderate goals of the movement. The existence of movement radicals helps to legitimate the demands of moderates in the eyes of both the public and the elites. But there is also a cost to be paid for such diversity. Issues and differences that appear trivial to outsiders may take on major importance to movement activists. Substantial time, energy, and resources may be spent on internecine battles over them.

The potential results of intramovement conflict are several. First, whatever time, energy, and resources are devoted to internal struggles are not available for the pursuit of gender system change (see Ferree and Hess, 1985). Second, otherwise sympathetic supporters, including many people who define themselves as part of the movement, may become exasperated and alienated from it over what they define as distractions or petty feuds. Third, all sense of a common cause may be lost, making alliances for the pursuit of common goals difficult if not impossible. Finally, if faced by organized opposition in the form of an antifeminist movement, a fragmented women's movement is less able to respond effectively to the challenge.

Countermovements generally coalesce around one clear issue: to resist or reverse change. Consensus around this issue is relatively easily maintained (Mottl, 1980, p. 627; Gamson, 1975, pp. 103–4). Change-oriented movements typically involve different perspectives on what requires change, how much change is desirable, and how change ought to be pursued. Consensus is, therefore, difficult to achieve or maintain. In general, cohesive groups win conflicts and achieve their goals more readily than disorganized ones. In his study of "challenging groups," Gamson found that less than one-fourth of those that experienced factionalism won new advantages, compared with 70% of those without factions (1975, p. 101). Therefore, in conflicts with an antifeminist movement, a women's movement is often disadvantaged, even if it is considerably larger and has more public support than its opposition.

Proposition 9.6. The more diversity in ideology, goals, and strategies within a women's movement, the more likely that internal conflict will erupt.

Proposition 9.7. The more a women's movement experiences internal conflict, the fewer resources activists devote to the pursuit of change goals, the more alienated movement adherents and members of the public become from the movement, and the more successful an antifeminist movement is likely to become in halting or reversing gender system change.

Perhaps in recognition of the self-defeating nature of internal conflict, women's movements often attempt to constrain or avoid it. In doing so, they face a dilemma. If they avoid conflict by focusing on one or a small number of the most widely agreed upon goals, they end up by losing sight of the general systemic problems of gender inequality. In the First Wave, large movements in the United States, Great Britain, and elsewhere virtually abandoned all goals but women's suffrage, an issue around which a large number of women could rally despite deep differences on other issues. Suffrage scarcely solved issues of gender inequity, yet because of the single-issue focus, such movements largely dissolved shortly after they achieved that goal. Many activists, especially those with the earliest involvement, had proposed a far more varied and radical agenda for change (see Chafetz and Dworkin, 1986, chap. 4), one that was sacrificed to achieve unity and wide public support.

If, on the other hand, a women's movement attempts to avoid conflict by maintaining the full range of diversity, two problems may emerge. First, its resources and energies may be spread too thinly, thereby reducing the probability that any major goals are achieved. Second, moderates and radicals will remain uncomfortable bedfellows. Many in each camp will come to abandon active involvement in the movement out of a desire not to be associated with the other. Almost regardless of what specific goals are pursued, activists from one extreme or the other are likely to see them as the wrong ones to emphasize. The result of an attempt to maintain diversity will tend to be a shrunken movement and/or one so fragmented as to be decreasingly effective over time in the achievement of central goals. Most Second Wave movements have attempted to maintain diversity after having experienced substantial conflict and fragmentation in their early years (see Chafetz and Dworkin, 1986, chap. 5). Within less than a decade after internecine battling occurred, these movements appear to have peaked and begun to shrink (Taylor, 1989, p. 485), and central goals (e.g., passage of the ERA) remain unachieved. Some observers now argue that, by the 1980s, the women's movement in the United States had been largely converted from a grass-roots effort to realize a feminist agenda of gender equity into an interest group lobbying for programs for women (Costain, 1982).

In summary, diversity is a mixed blessing for women's movements. In the short run, it improves the chances for accomplishing some, albeit moderate, goals. Over time, diversity tends to weaken the ability of such movements to sustain their following, to vigorously and successfully pursue central goals, and to fight off oppositional forces. Yet the price of eliminating diversity is to all but ensure that whatever goals may be achieved will be modest in their impact on gender inequality and to reduce the possibility of even that. Moreover, the elimination of diversity entails the end of the movement when its shrunken goals are met. The conclusion to be drawn from this discussion is that, over time, a given wave of a women's movement tends to experience internal conflict, and, regardless of whether it moves to increase homogeneity or maintain diversity, in the long run it will usually not be able to sustain high visibility and substantial grass-roots support to continue the struggle for gender equality.

PUBLIC APATHY

As noted earlier, in many nations, especially those that experienced large First Wave movements, public visibility and mass activism came to a halt shortly after the passage of women's suffrage. Moreover, some feminist scholars perceive a marked decline in visibility and grass-roots commitment in the 1980s, after nearly two decades of Second Wave activism. Younger women especially do not appear to be willing to devote their resources and energies to the cause of gender system change and equity (see Taylor, 1989).

Rossi (1982) describes a cyclical generational pattern to such activism. A first generation struggles for structural change and the development of gender consciousness. However, it is succeeded by a younger generation of women who experience new advantages gained by the efforts of the activists, which they take for granted. A yet later generation rediscovers gender inequity and develops an agenda designed to solve problems unresolved by earlier changes. The daughters of a generation of activists face different problems than did their mothers, precisely because the earlier activism helped to produce change (Ferree and Hess, 1985). Younger women may believe that "the women's movement had already achieved equal status for them, allowing them to either direct their attention to other issues or simply to get on with the work of building their careers and their families" (Boneparth and Stoper, 1988, p. 7). Further, as discrimination becomes more subtle and informal, in response to legal and policy changes that prohibit its formal and overt expression, younger women are less likely even to perceive it (Safilios-Rothschild, 1979; for a general discussion of generations and women's movement activism, see Schneider, 1988).

By failing to recruit younger women in large numbers, a women's movement gradually ages (e.g., see Rupp and Taylor's, 1987, description of feminist activists in the United States between the two main movement waves). It also shrinks as members of the activist generation gradually burn out, move on to other causes, or die. The remaining core keeps the issues alive, largely by lobbying and by maintaining fewer and smaller movement organizations. Rupp and Taylor describe this phase of movement history as "elite sustained" (1987). While the Second Wave in the United States has not reached this stage in 1990, it is probably headed in that direction.

The mass public, which supported many of the specific programs, policies, and legal changes sought by a women's movement at its zenith, also becomes increasingly apathetic over time. Ironically, public apathy results in substantial measure from the very successes of the movement. I argued that widespread public support for gender system change emanates from the fact that structural changes produce problems for a large number of women and for the men to whom they are related by intimate or familial ties. The rhetoric of a women's movement allows them to define the source of some of those problems in sociopolitical, cultural, and economic terms, and the solution as some measure of systemic change. To the extent that elites respond to those problems with new laws, policies, and programs, many members of the public come to feel that all that could be done has been done. After all, members of the public generally supported only some of the less radical demands made by the movement in the first place.

In addition, the negative latent consequences of gender system change discussed in the last chapter (e.g., women's double workday, increased divorce rates, the feminization of poverty, an increase in male violence against women) become increasingly apparent over time. Increasing awareness of problems may encourage many people to wonder if change has not been too extensive or rapid. With the passage of time, people begin to see what is being lost—the costs of change. New "social problems" are defined (e.g., latchkey children, poor-quality day care), often by the media and by antifeminist activists, and often in exaggerated form. Nonetheless, members of the public gradually become less enamored of gender system change—even if the extent of change has been more apparent than real.

In summary, both because of the (limited) successes of movement activists and because of problems created by the always uneven pace of social change in complex systems, the public becomes decreasingly committed to further change in the gender system. Organized antifeminist activism and two phenomena to be discussed in the next section often expedite a decline in public pressure and elite enthusiasm for further change. If the women's movement experiences factionalism and internal conflict, public apathy and movement shrinkage are even more likely to occur. However, even in the absence of these factors, public enthusiasm declines over time, and a women's movement loses its ability to recruit new members and begins the inexorable process of shrinking. The impetus for new policies, programs, and laws is thereby largely lost. How rapidly this occurs is, ironically, a function of how rapidly elites respond to demands for change. By rapidly responding to the least radical, but most strongly supported, demands, elites co-opt the movement, hastening its decline and an increase in public apathy concerning the issues promulgated by the movement.

Proposition 9.8. The more rapidly elites respond to demands for change promulgated by a women's movement and strongly supported by the public, the more rapidly members of the public and younger cohorts of women become apathetic to issues of gender system change and gender equality.

Finally, a substantial increase in public apathy produces two results. Those vested interest groups that had failed to become actively involved in the antifeminist movement in fear of antagonizing constituents may feel more free to do so. Their perception of the public relations cost of such activism declines. In this way, organized opposition to gender system change may be strengthened. Second, increased apathy reduces the pressure on elites, especially in the political realm, to make further changes—or even to enforce or fund those already made. Moreover, it does so at the very time that elites may be experiencing increased pressure from an antifeminist movement to halt or reverse change.

SOCIOPOLITICAL AND ECONOMIC FACTORS

Nations may experience one or both of two phenomena, one sociopolitical and one economic (exclusive of those that affect the demand for women in nondomestic roles), that further contribute to the slowing, halting, or reversal of the change process. These factors are related to those discussed in the previous sections, often serving to reinforce organized antifeminism and public apathy to gender system change.

Virtually all scholars who examine the rise of women's movements, in both waves and a variety of nations, note that they emerge and grow during periods of general social activism and reform efforts. Indeed, often the general "spirit of the times" or the prior emergence of other reformist and change-oriented movements are cited as a fundamental cause of the rise of a women's movement (see Chafetz and Dworkin, 1986, chap. 2, for a review of this argument). Dworkin and I rejected the argument that makes such prior movements causally fundamental to the emergence of women's movements. However, there is little doubt that the general sociopolitical climate of a given time and place constitutes a moderately important variable for understanding the extent of both public and elite support for the demands made by a women's movement. A general atmosphere supportive of change and reform helps to legitimate the movement and its demands. If a more conservative climate emerges—for whatever reason(s)—such support wanes. The result ranges from increasing apathy to further change to outright opposition not only to further changes but to those already in place. At a minimum, the emergence of a conservative climate contributes to a slowdown in the change process. In some cases (e.g., Nazi Germany and contemporary Iran) it results in reactionary policies that substantially reverse recent gains made by women. As Boneparth and Stoper suggest (1988, p. 3), a conservative or reactionary political climate compels women's movement organizations to divert their resources and energies from the pursuit of change to an attempt to resist efforts to turn back the clock.

Change toward a more conservative sociopolitical atmosphere may result from a generally adverse economic situation for the nation. The conservative reaction of the late 1970s and early 1980s is often attributed to the "stagflation" of those years. Likewise, the rise of Fascism in Germany is often traced in substantial measure to the severe inflation and high unemployment rates of the post-World War I years. Regardless of its sources, and whether it is related to a generally more conservative atmosphere, economic downturn is usually not hospitable to the development of new governmental programs on behalf of gender equity (Boneparth and Stoper, 1988, pp. 4–5; see also Dye, 1978, p. 306). New programs usually entail the expenditure of money. At a minimum, additional personnel must be paid (e.g., to enforce antidiscrimination legislation). Where new services (e.g., government-provided child care) or entitlements (e.g., family allowances) are involved, the additional government expenditures are quite substantial. In an expanding economy, rising government income may suffice to cover the additional costs without a tax increase. Moreover, tax increases are not as unpalatable when people's incomes are rising. However, in an era of inflation and/or recession (not to mention depression), government resources decline and people are loath to accept higher taxes. Therefore, both the public and government officials are generally reluctant to pass legislation that might entail more government expenditures. Indeed, the budgets for existing programs are often cut. Moreover, newer programs, which had less time to become entrenched either within the government bureaucracy or within public consciousness, are more likely to be cut than long-standing ones. Recent programmatic and legal gains made by women are, therefore, more vulnerable to cuts than long-standing programs such as social security, veterans' benefits, or farm subsidies. This logic applies to all levels of government: national, state or provincial, and local.

Proposition 9.9. The more conservative the general sociopolitical atmosphere of a nation becomes, the less supportive both elites and members of the public become to gender system change that reduces female disadvantage, which also includes the possibility of the reversal of some recent gains made by women.

Proposition 9.10. The greater the economic difficulties faced by a nation, the less inclined political elites are to adopt new policies, programs, and laws in support of gender equity, and the more inclined they are to cut the budgets of recently enacted programs on behalf of women.

CONCLUSION

Figure 9.2 summarizes the processes discussed in this chapter that appear to substantially slow, halt, or even reverse the impetus for change that decreases gender stratification. Over time, to the extent that a women's movement succeeds in achieving some of its goals, organized opposition arises, public apathy—especially among younger cohorts of women—increases, and the women's movement begins to shrink. In response, elites cease to support further gender system change and may even attempt to turn back the clock. The change process has reached its limits for a particular era and place. A new gender system has emerged, somewhat more egalitarian than the old, but still rife with inequities. The passage of time is required for that new system to stabilize and become accepted as "normal." Only then is it potentially possible for a new wave of activists to define the remaining inequities in a way that makes sense to a substantial proportion of the public. Between waves, the message of the handful of organiza-

218

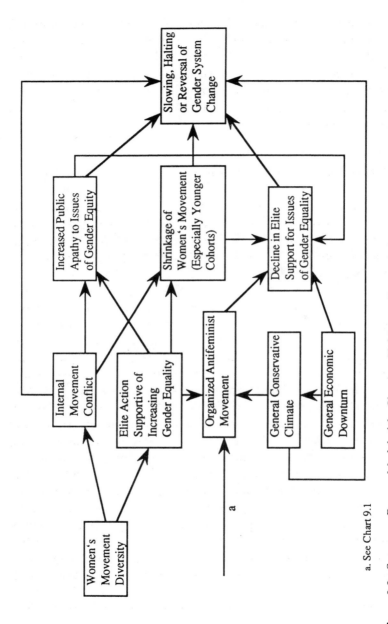

Figure 9.2. Summary Process Model of the Slowing, Halting, or Reversal of a Process of Gender System Change Toward Increased Equality

a. See Chart 9.1

tions and activists who maintain the vision of, and commitment to, bringing about a system of gender equality falls on largely deaf—if not hostile—ears. In short, gender system change, and the women's movements that support and pursue it, have a self-limiting quality. Finally, the slowdown or cessation is ironically induced largely by the achievement of (modest) changes that decrease gender inequality.

A Brief Digression About Movement Waves

At this point a cautious reader might ask how I could argue that women's movements inexorably wane, based at most on only two data points (one per movement wave), one of which has not yet ended. Such a reader might also ask how, in the absence of more waves, such a theory could possibly be tested.

A closer examination of the First Wave cases suggests that in many instances that wave appears unitary only in historical retrospect. First Wave movements in several nations (e.g., the United States, Great Britain, Germany, Japan) spanned from half to nearly three-quarters of a century. During that time, public support for them waxed and waned, and movement goals, ideologies, and goal achievement varied (see Chafetz and Dworkin, 1986, chap. 4). A closer examination of the histories of those cases could result in a description of at least two and possibly more "wavelets" within what is commonly referred to as the First Wave. In fact, Dworkin and I (1986, chap. 6, 1989) did divide First Wave movements in five nations into two phases based on a dramatic shift in ideology and/or size. A partial test of some of the ideas presented in this chapter could possibly be conducted by more closely examining the wavelets within those nations that experienced a relatively long and/or discontinuous First Wave movement. It is possible that since the early 1980s Second Wave activism has been in a temporarily quiescent period from which it will reemerge in a few years, that the first 15 years of this movement constituted only the first wavelet of what will prove to be a much longer wave.

CHAPTER TEN

Epilogue: The Issue of Elites

The major underlying theme of the preceding eight chapters has been that, *given a system of gender stratification*, women's collective opportunity to enhance their power resources is largely a function of the gender division of labor, which in turn responds primarily to forces outside their direct control. Changes in the nature of women's work, and the levels of rewards that accrue to their work, mostly reflect technological, economic, and demographic forces. To the extent that these forces are consciously controlled by willful human agency, it is by elite incumbents, who are overwhelmingly male. In short, in gender-stratified societies women constitute a pool of labor whose members are manipulatable by the powerful actors who fill roles that allow them to control dominant social institutions and organizations. I argued in Chapter 5 that equal representation for women among a society's elites constitutes the single most important change required to produce a system of gender equality. However, in the subsequent four chapters nothing was said about how that might be accomplished.

Nowhere in the contemporary world do women constitute more than a tiny minority of any nation's elites. Women, in substantial numbers, have risen to midlevel positions in recent years in many, especially advanced, industrial societies, but rarely to the top of major organizations. In political life, it has become commonplace to see women on school boards and in mayoral mansions (alongside blacks in the United States), just as these governmental levels have increasingly lost autonomy to higher governmental units (see Holter, 1972). Women political leaders are more scarce in high-level state and national governments. Those such as Golda Meir, Indira Gandhi, Corazon Aquino, and Margaret Thatcher, who have achieved national leadership, failed to pursue policies or programs of gender equity. They rose through the political ranks as classic tokens who subscribed to the values and priorities of their overwhelmingly male peers and superordinates (see Kanter, 1977).

Elites are usually vitally concerned with protecting—if not enhancing—their own positions. While, under certain circumstances discussed in earlier chapters, they may institute many kinds of laws, policies, and programs that aid women, they are not likely to countenance changes that substantially jeopardize their privileged status. Given the organizational resources at their disposal, they will usually be able to guard their status from perceived threats by nonelites of all kinds. In his study of 53 "challenging groups" seeking change, Gamson (1975, pp. 42–43) found that, of the 16 whose goals included displacing some or all of their elite antagonists, only 2 (12.5%) attained even minor success in the achievement of any organizational goals. In contrast, about two-thirds of the other 37 groups experienced at least some success in goal achievement. Political scientist T. J. Lowie has classified domestic policies into three types: distributive, regulatory, and redistributive. He argues that the third type generates the greatest amount of conflict and is the most difficult to achieve (as cited in Boneparth and Stoper, 1988, pp. 15–16). The equitable sharing of elite roles clearly involves the redistribution of power and perquisites and is, therefore, more likely than virtually any other goals sought by gender-conscious groups to elicit hostile reactions.

Equal access to elite roles constitutes the most difficult and intractable problem in achieving gender equality. Yet, without it, all other improvements in women's relative status remain incomplete, fragile, and easily lost. I have no very clear idea of how women can accomplish the attainment of elite roles but I will nonetheless tentatively present some suggestions concerning how greater gender equality in elite incumbency could come about.

The possibility of enhancing women's representation among elites rests upon their increasing control of resources due to their greater labor-force participation and upon the equitable division of household and familial labor (that is, upon the other two aspects of the gender division of labor discussed in Chapter 5). The latter is necessary if women are to be able to devote time and energy equal to that of men to pursuing and filling what are very demanding work roles. Corporate chief executive officers, university or foundation presidents, Senate or parliamentary leaders, and so on travel and entertain extensively and typically work long and odd hours. They require "wives," that is, people and/or services that take care of their personal maintenance and that of their children. At the very least, they cannot *be* "wives" doing those tasks for others. Either both men and women will have to be able and willing to readily purchase such services or both will have to share the equal "handicap" of doing them. Already, women in midlevel positions are able and apparently willing to purchase many of the services wives have traditionally provided. The provision of household labor is essentially a supply-side variable, that is, one that affects women's and men's relative availability for elite roles. As argued repeatedly, however, it is the demand side that really counts. At best, supply variables constitute necessary but not sufficient factors for change.

Why would male elites create a demand for women in their ranks? I assume that, no matter how small the population or how low the sex ratio, there will always be enough men available to assume elite roles. Nor will the number of such roles expand beyond the capacity of men to fill them. Elites are, after all, only a tiny minority of the male population.

To gain entrance in more than token numbers, women will probably have to employ their resources collectively and coercively. They will have to up the reward ante for male elites if they are included, and the cost ante if they continue to be excluded. Despite my assertion in earlier chapters that women's movements are highly limited in their ability to produce change directly, I think that to change the ante requires a mass women's movement willing to use such coercive tactics as boycotts and strikes. Well-organized, resource-enriched women could *outspokenly* refuse to give money to universities or religious organizations that do not meet a "quota" of female board members, administrators, and so on and could give generously of their funds to those that do. They could *outspokenly* boycott the products and services of companies on the same basis and purchase only from those that comply. They could form all-women unions—at a much higher rate than currently is the case—and strike for the same purpose. One example might be a teacher's strike, one nonnegotiable demand of which would be proportional representation of women (based on their percentage of all teachers) as principals and district administrators. Clerical staff, nurses, women in banking or insurance could do likewise. Any work setting where a large segment of the labor force is composed of women, regardless of the range of occupations in which they are employed, could potentially serve as a setting for such a strike. And today almost every organization employs a very substantial number of women in some capacity.

The Women's Political Caucus and several other organizations target candidates for support, financial and otherwise. This effort, already somewhat effective, would need to be stepped up considerably if political elite equality is to come about (see Papandreou, 1988). Where women run for office, they win about as often as men (Karnig and Walter, 1976; Bullock and Johnson, 1985). In order to run, especially for state or national office, extensive resources are required. Women have only begun to amass resources in recent years, and to date only some have been willing to commit them primarily on the basis of gender equity issues and candidates. Benze and Declercq (1985) found that, while male candidates for public office do have an advantage in fund-raising, during the 1970s women candidates substantially improved in their ability to raise funds. Other research indicates that the proportion of women in state legislatures is heavily contingent upon "the level of feminist activism and the resources this activism can provide to female candidates" (Volgy et al., 1986, p. 166).

At least two things have prevented women from more fully exploiting the kinds of tactics outlined above. First, gender-conscious women have had insufficient resources and have been too few in number to substantially affect the reward and cost ante of most elites most of the time. Beyond resources, a large number of women would have to become conscious of the need for *this particular kind of activism* on behalf of *this specific target*, and would have to be willing to commit themselves to it (Papandreou, 1988). I do not think that this will happen any time soon, for reasons explored in the last chapter. My guess is that, at best, it awaits the revival of mass women's movement activism, perhaps about 25–30 years from now (a possibility to be discussed at the end of this chapter). Such a movement would be composed, in the majority, of well-paid, well-educated, highly skilled women in the professions and midlevel management and administration. There should be a large number of such women by then. Regardless of rhetoric, the Second Wave has primarily been a struggle to gain entry for more than a token number of women precisely into those kinds of positions—and it has been quite successful. It required a First Wave, which was oriented chiefly to gaining access for women to public life and to the education that such access requires. After a period of time during which those gains in education and public access were consolidated and made part of "normal" social life, the remaining, and very substantial, gender inequities could become apparent to large numbers of women in several nations. The gains made by women during recent decades also require the passage of time to become fully accepted. A relatively stable but more gender egalitarian system than existed prior to the 1970s will have to seem "normal" and cease to cause substantial discussion and opposition (much as people eventually stopped debating women's access to a university education and women's suffrage). Only after this—still in 1990 newly emerging—gender system attains stability can it become widely apparent that inequities persist. Only then can an accurate picture of remaining inequities and their likely causes be developed. And only at that point can strategies and tactics be developed to combat the new, but still unequal, gender system.

It is certainly not a foregone conclusion that such a new wave of women's movement activism will occur, not to mention succeed. After all, the past history of gender stratification has not been one of linear "progress" or gradually decreasing gender stratification. To the extent that, as the Second Wave winds down, women are able to consolidate their gains in the labor force, if a new wave were to emerge, it would have to focus on the continuing dearth of women in the ranks of the elite; the continuing male control of macro-level power resources; the continuing dominance of androcentric social definitions and priorities, as expressed and reinforced by male elites. There would be few targets other than male dominance of elite roles available to explain women's continuing disadvantages. If this new wave were successful, then genuine gender equality could well be the result.

The job for feminists in coming years is much the same as the role played by surviving First Wave activists from about 1920 until the late 1960s in the United States, as described by Rupp and Taylor (1987). They need to keep alive some of the organizations—shrunken though they may become—the ideology, and the goals of feminism, maintaining as much pressure as possible at least on political elites. They must do this in an era when public support for such activism will be lacking and outright hostility from some quarters will confront them. It must be seen as a historical interlude—probably a necessary one—while an improved but imperfect gender system digests the changes brought about during the second half of the twentieth century. This is a thankless task that only a few dedicated women are likely to undertake. They cannot know when the time will be right for their ideals to once again move to center stage and inspire a new generation of activists. Many, perhaps most, will not even survive to witness a new wave of mass activism. But I believe that out of the millions who have had their imaginations ignited by, and have devoted the best part of their energies to, Second Wave activism and change, thousands will emerge to carry the torch into the future with determination and guarded optimism.

A PERSONAL DIGRESSION

In a fundamental way, my theoretical logic has led me to a conclusion that I find discomfiting. Many—perhaps most—feminists today think that contemporary industrial societies pay very little attention to the traditional feminine values of caring, nurturance, and human connectedness, to the detriment of, and risk to, all people on earth, and especially the needy and poor. They argue that women should be valued for those qualities and for their commitment to family relationships; that traditionally women's work in the home and in the labor force that expresses these values should be more highly valued and rewarded than currently is the case. My logic leads to an inescapable quandary. As long as men are more powerful than women, especially at the macro level, what women do and value will be relatively devalued according to general social definitions. Only in assuming nondomestic, and specifically elite, roles can women hope to contribute substantially to the formulation of general social values and policies. Yet in order to achieve such roles, more often than not women must sacrifice to a substantial degree those very values and behaviors that are often defined as distinctively feminine. To enter elite roles, they must resemble the elites already there; they must demonstrate that they share the values and priorities, as well as the behaviors, of their superordinates. Like other minority groups, women will not be able to be the equals of men without considerable sacrifice of what women have traditionally valued most highly; what, on the average, distinguishes women from men. To the extent that women's traditional values are distinct from those of men, in all likelihood they are an outgrowth of their subordination and the traditional gender division of labor. Equality usually entails assimilation, and traditional values rarely survive that process.

Having just been the pessimist, let me juxtapose that logic with another more optimistic possibility. The theory argues that, over time, gender differentiation, as produced by childhood engenderment, should decrease for both males and females. This decrease implies that, as females shed some of their traditional values and behaviors, males should assume them, and both should be more androgynous. Moreover, if women are once able to enter the ranks of the elite in more than token numbers, they can then support one another's values, reducing the necessity for "successful" women to think and act as pseudomen (see Kanter, 1977). In both of these ways traditional feminine values of human caring and relatedness may be preserved. Moreover, in the hands of the powerful, they should be much more instrumental in affecting the future of nations and the planet than left in the hands of the powerless. Stated in a different way, women and men cannot do different yet equally rewarded work unless those (elites) who establish dominant social definitions value the different contributions equally. In turn, equal valuation is unlikely until women share equally in elite roles. Ironically, it requires gender similarity in elite incumbency in order for gender differences in other aspects of the gender division of labor to be equally valued and rewarded.

Many radical feminists reject the entire notion of power and elites as part of a future society based on feminist values. They define such inequality as the product of male dominance (patriarchy) and, therefore, as a central target to be eliminated. I might wish to agree with them ideologically, but sociologically I see no chance that human societies will return to substantial social egalitarianism. Nowhere other than in non-surplus-producing, technologically very simple, societies has a system lacking elites and structured inequality existed. Such societies have been all but wiped out by technologically and socially more complex ones. Short of a holocaust that returns us to subsistence living in a world where the vast majority of the human population has died, I see no realistic likelihood that the earth will again experience such a social form (other than in small, "experimental" communities). The sheer number of human beings, and the dense concentrations in which most live, seem to necessitate forms of social organization that include a hierarchy of authority. Egalitarian societies have always been tiny and relatively isolated. The apparent human desire to improve the material standard of living beyond the minimal level, which is still characteristic of most of the world's peoples, means that those technologies and forms of economic organization that produce most will tend to be adopted wherever the collectivity is able to do so. Now and in the foreseeable future, these too appear to entail hierarchy, regardless of the form of political economy. High-tech involves a knowledge elite; mass production, an administrative one. Differences in authority, not to mention other forms of inequality, could undoubtedly be substantially mitigated, but it is doubtful that they can be eliminated in any reasonably foreseeable future.

Elites will exist for the foreseeable future. The issues are then: Who composes the elite and what kind of policies do they pursue? For the sake of gender equity, women must constitute their fair share—about half—of those who occupy elite roles. For the sake of the future of our species and planet, traditional feminine values (as described, for instance, by Gilligan, 1982; Chodorow, 1978; Johnson, 1988) must be incorporated into the policies pursued by elites. Gender equality in elite role incumbency and the incorporation of traditional feminine values into elite policy formation must be the central agenda items for the next round of change activism devoted to gender equality.

WHAT MIGHT THE FUTURE HOLD?
TWO SCENARIOS

In this, the concluding section, two alternative scenarios are offered of what the future might hold in terms of gender stratification in advanced industrial societies, specifically the United States.

The Optimistic Scenario

The first scenario assumes, at worst, periodic recessions of no more than moderate length and depth, but no sustained and deep economic downturn. This is the optimistic scenario. Reasonably well-paid, unionized, and mostly traditionally male jobs in the secondary sector will continue to decrease as a proportion of the paid labor force as a result of both automation and the export of factories to low-labor-cost nations. Until about the year 2000, entry-level demand will outstrip the supply of young workers, who are members of the "baby bust" cohort (those born between about 1964 and 1980). Service sector (tertiary) jobs will continue to expand, but even if the rapid expansion rate of the past few decades fails to continue, the small cohort size should result in widespread labor-force opportunities for young women. Between 2010 and 2020, the large baby boom cohort will begin to retire, and by 2035 the entire cohort will have retired. The departure of the baby boom generation from the labor force will help to sustain high levels of labor-force demand, expediting the career mobility of the baby bust cohort and probably easing the problems of the larger "echo boom" cohort born after 1980. Moreover, given the small size of the baby bust cohort, the generation following the echo boom should be relatively small, especially if baby bust women, experiencing ample job opportunities, restrict their fertility. Therefore, women should continue to face considerable opportunity to engage in extradomestic work well into the next century.

Tertiary sector jobs span the pay, prestige, and skill-level continua. They range from poorly paid, low-skilled jobs (e.g., in retail sales and personal services) to highly rewarded, prestigious, and highly skilled occupations in technical and scientific areas, the professions, finance, administration, and so on. With an aging population, the fields of medicine, leisure, and gerontology will burgeon. Most of these fields have already provided substantially improved opportunities for women, who have, however, continued to shy away from highly technical areas such as engineering and computer design or repair. Women should be able to hold their own in those tertiary occupations they have already penetrated or have long dominated, and move into many others, because labor demand will outstrip the capacity of men to meet it.

In the optimistic scenario, continued high demand for women's extradomestic labor will enhance trends toward decreasing gender social definitions and gender differentiation, and in general serve to further reduce gender stratification. Given the small size of the baby bust cohort, educated women of that generation may constitute the first to gain significant access to elite roles. Widespread entrance into elite roles could occur as they enter midlife, beginning around 2010–15. If (as is likely) they fail to gain entry into the ranks of the elites in substantial numbers, well-educated, career-oriented, female labor-force participants of this cohort might constitute the central agents of a new wave of women's movement activism. They would have experienced the great optimism that comes with beginning their careers during a period of labor shortage, only to find their paths upward thwarted in midcareer by their gender. As previously suggested, it is possible to view many of the activists and followers of the Second Wave as seeking paths *into* highly rewarded occupations. Merely "arriving" is quite satisfying. For a future generation, entry will be taken for granted and not be enough, especially if early in their careers women foresaw yet greater opportunity.

The Pessimistic Scenario

The depressing scenario assumes long-term, serious economic problems that result in a more than temporary reduction in the overall demand for labor. Prolonged and severe economic downturn could result from increasingly successful foreign competition for markets (external and internal), from global economic phenomena, from the burden of national debt, or from some other cause(s). Coupled with a decrease in jobs in the heavily male manufacturing occupations, and despite smaller working-aged cohorts, women would be disproportionately squeezed out of the labor force. In this scenario, under- and unemployed men invade female-dominated occupations in the tertiary sector while using their macro power to resist female incursion into male-dominated sectors. Increasingly deprived of extradomestic work opportunities, women rapidly experience a loss of power resources and gender stratification increases.

CONCLUSION

Demography is on the side of women in the coming decades. The more time passes before a serious economic setback occurs, the more likely women will have become firmly entrenched in the labor force and perhaps in elite roles. Such entrenchment would result in a more gender-equal sharing of the effects of economic hardship in the event of prolonged and deep economic downturn. Already, in the recession of the early 1980s, for the first time the male unemployment rate was somewhat higher than the female rate in the United States. If serious economic decline occurs soon, the clock is likely to be set back, and the gender system will resemble more that of 1950 than that of the 1970s and 1980s. Until women consolidate their power, they constitute an expendable labor force to be used according to the perceived needs and interests of mostly male elites. The key to the consolidation of power is the continued presence of most women in the labor force and their movement in more than token numbers into the ranks of elite gatekeepers, resource and opportunity distributors, and social definition makers. It remains to be seen if this will occur.

References

Acker, Joan. 1987. "Sex Bias in Job Evaluation: A Comparable Worth Issue." Pp. 183–96 in *Ingredients for Women's Employment Policy*, edited by Christine Bose and Glenna Spitze. Albany: State University of New York Press.

Adam, Barry. 1987. *The Rise of a Gay and Lesbian Movement*. Boston: Twayne.

Almquist, Elizabeth. 1987. "Labor Market Gender Inequality in Minority Groups." *Gender & Society* 1(4):400–414.

Arizpe, Lourdes. 1977. "Women in the Informal Labor Sector: The Case of Mexico City." *Signs* 3:25–37.

Bacchi, Carol Lee. 1983. *Liberation Defined?* Toronto: University of Toronto Press.

Bámdád, Badr al-Moluk. 1977. *From Darkness into Light: Women's Emancipation in Iran*, edited and translated by F.R.C. Bagley. Hicksville, NY: Exposition.

Banks, Olive. 1981. *Faces of Feminism: A Study of Feminism as a Social Movement*. New York: St. Martin's.

Barron, R. D. and G. M. Norris. 1976. "Sexual Divisions and the Dual Labour Market." Pp. 47–69 in *Dependence and Exploitation in Work and Marriage*, edited by Diana Leonard Barker and Sheila Allen. London: Longman.

Bell, Colin and Howard Newby. 1976. "Husbands and Wives: The Dynamics of the Deferential Dialectic." Pp. 152–68 in *Dependence and Exploitation in Work and Marriage*, edited by Diana Barker and Sheila Allen. London: Longman.

Beller, Andrea. 1982. "Trends in Occupational Segregation by Sex: 1960–1990." Mimeographed.

Bennholdt-Thomsen, Veronika. 1984. "Towards a Theory of the Sexual Division of Labor." Pp. 252–70 in *Households and the World Economy*, edited by Joan Smith, Immanuel Wallerstein, and Hans Dieter Evers. Beverly Hills, CA: Sage.

Benze, James and Eugene Declercq. 1985. "The Importance of Gender in Congressional and Statewide Elections." *Social Science Quarterly* 66(December): 954–63.

Berch, Bettina. 1982. *The Endless Day: The Political Economy of Women and Work*. New York: Harcourt Brace Jovanovich.

Bergom-Larsson, Maria. 1982. "Women and Technology in the Industrialized Countries." Pp. 29–75 in *Scientific-Technological Change and the Role of Women in Development*, edited by P. D'Onofrio-Flores and S. Pfafflin. Boulder, CO: Westview.

Berk, Richard A. and Sarah F. Berk. 1979. *Labor and Leisure at Home*. Beverly Hills, CA: Sage.

Berk, Sarah Fenstermaker. 1985. *The Gender Factory.* New York: Plenum.

Beuf, A. 1974. "Doctor, Lawyer, Household Drudge." *Journal of Communications* 24:142–45.

Blau, Francine. 1978. "The Data on Women Workers, Past, Present and Future." Pp. 29–62 in *Women Working,* edited by A. Stromberg and S. Harkess. Palo Alto, CA: Mayfield.

Blau, Peter M. 1964. *Exchange and Power in Social Life.* New York: John Wiley.

Blumberg, Rae Lesser. 1978. *Stratification: Socioeconomic and Sexual Inequality.* Dubuque, IA: William C Brown.

_____. 1979. "A Paradigm for Predicting the Position of Women: Policy Implications and Problems." Pp. 113–42 in *Sex Roles and Social Policy,* edited by Jean Lipman-Blumen and Jessie Bernard. Beverly Hills, CA: Sage.

_____. 1984. "A General Theory of Gender Stratification." Pp. 23–101 in *Sociological Theory, 1984,* edited by Randall Collins. San Francisco: Jossey-Bass.

_____. 1988. "Income Under Female Versus Male Control: Hypotheses from a Theory of Gender Stratification and Data from the Third World." *Journal of Family Issues* 9(March):51–84.

_____. Forthcoming-a. *Women and the Wealth of Nations: Theory and Research on Global Development.* New York: Praeger.

_____. Forthcoming-b. "As You Sow, so Shall You Reap: Updating a Structural Analysis of Sexual Stratification in the Kibbutz." *Gender & Society.*

Boneparth, Ellen and Emily Stoper. 1988. "Introduction: A Framework for Policy Analysis." Pp. 1–19 in *Women, Power and Policy,* edited by E. Boneparth and E. Stoper. New York: Pergamon.

Boserup, Ester. 1970. *Women's Role in Economic Development.* New York: St. Martin's.

Bouchier, David. 1984. *The Feminist Challenge: The Movement for Women's Liberation in Britain and the USA.* New York: Schocken.

Bourguignon, Erika. 1980. "Introduction and Theoretical Considerations." Pp. 1–15 in *A World of Women,* edited by E. Bourguignon. New York: Praeger.

Boxer, Marilyn. 1982. "First Wave Feminism in Nineteenth-Century France: Class, Family, and Religion." *Women's Studies International Forum* 5(6):551–59.

Boxer, Marilyn and Jean Quataert. 1978. *Socialist Women: European Socialist Feminism in the Nineteenth and Early Twentieth Centuries.* New York: Elsevier-North Holland.

Brownmiller, Susan. 1975. *Against Our Will: Men, Women and Rape.* New York: Bantam.

Bullock, Charles and Loch Johnson. 1985. "Sex and the Second Primary." *Social Science Quarterly* 66(December):933–44.

Bullough, Bonnie. 1974. "Some Questions About the Past and the Future." Chap. 13 in *The Subordinate Sex: A History of Attitudes About Women,* edited by Vern Bullough. New York: Penguin.

Burris, Val. 1983. "Who Opposed the ERA? An Analysis of the Social Bases of Antifeminism." *Social Science Quarterly* 64:305–17.

Cahill, Spencer. 1983. "Reexamining the Acquisition of Sex Roles: A Symbolic Interactionist Approach." *Sex Roles* 9(1):1–15.

Callaway, Helen. 1987. "Survival and Support: Women's Forms of Political

Action." Pp. 214–29 in *Women and Political Conflict: Portraits of Struggle in Times of Crisis*, edited by Rosemary Ridd and H. Callaway. New York: New York University Press.

Carden, Maren L. 1974. *The New Feminist Movement*. New York: Russell Sage.

Chafe, William. 1972. *The American Woman*. New York: Oxford University Press.

Chafetz, Janet Saltzman. 1978. *Masculine/Feminine or Human?* 2nd ed. Itasca, IL: F. E. Peacock.

————. 1980. "Conflict Resolution in Marriage: Toward a Theory of Spousal Strategies and Marital Dissolution Rates." *Journal of Family Issues* 1(3):397–421.

————. 1984. *Sex and Advantage: A Comparative, Macro-Structural Theory of Sex Stratification*. Totowa, NJ: Rowman & Allanheld.

————. 1988a. *Feminist Sociology: An Overview of Contemporary Theories*. Itasca, IL: F. E. Peacock.

————. 1988b. "The Gender Division of Labor and the Reproduction of Female Disadvantage: Toward an Integrated Theory." *Journal of Family Issues* 9(1):108–31.

————. 1989. "Gender Equality: Toward a Theory of Change." In *Feminism and Sociological Theory*, edited by Ruth Wallace. Beverly Hills, CA: Sage.

Chafetz, Janet Saltzman and A. Gary Dworkin. 1984. "Board Room and Laundry Room: Similar Pressures on Homemakers, Professionals, Managers and Administrators." *Free Inquiry in Creative Sociology* 12(May):47–50.

————. 1986. *Female Revolt: Women's Movements in World and Historical Perspective*. Totowa, NJ: Rowman & Allanheld.

————. 1987. "In the Face of Threat: Organized Antifeminism in Comparative Perspective." *Gender & Society* 1(March):33–60.

————. 1989. "Action and Reaction: An Integrated, Comparative Perspective on Feminist and Antifeminist Movements." In *Cross-National Research in Sociology*, edited by Melvin Kohn. Beverly Hills, CA: Sage.

Chincilla, Norma. 1977. "Industrialization, Monopoly Capitalism, and Women's Work in Guatemala." *Signs* 3:38–56.

Chodorow, Nancy. 1978. *The Reproduction of Mothering: Psychoanalysis and the Sociology of Gender*. Berkeley: University of California Press.

Coleman, Marion Tolbert. 1988. "The Division of Household Labor: Suggestions for Future Empirical Consideration and Theoretical Development." *Journal of Family Issues* 9(March):132–48.

Collins, Randall. 1972. "A Conflict Theory of Sexual Stratification." In *Family, Marriage, and the Struggle of the Sexes*, edited by Hans Peter Dreitzel. New York: Macmillan.

————. 1975. *Conflict Sociology: Toward an Explanatory Science*. New York: Academic Press.

Coltrane, Scott. 1988. "Father-Child Relationships and the Status of Women: A Cross-Cultural Study." *American Journal of Sociology* 93(March):1060–95.

Condon, Jane. 1985. *A Half Step Behind*. New York: Dodd, Mead.

Conover, Pamela and Virginia Gray. 1983. *Feminism and the New Right Conflict over the American Family*. New York: Praeger.

Constantinople, Anne. 1979. "Sex-Role Acquisition: In Search of the Elephant." *Sex Roles* 5(2):121–33.

Cook, Alice and H. Hayashi. 1980. *Working Women in Japan*. Ithaca, NY: Cornell University Press.

Coser, Lewis. 1956. *The Functions of Social Conflict*. London: Free Press of Glencoe.

Coser, Rose Laub. 1975. "Stay Home Little Sheba: On Placement, Displacement and Social Change." *Social Problems* 22(April):470–80.

———. 1986. "Cognitive Structure and the Use of Social Space." *Sociological Forum* 1(Winter):1–26.

Coser, Rose Laub and Gerald Rokoff. 1982. "Women in the Occupational World: Social Disruption and Conflict." Pp. 39–53 in *Women and Work*, edited by R. Kahn-Hut, A. Kaplan Daniels, and R. Colvard. New York: Oxford University Press. [First published in 1971 in *Social Problems* 18(Spring):535–54]

Costain, Anne. 1982. "Representing Women: The Transition from Social Movement to Interest Group." Pp. 19–37 in *Women, Power and Policy*, edited by E. Boneparth and E. Stoper. New York: Pergamon.

Coverman, Shelley and Joseph F. Sheley. 1986. "Men's Housework and Child-Care Time, 1965–1975." *Journal of Marriage and the Family* 48:413–22.

Cramer, James C. 1980. "Fertility and Female Employment: Problems of Causal Direction." *American Sociological Review* 45(April):167–90.

Croll, Elizabeth. 1978. *Feminism and Socialism in China*. London: Routledge & Kegan Paul.

———. 1986. "Rural Production and Reproduction: Socialist Development Experiences." Pp. 224–52 in *Women's Work: Development and the Division of Labor by Gender*, edited by Eleanor Leacock and Helen Safa. South Hadley, MA: Bergin & Garvey.

Curtis, Richard. 1986. "Household and Family in Theory on Inequality." *American Sociological Review* 51(April):168–83.

Dill, Bonnie Thornton. 1983. "Race, Class, and Gender: Prospects for an All-Inclusive Sisterhood." *Feminist Studies* 9:131–49.

Dodds, Dinah. 1982. "Extra-Parliamentary Feminism and Social Change in Italy, 1971–1980." *International Journal of Women's Studies* 5(2):148–60.

D'Onofrio-Flores, Pamela and Sheila Pfafflin, eds. 1982. *Scientific-Technological Change and the Role of Women in Development*. Boulder, CO: Westview.

Dye, Thomas. 1978. *Understanding Public Policy*. 3rd ed. Englewood Cliffs, NJ: Prentice-Hall.

Easterlin, Richard. 1987. *Birth and Fortune*. 2nd ed. Chicago: University of Chicago Press

Easton, Barbara. 1976. "Industrialization and Femininity: A Case Study of Nineteenth Century New England." *Social Problems* 23(April):389–401.

Ehrenreich, Barbara. 1982. "Defeating the ERA: A Right-Wing Mobilization of Women." *Journal of Sociology and Social Welfare* 9(3):391–98.

Eisenstein, Zillah. 1979. "Developing a Theory of Capitalist Patriarchy and Socialist Feminism" and "Some Notes on the Relations of Capitalist Patriarchy." Pp. 5–55 in *Capitalist Patriarchy and the Case for Socialist Feminism*, edited by Zillah Eisenstein. New York: Monthly Review Press.

Ellovich, Risa. 1980. "Dioula Women in Town: A View of Intra-Ethnic Variation (Ivory Coast)." Pp. 87–103 in *A World of Women*, edited by Erika Bourguignon. New York: Praeger.

England, Paula. Forthcoming. "A Feminist Critique of Rational-Choice Theories: Implications for Sociology." *The American Sociologist.*

England, Paula and George Farkas. 1986. *Households, Employment and Gender: A Social, Economic and Demographic View.* New York: Aldine.

England, Paula and Barbara Stanek Kilbourne. Forthcoming. "Markets, Marriages, and Other Mates." In *Beyond the Marketplace: Rethinking Society and Economy,* edited by Roger Friedland and Sandy Robertson. New York: Aldine.

Epstein, Barbara L. 1981. *The Politics of Domesticity.* Middletown, CT: Wesleyan University Press.

Epstein, Cynthia Fuchs. 1988. *Deceptive Distinctions: Sex, Gender, and the Social Order.* New Haven, CT: Yale University Press.

Etienne, Mona and Eleanor Leacock. 1980. "Introduction." Pp. 1–24 in *Women and Colonization: Anthropological Perspectives,* edited by M. Etienne and E. Leacock. New York: Praeger.

Evans, Richard J. 1976. *The Feminist Movement in Germany, 1894–1933.* London: Sage.

———. 1977. *The Feminists: Women's Emancipation Movements in Europe, America, and Australasia, 1840–1920.* London: Croom Helm.

Everett, Jana M. 1979. *Women and Social Change in India.* New York: St. Martin's.

Faderman, Lillian. 1989. "A History of Romantic Friendship and Lesbian Love." Pp. 26–31 in *Gender in Intimate Relationships: A Microstructural Approach,* edited by B. Risman and P. Schwartz. Belmont, CA: Wadsworth.

Featherman, D. L. and R. Hauser. 1976. "Sexual Inequalities and Socioeconomic Achievement in the U.S. 1962–1973." *American Sociological Review* 41:462–83.

Ferguson, Kathy. 1980. *Self, Society, and Womankind.* Westport, CT: Greenwood.

Ferree, Myra Marx and Beth Hess. 1985. *Controversy and Coalition: The New Feminist Movement.* Boston: G. K. Hall.

Fishman, Pamela. 1982. "Interaction: The Work Women Do." Pp. 170–80 in *Women and Work: Problems and Perspectives,* edited by R. Kahn-Hut, A. Kaplan Daniels, and R. Colvard. New York: Oxford University Press.

Flexner, Eleanor. 1975. *Century of Struggle: The Woman's Rights Movement in the United States.* Rev. ed. Cambridge, MA: Belknap Press.

Foreman, Ann. 1977. *Femininity as Alienation: Women and the Family in Marxism and Psychoanalysis.* London: Pluto.

Fox, Greer Litton. 1977. " 'Nice Girl': Social Control of Women Through a Value Construct." *Signs* 2(4):805–17.

Fox, Mary Frank and Sharlene Hesse-Biber. 1984. *Women at Work.* Palo Alto, CA: Mayfield.

Freeman, Jo. 1975. *The Politics of Women's Liberation.* New York: David McKay.

Friedan, Betty. 1963. *The Feminine Mystique.* New York: Dell.

Friedl, Ernestine. 1975. *Women and Men: An Anthropologist's View.* New York: Holt, Rinehart & Winston.

Gale, Richard. 1986. "Social Movements and the State: The Environmental Movement, Countermovement, and Government Agencies." *Sociological Perspectives* 29:202–40.

Game, Ann and Rosemary Pringle. 1983. *Gender at Work.* Sydney: Allen & Unwin.

Gamson, William. 1975. *The Strategy of Social Protest.* Homewood, IL: Dorsey.

Gelb, Joyce and Marian Palley. 1982. *Women and Public Policies*. Princeton, NJ: Princeton University Press.

Gershuny, J. I. and I. D. Miles. 1983. *The New Service Economy*. New York: Praeger.

Giele, Janet Zollinger. 1978. *Women and the Future: Changing Sex Roles in Modern America*. New York: Free Press.

Gilligan, Carol. 1982. *In a Different Voice*. Cambridge, MA: Harvard University Press.

Glass, Jennifer. 1988. "Job Quits and Job Changes: The Effects of Young Women's Work Conditions and Family Factors." *Gender & Society* 2(2):228–40.

Goffman, Irving. 1977. "The Arrangement Between the Sexes." *Theory and Society* 4(3):301–31.

Grimshaw, Patricia. 1972. *Women's Suffrage in New Zealand*. Wellington: Consolidated.

Guttentag, Marcia and Paul Secord. 1983. *Too Many Women? The Sex Ratio Question*. Beverly Hills, CA: Sage.

Haavind, Hanne. 1984. "Love and Power in Marriage." Pp. 136–67 in *Patriarchy in a Welfare Society*, edited by Harriet Holter. Oslo: Universitetsforlaget.

Harris, Louis. 1987. *Inside America*. New York: Vintage.

Harris, Marvin. 1978. *Cannibals and Kings: The Origins of Cultures*. London: Collins.

Harrison, Brian. 1978. *Separate Spheres: The Opposition to Women's Suffrage in Britain*. London: Croom Helm.

Hartmann, Betsy. 1987. *Reproductive Rights and Wrongs*. New York: Harper & Row.

Hartmann, Heidi. 1979. "Capitalism, Patriarchy, and Job Segregation by Sex." Pp. 206–47 in *Capitalist Patriarchy and the Case for Socialist Feminism*, edited by Z. Eisenstein. New York: Monthly Review Press.

————. 1984. "The Unhappy Marriage of Marxism and Feminism: Towards a More Progressive Union." Pp. 172–89 in *Feminist Frameworks: Alternative Theoretical Accounts of the Relations Between Women and Men*, edited by Alison Jaggar and Paula Rothenberg. New York: McGraw-Hill.

Heitlinger, Alena. 1979. *Women and State Socialism: Sex Inequality in the Soviet Union and Czechoslovakia*. Montreal: McGill-Queens University Press.

Henley, Nancy. 1977. *Body Politics: Power, Sex, and Nonverbal Communication*. Englewood Cliffs, NJ: Prentice-Hall.

Hertz, Rosanna. 1986. *More Equal than Others: Women and Men in Dual-Career Marriages*. Berkeley: University of California Press.

Herzog, A. Regula and Jerald G. Bachman. 1982. *Sex Role Attitudes Among High School Seniors: Views About Work and Family Roles*. Ann Arbor, MI: Institute for Social Research.

Holter, Harriet. 1970. *Sex Roles and Social Structure*. Oslo: Universitetsforlaget.

————. 1972. "Sex Roles and Social Change." Pp. 331–43 in *Toward a Sociology of Women*, edited by Constantina Safilios-Rothschild. Lexington, MA: Xerox College Publications.

Homans, George. 1961. *Social Behavior: Its Elementary Forms*. New York: Harcourt Brace Jovanovich.

Hood, Jane. 1983. *Becoming a Two-Job Family*. New York: Praeger.

Howard, Jeanne. 1982. "Our Own Worst Enemies: Women Opposed to Woman Suffrage." *Journal of Sociology and Social Welfare* 9:436–74.

Howell, Nancy. 1976. "The Population of the Dobe Area !Kung." In *Kalahari Hunter-Gatherers*, edited by R. B. Lee and I. DeVore. Cambridge, MA: Harvard University Press.

Huber, Joan. 1976. "Toward a Sociotechnological Theory of the Women's Movement." *Social Problems* 23(April):371-88.

——. 1988. "A Theory of Family, Economy and Gender." *Journal of Family Issues* 9(1):9-26.

Huber, Joan and Glenna Spitze. 1980. "Considering Divorce: An Expansion of Becker's Theory of Marital Stability." *American Journal of Sociology* 86(July):75-89.

——. 1983. *Sex Stratification: Children, Housework, and Jobs*. New York: Academic Press.

Huet, Maryse. 1982. "La Progression de l'Activite Feminine est-elle Irreversible?" *Economie et Statistique* 143:3-17.

Izraeli, Dafna. 1981. "The Zionist Women's Movement in Palestine, 1911-1927: A Sociological Analysis." *Signs* 7(1):87-114.

Jackson, Robert Max. 1989. "The Reproduction of Parenting." *American Sociological Review* 54(April):215-32.

Jacobs, Monica. 1978. "Civil Rights and Women's Rights in the Federal Republic of Germany Today." *New German Critique* 13(Winter):165-74.

Jancar, Barbara Wolfe. 1978. *Women Under Communism*. Baltimore: Johns Hopkins University Press.

Jencks, Christopher, Lauri Perman, and Lee Rainwater. 1988. "What Is a Good Job? A New Measure of Labor-Market Success." *American Journal of Sociology* 93(May):1322-57.

Jenkins, J. Craig. 1983. "Resource Mobilization Theory and the Study of Social Movements." *Annual Review of Sociology* 9:527-53.

Johnson, Kay Ann. 1978. *Women, the Family and Peasant Revolution in China*. Chicago: University of Chicago Press.

Johnson, Miriam. 1988. *Strong Mothers, Weak Wives: The Search for Gender Equality*. Berkeley: University of California Press.

Jones, Jo Ann and Rachel A. Rosenfeld. 1989. "Women's Occupations and Local Labor Markets: 1950 to 1980." *Social Forces* 67:668-92.

Jump, Teresa and Linda Hass. 1987. "Fathers in Transition: Dual-Career Fathers Participating in Child Care." Pp. 98-114 in *Changing Men: New Directions in Research on Men and Masculinity*, edited by Michael Kimmel. Beverly Hills, CA: Sage.

Jusenius, Carol. 1976. "Economics" (Review essay). *Signs* 2:177-89.

Kandiyoti, Deniz. 1988. "Bargaining with Patriarchy." *Gender & Society* 2(3):274-90.

Kanter, Rosabeth Moss. 1977. *Men and Women of the Corporation*. New York: Basic Books.

Karnig, Alberd and B. Oliver Walter. 1976. "Elections of Women to City Councils." *Social Science Quarterly* 56(March):605-13.

Katz, Phyllis. 1979. "The Development of Female Identity." *Sex Roles* 5(2):155-78.

Kessler, Suzanne and Wendy McKenna. 1978. *Gender: An Ethnomethodological Approach*. New York: John Wiley.

King, A. G. 1978. "Industrial Structure, the Flexibility of Working Hours, and

Women's Labor Force Participation." *Review of Economics and Statistics* 60:399–407.

Kohn, Melvin and Carmi Schooler. 1983. "Occupational Experience and Psychological Functioning: An Assessment of Reciprocal Effects." In *Work and Personality: An Inquiry into the Impact of Social Stratification,* edited by M. Kohn and C. Schooler. Norwood, NJ: Ablex.

Koyama, Takoshi. 1961. *The Changing Social Position of Women in Japan.* Paris: UNESCO.

Lakoff, Robin. 1975. *Language and Woman's Place.* New York: Harper Colophon.

Lapidus, Gail W. 1977. "Sexual Equality in Soviet Policy: A Developmental Perspective." Pp. 115–38 in *Women in Russia,* edited by D. Atkinson, A. Dallin, and G. W. Lapidus. Stanford, CA: Stanford University Press.

Leacock, Eleanor Burke. 1978. "Introduction." Pp. ix–xxiv in *Women in Class Society,* edited by Heleieth Saffioti. New York: Monthly Review Press.

Lenski, Gerhard. 1966. *Power and Privilege: A Theory of Social Stratification.* New York: McGraw-Hill.

Lever, Janet. 1976. "Sex Differences in the Games Children Play." *Social Problems* 23–24(April):478–87.

Lewis, Michael and Marsha Weinraub. 1979. "Origins of Early Sex-Role Development." *Sex Roles* 5(2):135–53.

Lipman-Blumen, Jean. 1976. "Toward a Homosocial Theory of Sex Roles: An Explanation of the Sex Segregation of Social Institutions." *Signs* 1(Spring):15–31.

———. 1984. *Gender Roles and Power.* Englewood Cliffs, NJ: Prentice-Hall.

Lorber, Judith, Rose Coser, Alice Rossi, and Nancy Chodorow. 1981. "On *The Reproduction of Mothering*: A Methodological Debate," *Signs* 6(Spring):482–514.

Lorence, Jon. 1988. "Growth in Service Sector Employment and MSA Gender Earnings Inequality: 1970–1980." Paper presented at the American Sociological Association Meetings, Atlanta.

Lorenzen, Maryvonne. 1986. *A Comparative Study of Women's Labor Force Status in Three Industrialized Countries.* M.A. thesis, University of Houston.

Luker, Kristin. 1984. *Abortion and the Politics of Motherhood.* Berkeley: University of California Press.

Marshall, Susan. 1985. "Ladies Against Women: Mobilization Dilemmas of Antifeminist Movements." *Social Problems* 32:348–62.

Martin, M. Kay and Barbara Voorhies. 1975. *Female of the Species.* New York: Columbia University Press.

Martin, Steven, Robert Arnold, and Ruth Parker. 1988. "Gender and Medical Socialization." *Journal of Health and Social Behavior* 29(December):333-43.

Martin, Susan. 1980. *Breaking and Entering: Policewomen on Patrol.* Berkeley: University of California Press.

Massey, Douglas, Rafael Alarcon, Jorge Durand, and Humberto Gonzalez. 1986. *Return to Aztlan: The Social Process of International Migration from Western Mexico.* Berkeley: University of California Press.

Mayo, Clara and Nancy Henley. 1981. "Nonverbal Behavior: Barrier or Agent for Sex Role Change?" Pp. 3–13 in *Gender and Nonverbal Behavior,* edited by C. Mayo and N. Henley. New York: Springer-Verlag.

Mazumdar, Vina. 1979. *Symbols of Power.* New Delhi: Allied.

McConnell-Ginet, Sally. 1978. "Intonation in a Man's World." *Signs* 3(Spring):541–59.

Meissner, Martin. 1977. "Sexual Division of Labor and Leisure." In *Women in Canada,* edited by M. Stephenson. Toronto: Women's Educational Press.

Michael, Robert. 1985. "Consequences of the Rise in Female Labor Force Participation Rates: Questions and Probes." *Journal of Labor Economics* 3(1, part 2):s117–46.

Michel, Andree. 1985. "France." Pp. 112–23 in *Women Workers in Fifteen Countries,* edited by J. Farley. New York: IRL Press.

Miller, Joanne, Carmi Schooler, Melvin Kohn, and Karen Miller. 1983. "Women and Work: The Psychological Effects of Occupational Conditions." In *Work and Personality: An Inquiry into the Impact of Social Stratification,* edited by M. Kohn and C. Schooler. Norwood, NJ: Ablex.

Mitchinson, Wendy. 1981. "The Woman's Christian Temperance Union: A Study in Organization." *International Journal of Women's Studies* 4(2):143–56.

Moore, Kristin and I. Sawhill. 1978. "Implications of Women's Employment for Home and Family Life." Pp. 29–62 in *Women Working,* edited by A. Stromberg and S. Harkess. Palo Alto, CA: Mayfield.

Mottl, Tahi L. 1980. "The Analysis of Countermovements." *Social Problems* 27:620–35.

Murray, G. F. and M. D. Alvarez. 1975. "Haitian Bean Circuits: Cropping and Trading Maneuvers Among a Cash-Oriented Peasantry." In *Working Papers in Haitian Culture and Society,* edited by S. W. Mintz. New Haven, CT: University Antilles Research Program.

Nashat, Guity. 1983. *Women and Revolution in Iran.* Boulder, CO: Westview.

Nielsen, Joyce. 1978. *Sex in Society: Perspectives on Stratification.* Belmont, CA: Wadsworth.

Niethammer, Carolyn. 1981. "Report on the Conference of Women's Contribution to Food Production and Rural Development in Africa." *The Women and Food Information Network Newsletter* 3(December).

Oakley, Ann. 1974. *Woman's Work.* New York: Vintage.

Ogburn, William F. 1927. *Social Change with Respect to Culture and Original Nature.* New York: Viking.

O'Kelly, Charlotte G. 1980. *Women and Men in Society.* New York: Van Nostrand.

O'Kelly, Charlotte and L. Carney. 1986. *Women and Men in Society.* 2nd ed. Belmont, CA: Wadsworth.

O'Neill, June. 1985. "The Trend in Male-Female Wage Gap in the United States." *Journal of Labor Economics* 3(1, part 2):s91–s116.

Oppenheimer, Valerie K. 1970. *The Female Labor Force in the United States.* Berkeley: University of California Press.

Ortner, Sherry B. 1974. "Is Female to Male as Nature Is to Culture?" In *Woman, Culture and Society,* edited by Michelle Rosaldo and Louise Lamphere. Stanford, CA: Stanford University Press.

Papandreou, Margarita. 1988. "Foreword: Feminism and Political Power." Pp. xi–xix in *Women, Power and Policy,* edited by E. Boneparth and E. Stoper. New York: Pergamon.

Papanek, Hanna. 1977. "Development Planning for Women." *Signs* 3:14–21.
Parker, Seymour and Hilda Parker. 1979. "The Myth of Male Superiority: Rise and Demise." *American Anthropologist* 81(2):289–309.
Philipp, Thomas. 1978. "Feminism and Nationalist Politics in Egypt." Pp. 277–94 in *Women in the Muslim World*, edited by L. Beck and N. Keddie. Cambridge, MA: Harvard University Press.
Piore, Michael J. 1979. *Birds of Passage: Migrant Labor and Industrial Societies*. Cambridge: Cambridge University Press.
Pohli, Carol. 1983. "Church Closets and Back Doors: A Feminist View of Moral Majority Women." *Feminist Studies* 9(Fall):529–58.
Polk, Barbara Bovee and Robert Stein. 1972. "Is the Grass Greener on the Other Side?" Pp. 14–23 in *Toward a Sociology of Women*, edited by Constantina Safilios-Rothschild. Lexington, MA: Xerox College Publications.
Poole, Keith and L. Harmon Zeigler. 1985. *Women, Public Opinion and Politics: The Changing Political Attitudes of American Women*. New York: Longman.
Rebecca, Meda, Robert Hefner, and Barbara Oleshansky. 1976. "A Model of Sex-Role Transcendence." Pp. 90–97 in *Beyond Sex-Role Stereotypes: Readings Toward a Psychology of Androgyny*, edited by Alexandra Kaplan and Joan Bean. Boston: Little, Brown.
Reskin, Barbara. 1988. "Bringing Men Back In: Sex Differentiation and the Devaluation of Women's Work." *Gender & Society* 2(1):58–81.
Reskin, Barbara and Polly Phipps. 1988. "Women in Male-Dominated Professional and Managerial Occupations." Pp. 190–205 in *Women Working: Theories and Facts in Perspective*, edited by A. H. Stromberg and S. Harkess. 2nd ed. Mountain View, CA: Mayfield.
Reskin, Barbara and Patricia Roos. 1987. "Status Hierarchies and Sex Segregation." Pp. 3–21 in *Ingredients for Women's Employment Policy*, edited by Christine Bose and Glenna Spitze. Albany: State University of New York Press.
Ridd, Rosemary and Helen Callaway, eds. 1987. *Women and Political Conflict: Portraits of Struggle in Times of Crisis*. New York: New York University Press.
Risman, Barbara. 1987. "Intimate Relationships from a Microstructural Perspective: Men Who Mother." *Gender & Society* 1(1):7–32.
Ritzer, George and D. Walczak. 1986. *Working: Conflict and Change*. Englewood Cliffs, NJ: Prentice-Hall.
Robins-Mowry, Dorothy. 1983. *The Hidden Sun: Women of Modern Japan*. Boulder, CO: Westview.
Rossi, Alice. 1982. *Feminists in Politics*. New York: Academic Press.
Rowbotham, Sheila. 1976. *Hidden From History: Rediscovering Women in History from the 17th Century to the Present*. New York: Vintage.
Rubin, Gayle. 1975. "The Traffic in Women: Notes on the 'Political Economy' of Sex." In *Toward an Anthropology of Women*, edited by R. Reiter. New York: Monthly Review Press.
Rupp, Leila. 1977. "Mother of the Volk: The Image of Women in Nazi Ideology." *Signs* 3:362–79.
Rupp, Leila and Verta Taylor. 1987. *Survival in the Doldrums: The American Women's Rights Movement, 1945 to the 1960s*. New York: Oxford University Press.
Sacks, Karen. 1974. "Engels Revisited: Women, the Organization of Production,

and Private Property." Pp. 207–22 in *Woman, Culture, and Society*, edited by Michelle Rosaldo and Louise Lamphere. Stanford, CA: Stanford University Press.

Saffioti, Heleieth. 1978. *Women in Class Society*. New York: Monthly Review Press.

————. 1986. "Technological Change in Brazil: Its Effects on Men and Women in Two Firms." Pp. 109–35 in *Women and Change in Latin America*, edited by June Nash and Helen Safa. South Hadley, MA: Bergin & Garvey.

Safilios-Rothschild, Constantina. 1979. "Women as Change Agents: Toward a Conflict Theoretical Model of Sex Role Change." Pp. 287–301 in *Sex Roles and Social Policy*, edited by Jean Lipman-Blumen and Jessie Bernard. Beverly Hills, CA: Sage.

Sanday, Peggy Reeves. 1974. "Female Status in the Public Domain." Pp. 189- 206 in *Women, Culture, and Society*, edited by Michelle Rosaldo and Louise Lamphere. Stanford, CA: Stanford University Press.

————. 1981. *Female Power and Male Dominance: On the Origins of Sexual Inequality*. Cambridge: Cambridge University Press.

Sattel, Jack. 1976. "The Inexpressive Male: Tragedy or Sexual Politics." *Social Problems* 23–24(April):469–77.

Sauter-Bailliet, Theresia. 1981. "The Feminist Movement in France." *Women's Studies International Quarterly* 4(4):409–20.

Schlegel, Alice. 1977. "Toward a Theory of Sexual Stratification" and "An Overview." Pp. 104 and 344–57 in *Sexual Stratification: A Cross-Cultural View*, edited by A. Schlegel. New York: Columbia University Press.

Schlossberg, Nancy and Jane Goodman. 1971–72. "A Woman's Place: Children's Sex Stereotyping of Occupations." *Vocational Guidance Quarterly* 20:266–70.

Schneider, Beth. 1988. "Political Generations and the Contemporary Women's Movement." *Sociological Inquiry* 58(1):4–21.

Schur, Edwin. 1984. *Labeling Women Deviant: Gender, Stigma, and Social Control*. New York: Random House.

Schwartz, Janet. 1980. "Women Under Socialism: Role Definitions of Soviet Women." *Social Forces* 58(September).

Scott, Hilda. 1979. "Women in Eastern Europe." Pp. 177–97 in *Sex Roles and Social Policy*, edited by Jean Lipman-Blumen and Jessie Bernard. Beverly Hills, CA: Sage.

Semyonov, Moshe and Richard Scott. 1983. "Industrial Shifts, Female Employment, and Occupational Differentiation." *Demography* 20:163–76.

Shah, Nasra and Peter Smith. 1984. "Migrant Women at Work in Asia." Pp. 297–322 in *Women in the Cities of Asia: Migration and Urban Adaptation*, edited by James Fawcett, S. E. Khoo, and P. Smith. Boulder, CO: Westview.

Shelton, Beth Ann and Juanita Firestone. 1989. "Household Labor Time and the Gender Gap in Earnings." *Gender & Society* 3(March):105–12.

Siegel, C.L.F. 1973. "Sex Differences in Occupational Choice of Second Graders." *Journal of Vocational Behavior* 3:15–19.

Sievers, Sharon L. 1983. *Flowers in Salt: The Beginnings of Feminist Consciousness in Modern Japan*. Stanford, CA: Stanford University Press.

Simmons, Alan B. and Jean E. Turner. 1976. "The Socialization of Sex-Roles and Fertility Ideas: A Study of Two Generations in Toronto." *Journal of Comparative Family Studies* 7:255–71.

Smith, Peter, Siew-Ean Khoo, and Stella Go. 1984. "The Migration of Women to Cities: A Comparative Perspective." Pp. 15–35 in *Women in the Cities of Asia: Migration and Urban Adaptation,* edited by James Fawcett, S. E. Khoo, and P. Smith. Boulder, CO: Westview.

Smith-Rosenberg, Carroll. 1989. "The Female World of Love and Ritual: Relations Between Women in Nineteenth-Century America." Pp. 229–35 in *Feminist Frontiers II: Rethinking Sex, Gender, and Society,* edited by L. Richardson and V. Taylor. New York: Random House.

South, Scott and Katherine Trent. 1988. "Sex Ratios and Women's Roles: A Cross-National Analysis." *American Journal of Sociology* 93(March):1096–1115.

Spiro, Melford. 1979. *Gender and Culture: Kibbutz Women Revisited.* New York: Schocken.

Spitze, Glenna and Scott South. 1985. "Women's Employment, Time Expenditure, and Divorce." *Journal of Family Issues* 6(September):307–29.

Steinberg, Ronnie and Alice Cook. 1988. "Policies Affecting Women's Employment in Industrial Countries." Pp. 307–28 in *Women Working: Theories and Facts in Perspective,* edited by A. H. Stromberg and S. Harkess. 2nd ed. Mountain View, CA: Mayfield.

Stewart, Abigail, M. Brinton Lykes, and Marianne LaFrance. 1982. "Educated Women's Career Patterns: Separating Social and Developmental Changes." *Journal of Social Issues* 38:97–117.

Stites, Richard. 1980. "The Women's Liberation Issue in Nineteenth Century Russia." Pp. 21–39 in *Women in Eastern Europe and the Soviet Union,* edited by T. Yeddin. New York: Praeger.

Stockard, Jean, Alphons Van De Kragt, and Patricia Dodge. 1988. "Gender Roles and Behavior in Social Dilemmas: Are There Sex Differences in Cooperation and in its Justification?" *Social Psychology Quarterly* 51(June):154–63.

Stolzenberg, Ross and Linda Waite. 1977. "Age, Fertility Expectations and Plans for Employment." *American Sociological Review* 42(October):769–83.

Strasser, Susan. 1982. *Never Done: A History of American Housework.* New York: Pantheon.

Summers, Anne. 1975. *Damned Whores and God's Police: The Colonization of Women in Australia.* Ringwood, Australia: Allen Lane.

Taylor, Verta. 1989. "The Future of Feminism: A Social Movement Analysis." Pp. 473–88 in *Feminist Frontiers II: Rethinking Sex, Gender, and Society,* edited by L. Richardson and V. Taylor. New York: Random House.

Thadani, Veena and Michael Todaro. 1984. "Female Migration: A Conceptual Framework." Pp. 36–59 in *Women in the Cities of Asia: Migration and Urban Adaptation,* edited by James Fawcett, S. E. Khoo, and P. Smith. Boulder, CO: Westview.

Thomas, P. 1964. *Indian Women Through the Ages.* Bombay: Asia Publishing House.

Thornton, Arland, Duane Alwin, and Donald Camburn. 1983. "Causes and Consequences of Sex-Role Attitudes and Attitude Change." *American Sociological Review* 48(April):211–27.

Treiman, Donald and Heidi Hartmann. 1981. *Women, Work, and Wages.* Washington, DC: National Academy Press.

Tremaine, Leslie, Candace G. Schau, and Judith W. Busch. 1982. "Children's Occupational Sex-Typing." *Sex Roles* 8(7):691-710.

Trey, J. E. 1972. "Women in the War Economy—World War II." *Review of Radical Economics* 4(July):1-17.

Urquhart, Michael. 1984. "The Employment Shift to Services: Where Did It Come From?" *Monthly Labor Review* 107(4):15-22.

U.S. Bureau of the Census. 1976. *Statistical Abstract of the United States.* Washington, DC: Government Printing Office.

Vasquez de Miranda, Glaura. 1977. "Women's Labor Force Participation in a Developing Society: The Case of Brazil." *Signs* 3:261-74.

Vogel, Lise. 1983. *Marxism and the Oppression of Women: Toward a Unitary Theory.* New Brunswick, NJ: Rutgers University Press.

Volgy, Thomas, John Schwarz, and Hildy Gottlieb. 1986. "Female Representation and the Quest for Resources: Feminist Activism and Electoral Success." *Social Science Quarterly* 67(1):156-68.

Waller, Willard. [1938] 1951. *The Family,* revised by Reuben Hill. New York: Dryden.

Ward, Kathryn. 1984. *Women in the World-System: Its Impact on Status and Fertility.* New York: Praeger.

Ward, Kathryn and Jane Weiss. 1982. "A Competitive Model of Women's Labor Force Participation in the U.S.: 1940-78." Paper presented at the American Sociological Association Meetings.

Webley, Irene. 1980. "Some of My Best Friends Are Housewives?" Paper presented at the meetings of the Australian Political Studies Association, Canberra, August 27-29.

Weitzman, Lenore J. 1987. *The Divorce Revolution.* Paperback ed. New York: Free Press.

West, Candace and Don Zimmerman. 1977. "Women's Place in Everyday Talk: Reflections on Parent-Child Interaction." *Social Problems* 24(June):521-29.

———. 1987. "Doing Gender." *Gender & Society* 1:125-51.

White, Merry. 1987. *The Japanese Educational Challenge: A Commitment to Children.* New York: Free Press.

Whyte, Martin King. 1978. *The Status of Women in Preindustrial Societies.* Princeton, NJ: Princeton University Press.

Wilkie, Jane Riblett. 1988. "Marriage, Family Life, and Women's Employment." Pp. 149-66 in *Women Working: Theories and Facts in Perspective,* edited by A. H. Stromberg and S. Harkess. 2nd ed. Mountain View, CA: Mayfield.

Zald, Mayer and John McCarthy. 1979. *The Dynamics of Social Movements.* Cambridge, MA: Winthrop.

Zanna, Mark, Faye Crosby, and George Loewenstein. 1987. "Male Reference Groups and Discontent Among Female Professionals." Pp. 28-41 in *Women's Career Development,* edited by Barbara Gutek and Laurie Larwood. Newbury Park, CA: Sage.

Zimmer, Lynn. 1987. "How Women Reshape the Prison Guard Role." *Gender & Society* 1(4):415-31.

Zwemer, Samuel M. and S. Zwemer. 1926. *Moslem Women.* Brattleboro, VT: Vermont Printing Co.

Index

About the Author

Janet Saltzman Chafetz is Professor of Sociology at the University of Houston, where she has been since 1971. She completed her Ph.D. at the University of Texas, Austin, in 1969. Emerging from graduate school just as the women's movement was gaining widespread visibility, she was one of a relatively small but rapidly growing number of feminists who worked to establish the area of gender sociology in the late 1960s and early 1970s. Her 1974 undergraduate text—*Masculine/Feminine or Human?*—was among the first available in the discipline. During the past decade her work has reflected her dual interests in sociological theory and in gender stratification. In 1988 she published an overview of contemporary feminist theories in sociology (*Feminist Sociology*). Her 1984 book, *Sex and Advantage*, was a general theory explaining cross-cultural variation in the extent of gender stratification. She considers this book to be a companion to that work, in that it attempts to explain how, once in existence, systems of gender stratification are maintained and, especially, how they change. Along with A. G. Dworkin, she has also published several papers and a book (*Female Revolt*, 1986) that attempt to explain why women's movements and antifeminist movements emerge and grow in specific times and places. Her theoretical work, including this book, has been cross-culturally and historically sweeping in an explicit attempt to perceive theoretical uniformities underlying the concrete details unique to specific times and places.